BRITAIN, THE COLD WAR AND YUGOSLAV UNITY, 1941–1949

For my Mother
and to the memory of my Father

Britain, the Cold War and Yugoslav Unity, 1941–1949

Ann Lane

SUSSEX
ACADEMIC
PRESS

First published 1996 in Great Britain by

SUSSEX ACADEMIC PRESS
18 Chichester Place
Brighton BN2 1FF, United Kingdom

and in the United States of America by
SUSSEX ACADEMIC PRESS
c/o International Specialized Book Services, Inc.
5804 N.E. Hassalo St.
Portland, Oregon 97213-3644
USA

British Library Cataloguing in Publication Data
A CIP catalogue record for this book is available from the British Library.

ISBN 1–898723 27 3 (hardcover)

Printed and bound by Biddles Ltd, Kings's Lynn and Guildford

Contents

Foreword by Geoffrey Warner

Developments in the former Yugoslavia since the death of its Communist leader, Marshal Tito, in 1980 have not unnaturally led to a great deal of speculation as to whether what has occurred could have been avoided if different policies had been pursued, particularly by the western powers, at the time when Tito was endeavouring to create the conditions for his post-World War II seizure of power. In particular, it has been alleged by a number of historians, journalists and former participants in events that the decision by Britain and the United States in 1943 to switch their support from the Chetnik guerrillas under General Draza Mihailovic to the Communist partisans under Tito was a colossal blunder, brought about by a combination of ignorance and deliberate deception on the part, not only of Tito, but also of Communists and fellow-travellers in the allied camp. If only Tito had been seen for what he was, the argument runs, things might have turned out differently.

Not the least of the merits of Ann Lane's book is that it brings some much needed balance and sanity into this debate. She demonstrates that there were no illusions, in London in any rate, as to the nature of Tito's partisan movement and that the decision to support it was not taken as a result of disinformation supplied by Communists in S.O.E. It was taken because the best intelligence (including decoded enemy messages) indicated that the partisans were doing more to damage the Germans than the Chetniks and because the number one priority of the British government was to win the war against Hitler.

To have supported Mihailovic, as the critics of British policy favour, might well have led to a prolongation of the war. Was this a price they think was worth paying? It is by no means certain, moreover, that such a policy would have settled the outcome of the struggle for power inside Yugoslavia in the west's favour, as they imply. One of the factors underlying British policy, as Dr Lane makes clear, was a fear that the situation in post-war Yugoslavia would come to resemble that in pre-war Spain. Interestingly enough, the same anxiety preoccupied President Roosevelt in respect of China, where there was a similar internal conflict between Communists and anti-Communists running parallel with resistance to foreign aggression and occupation, in this case by Japan. The Americans chose to support the anti-Communists in China, but it did not do them much good. Intervention in other countries' civil wars is a perilous enterprise at the best of times; it is even worse if you back the losing side.

Another parallel between the victorious Communist regimes in Yugoslavia and China is that both of them subsequently broke with their Soviet patron to the accompaniment of considerable acrimony. Dr Lane shows that there were those in the British policy-making establishment – notably Brigadier Fitzroy Maclean [and Colonel Willim Deakin?] – who always regarded this as a possibility in the case of Yugoslavia, which makes the decision to support Tito more far-seeing than might otherwise appear.

Tito's hard-line Communism in the immediate aftermath of World War II, however, gave no indication of an imminent break with Moscow. Indeed, Dr Lane cites a Foreign Office evaluation of early 1948 to the effect that Yugoslavia was 'undoubtedly the prize pupil of east European states within the Soviet orbit' and that Tito had 'largely been entrusted [by Moscow] with the responsibility of consolidating eastern Europe'. The fact that London picked up no hint of the growing tension between Yugoslavia and the Soviet Union until the crisis broke in June 1948 clearly shows the limitations of western intelligence concerning the Communist bloc in the early Cold War years.

After Yugoslavia's break with the Soviet Union Britain moved only gradually towards a policy of 'keeping Tito afloat'. The government had to be sure, as Dr Lane points out, that the rift was permanent and that Tito would not be overthrown by a Stalinist conspiracy. It also had to keep in step with the United States, which was alone in a position to provide much in the way of financial and economic assistance to the Yugoslav regime. Nevertheless, it was the British who, as a result of conversations between Fitzroy Maclean and Tito in May 1949, secured the valuable *quid pro quo* of a cessation of Yugoslav support for the Communist guerrillas in Greece.

Dr Lane concludes that, far from being a disaster, British policy towards Yugoslavia during and after World War II turned out quite successful. '[T]he emergence of the Cold War in Europe', she writed, 'had made an independent Yugoslavia more valuable to the west than could have been envisaged in 1943–44 . . . With Belgrade's neutrality, Italy could be defended against attack at the Ljubljana Gap, her natural point of defence, rather than on the Venetian Plain; Greece could be defended in the upper Varda Valley rather than at Salonika; the thirty-three divisions of the Yugoslav army were neutralised . . . The purpose of British wartime policy – the search for stability and order in a notoriously troublesome and dangerous region – had been achieved.'

Even though this state of affairs was probably as much the result of Stalin's folly as of Britain's wisdom, it seems to me that the central thrust of Dr Lane's argument cannot be gainsaid. It will of course be maintained that the Tito regime did not solve the problem of Yugoslavia's internal divisions and may even have exacerbated them. Dr Lane concedes the point, but this does not undermine her central thesis. The critics of British policy need to show that their alternative was not only practicable, but would also have solved both the problem of Balkan security during the Cold War and that of Yugoslavia's internal divisions. This they have conspicuously failed to do, not least because, unlike Dr Lane, they tend to allow their preoccupation with the present to distort their view of the past.

Foreword by Christopher Cviic

The Yugoslav federation, which Marshal Tito and his Communist Partisans set up at the end of the Second World War, is now no more and is unlikely to be resurrected. To the outside world, this second Yugoslavia had looked much more sturdy and successful than its sickly monarchist predecessor, leading most (though not quite all) professional observers to conclude that Yugoslavia was here to stay – 'survivor', however 'improbable', as one of them put it. There was a strong element of interest involved here. Most of the outside world, including Yugoslavia's neighbours, found Yugoslavia useful as a factor of stability – so much so that at times it did look as though Yugoslavia was almost more important to outsiders than to those living in it.

Not surprisingly, the sudden death of a state that had for decades been an important player on the international stage has, predictably, prompted the question whether its demise had been 'inevitable'. The question, though not beloved of professional historians – and unlikely ever to be satisfactorily answered (how does one define inevitability in the first place?) – is nevertheless sure to continue to be raised. This is no bad thing because the study of ex-Yugloslavia is important and deserves to be encouraged. Its dramatic history – not least its violent break-up in 1991 and what followed it – teaches important lessons for other regions of Europe and the world outside Europe. Those lessons should not be neglected. In any case, neglect is unlikely.

Many of the problems which the setting up of Yugoslavia in 1918 and its restoration in 1944–45 was supposed to resolve but in the end did not (and possibly even made worse) are still there. It is to be hoped – as the old *Manchester Guardian* used to start its leading articles – that the new framework of ex-Yugoslav successor states will allow for clearer and, ultimately, more harmonious relations among the various nationalities that had not so long ago lived within Yugoslavia. However, in the light of what has happened since 1991 in Bosnia and Croatia, in particular, a happy outcome is by no means a foregone conclusion – certainly not without a good deal of constructive help from outside. How this help is offered – and to whom – will inevitably reflect the often very different interests of the various states and international agencies involved. There will be serious dilemmas not only for the outside powers but also for the domestic players. What is deemed good for the outsiders will not necessarily always be seen as good for, and acceptable to, the locals – and vice versa.

The situation is not new. Reconciling outside and domestic concerns has never been easy in this complicated region. A rough but workable balance between domestic and external interests in the context of an East–West stand-off appeared to be struck after Tito's expulsion in 1948 from the Soviet bloc and held till his death in 1980 and for a while beyond. But the bill for those stable decades Yugoslavia spent in the grip of the Cold War corset came in 1991 in the shape of various accumulated grievances suddenly exploding. An attempt is now in progress to strike a new power balance in South-Eastern Europe in the very much more complicated conditions of the post-Cold War period.

Britain, which has been one of the key influences in the region during most of our century, is once again an important player, both in the Nato and the EU contexts. British and other western policy-makers searching for clues and, even more important, pitfalls in the huge post-Dayton joint operation by NATO, the European Union and other Western institutions – and, indeed, anybody interested in the region – should with profit read Dr Ann Lane's carefully researched and meticulously documented study of Britain's involvement in the region covering the crucial period between 1941 and 1949. One of the great merits of this highly instructive work is that, by calmly establishing the facts ('how it really was'), it simultaneously kills off a number of myths about that period. In that sense, it should serve as a model for those setting out to write about the more recent events involving ex-Yugoslavia.

Christopher Cviic
The Royal Institute of International Affairs – London
January 1996

Acknowledgements

In writing this book I have incurred many obligations, and I am happy to take this opportunity to thank those who have helped in its preparation. I am particularly grateful to Donald Cameron Watt who encouraged and guided my post-graduate research and who first suggested British relations with Yugoslavia to me as a possible subject of research. The Graduate School of the London School of Economics and Political Science and the British Library of Political and Economic Science provided research grants which facilitated my research. The great bulk of the book is based on documents in the Public Record Office at Kew which are quoted by permission of H.M. Stationery Office.

I owe a great debt to friends as well as to some former colleagues, and would mention in particularly Eleanor Breuning, Keith Hamilton and Geoffrey Warner, who read this draft in various stages of completion and whose wise and tactful comments have saved me from a number of errors and wrought many improvements to the text. It goes without saying that they bear no responsibility for the imperfections which remain. I am also indebted to Christopher Cviic and the late Robert Cecil for enthusiastic support of my endeavours, and to Michael Dockrill and Richard Langhorne who encouraged me to produce this work for publication. Thanks are also due to Anthony Grahame, my editor at Sussex Academic Press.

Those who have given their time to talk to me about these events are referred to in the bibliography: I would like to make a collective thank you both for their knowledge and, on occasion, for the hospitality of their homes which made the research a pleasant task. My appreciation to them all. In addition, I have been fortunate enough to have had the benefit over the years of many informal conversations with eye-witnesses and in this regard I would like to thank Ralph Bennett, the late Lord Brimelow, David Floyd, Sir Alexander Glen, Sir Frank Roberts, and Sir Denis Wright. Perhaps my greatest debt in this regard is to Sir William Deakin who not only encouraged my doctoral work and gave me access to unpublished papers, but has remained a valued source of academic wisdom and friendship over many years.

Ann Lane
London, November 1995

Introduction

This book is a history of British policy towards Yugoslavia following the collapse of the Yugoslav state in April 1941, and the reorientation of western policies towards post-war Yugoslavia which ensued upon the latter's expulsion from the Cominform in 1948. The break up of Yugoslavia in 1991 has cast this period in a new perspective: recent events have, in revealing the fragility of South Slav unity, led scholars to reconsider those factors, internal and external, which previously underpinned order in a region fissured ethnically, politically, religiously and geographically. They have also raised questions about the conduct of the great powers in Yugoslavia: why, for instance, had Britain become involved in what was essentially a Balkan civil war in the years 1941–5? How far was her contribution towards Tito's accession to power and later her support of Yugoslav neutrality in cold war Europe a conscious bid for stability in an intrinsically and historically unstable region? Did Yugoslav unity matter to the British?

The short answer to this last question must be yes. A civil war in the Balkans following the Second World War was unthinkable. Moreover, there was a precedent: the lessons of the Spanish civil war, which in the 1930s had divided Europeans both internationally, and within individual states, was, as the British records show, a danger ever present in the minds of officials and their political masters as they sought to grapple with the challenges mounted by the Balkans in this period.

There were other questions too, with which the British felt intimately connected. Chief among these was Greece. Britain had sought to guarantee Greek neutrality in 1939, a guarantee which was little more realistic than that given to Poland but which the British had nonetheless sought to back with military action in 1941. The re-establishment of the pro-British Greek monarchy after the war was an axiom of British policy and Winston Churchill never left his allies in any doubt that it was in British minds immutable. There was a similar concern for post-fascist Italy. Underlying these maxims was the perennial British preoccupation with the European balance of power. With Germany defeated and France critically weakened by the war, it was clear in London that Britain would be vying for domination on the continent with Soviet Russia. Although it took the experiences of 1945–6 for the British to grasp the meaning of Soviet hegemony in her sphere of influence, and longer still to evolve mechanisms for dealing with the challenges this posed, the British were aware from the earliest days of the Anglo-Soviet alliance of its potential significance for international politics.

Britain was still, even in the immediate aftermath of war, determined to maintain her pre-eminence in the Mediterranean. This preoccupation was driven by her interest in the Middle East, and in particular the oil resources under the Persian Gulf, and, still a maritime power at heart, by her need for access to the sea route through the Suez Canal to the Indian Ocean.

British policy in the Balkans during and immediately after the Second World War must be seen both in this context and in that of the related problem of the expansion of Soviet influence. In Britain, the Balkans had been seen since the nineteenth century as a buffer between Russian and British spheres of influence. This approach had been a central pivot of her bolstering of the Ottoman Empire throughout the nineteenth century and its immutability seemed ingrained on the British psyche. The collapse of the Ottoman Empire, followed by that of Austria–Hungary during the First World War had, however, spawned the emergence of smaller independent states whose populations were an uneasy conglomeration of peoples of widely differing political, cultural and religious traditions; the inter-war years had already revealed how difficult it was for these to settle peaceably together in the absence of a unifying imperial power.

During the 1930s, as Yugoslavia lurched from one political crisis to the next, Britain had hesitantly supported the French lead in their attempts to encourage the formation of Balkan alliances designed to discourage revisionism and outside aggression. These policies failed precisely because each of the Balkan states was unshakeably convinced of the righteousness of its territorial claims against the others. Another idea with which the British and French experimented in the inter-war period was that of Balkan Federation or some form of broader South Slav Union embracing Bulgaria. Interestingly, this was an idea that was being separately promoted by the Comintern which perceived the Yugoslav state as an instrument of imperial domination. The notion of federation was based on the idea that unity could be moulded in this region by promoting umbrella cover more effectively than through a system alliances which required the states concerned to accept their boundaries as determined and recognised by the Peace conference which followed the First World War. But the spirit of nationalism, which had been exploited to create these new Balkan states, proved too potent a force for any sort of normalisation of relations between them, or even between subject peoples within them. When war came to the Balkans in 1941, the Balkan peoples were ready to fight – not Germans, or Italians, but each other. In Yugoslavia unspeakable atrocities were committed by elements of some national groupings against the others. Further antagonism was generated by the Axis policy of fuelling Bulgaria's revisionist, and expansionist ambitions at Yugoslav expense. The division of Yugoslavia which followed upon her capitulation on 17 April 1941, the persecutions, the forced population transfers and, indeed, mass genocide, all had a shattering effect on the native peoples. The legacy of the inter-war period, combined with the damage done by the occupation, turned Yugoslavia into a battle ground for rival forces which seized the occasion for a power struggle. It was with this that the Allies, and in particular the British and Russians, steadily became embroiled: two resistance movements were supported, although these were at war with each other; there was also a government-in-exile and a King whose ultimately futile efforts to impose his will on Yugoslav politics became a pathetic side-show to the internecine vengeance being worked out in Yugoslavia itself. It is hardly surprising that it is difficult to trace a consistent line in either British or Soviet policy towards this region during this period.

However, the Second World War also provided an opportunity to recreate Yugoslavia, a fact which was not lost on the various political groupings who now evolved strategies from which they hoped to make political profit. While the Serbs were inclined towards a policy of compromise with the occupiers, which seemed to offer a chance of preserving the Serb state, the other national groups were only too ready to embrace a new form of political organisation.

Tito succeeded in bringing about his political revolution because he understood what the broad majority wanted – stability and protection from traditional enemies. But he also brought communism, and initially this meant allegiance to Moscow and broad conformity with the foreign-policy dictates of the Kremlin.

It was a quirk of fate that the very qualities that enabled Tito to seize power and unite Yugoslavia in 1944–46 were those which also led rapidly to his quarrel with Stalin in 1948 – and subsequently to the successful stabilisation of Yugoslavia as a neutral state in cold war Europe. As a man whose character combined the advantages of independent judgement with the energy derived from personal ambition, Tito's potential both as a unifier of Yugoslavia and protector of his country's right to self-determination was noted by British representatives who came into contact with him during the war. The British were not without hope that Tito's nationalism would triumph over his allegiance to communism and that war-time co-operation with the Partisans could be translated into a working relationship with a Tito-led regime in the post-war period. The paranoia and resulting overbearance which emanated from Moscow in the late 1940s, created an atmosphere in the Soviet camp in which British prognostications could be proven correct. Once Yugoslavia had separated from the Soviet bloc following her expulsion from the Cominform in July 1948, she moved hesitantly towards a position of western-sponsored neutrality: while western economic support assisted the Tito regime to remain in power, thus fulfilling the western objectives of security and stability in the Balkans, Yugoslav neutrality, which marked the dawn of non-alignment in a world already polarised by cold war, demonstrated the viability of a 'third way' between communism and western style capitalism. Tito defined Yugoslavia, and his international role, in these terms and at the same time adapted the communist system to justify both Yugoslavia's own road to socialism, and also her independence of Moscow. He might not have succeeded without western finance: the importance of the cold war framework of international relations for Yugoslav unity, and in particular the value of western economic aid, is indicated by the timing of Yugoslavia's implosion which followed closely upon the collapse of the Warsaw Pact. Paradoxically, through dependence on supra-national communism adapted to Yugoslav needs, combined with the myth-making which grew out of war-time resistance, the Tito era also placed in suspended animation the bitter legacies of the war, and thus postponed the bloodletting which followed Croatian secession from the Yugoslav federation in 1991.

This myth-making – essentially the business of controlling history for political ends – has inevitably had a considerable impact on the historiography of Yugoslavia and also of British policy in that region. Within Yugoslavia, apologists for the regime worked hard to elaborate on the romance of Partisan resistance in order to create a national sense of virtue above ethnic or religious rivalries, while also legitimating the post-war regime. The partisan mythology was also useful in identifying communist Yugoslavia's demonology through the technicality of 'collaboration': it provided a convenient yardstick by which to measure the individual's loyalty to the new socialist republic.[1]

Outside Yugoslavia, these myths were unintentionally strengthened by the memoirs of those who had played a role in the shaping of policy or its execution, and herein lies one of several hazards to historians who seek an objective interpretation of British involvement in Yugoslavia in this period, since the participants were inclined to identify (not unnaturally) with the resistance groups to which they were sent.[2] This had a distorting effect especially since Yugoslav resistance reflected the deep-seated racial, religious and political tensions within Yugoslav society while also acting as a cover for an ideologically motivated civil war. The second (and perhaps more fundamental) difficulty for the historian of British policy towards Yugoslavia in this period is the absence of a complete official record: this is a direct consequence of the clandestine nature of Britain's involvement during the war, both through the Secret Intelligence Service (SIS), which was perhaps not of first importance, and of the Special Operations Executive (SOE). The most intact record is that preserved in the Foreign Office archive and in this fact may be found some explanation of subsequent misunderstandings.[3] Furthermore, the cold war itself encouraged the publication in the west of quasi-scholarly accounts which sought to justify the Tito regime and in particular its virtues over that of the Soviet system, from the western viewpoint.[4] However, there was by the end of the 1970s a growing body of dissenters from this literature and since the death of Tito in 1980 a revisionist thesis has matured, both in Britain and also within Yugoslavia, which seeks to advance a more critical appreciation of Tito's rise to power and the British contribution to this process.[5] Despite its at times polemical nature, this revisionism has stimulated a re-examination of the scholarly debate about the

British role in Yugoslavia, a process which gained further impetus as a consequence of the end of the cold war and the break-up – or breakdown – of the Yugoslav state.

The overarching preoccupation for Britain in this region during the 1940s was the search for stability. There was before the war a tacit acknowledgement that the inter-war solution to the Balkan question was unsatisfactory, unstable and possibly ultimately unworkable. This is seen in the spasmodic discussion of the notion of Balkan federation, viewed by the British as a good thing to be actively encouraged when Hitler threatened the peace of Europe, but later as a hazard to regional stability. There was also a feeling in London, well before the war's end, that Russian domination of the region, while in one sense inevitable, should not, if Britain was to maintain her role as a European Great Power, be accepted without challenge. In pursuing a policy of maintaining a foothold in the Balkans, of keeping the economic door open and of refusing to acquiesce without comment in the establishment of a Soviet security zone in south-east Europe she was, as one senior Foreign Office official wrote in July 1945,[6] at once seeking to protect her own security interests in the Mediterranean, and asserting her right as a Great Power to have a say in the future of the whole of Europe.

1

Britain in Search of an Ally, 1939–1942

When war broke out in Europe 1939, Yugoslavia[1] was in a state of potential revolution. Since King Alexander's dismissal of the Skupstina – the Yugoslav parliament – on 6 January 1929, Yugoslav politics had been characterised by an uneasy dictatorship by the Serbs through the mechanism of the Serbian Karadjeordjevic monarchy supported by the Serbian army. Yugoslavia, a polyglot state formed at the end of the First World War out of Serbia, its war-time ally, Montenegro and the South Slav lands of the former Habsburg monarchy was a conglomeration of nationalities, religions, languages and traditions. To varying degrees, depending on the development of their political consciousness, the non-Serbs were resistant to and resentful of Serbian domination in the name of a Yugoslav state. While the Slovenes welcomed Yugoslavia as a means of protecting their interests from Italian revisionism, and whose geographical location, separate language and institutions in turn gave them some insulation against Serbianisation, the Croats were much less satisfied. Croatia shared not only a border with Serbia, but also had a very similar language and, moreover, a substantial ethnic Serb minority within her frontiers. Furthermore, the Croats had enjoyed relative autonomy within Austria–Hungary after the Ausgleich of 1867, and quickly came to feel particularly aggrieved at their subordination in the post-1919 state to Serb culture.

The strains of the inter-war period created by the multiplicity of traditions, the world economic crisis and the emergence of totalitarian ideologies, imposed stress on the uneasy conglomeration of peoples who were, for want of an alternative encompassed within a common frontier and governed in the name of the three principal races of Serbs, Croats and Slovenes, by the Serbian constitutional monarchy. However, the peoples of Yugoslavia failed in the inter-war period to develop into consocialisation, and increasingly the alternative patterns for the organisation of government and society offered by fascism and communism came to be seen as attractive to the Yugoslav malcontents. The royalist government attempted to resist these forces for change; the Yugoslav state as constituted, suited the Serbs and, lacking a consensus of support, they resorted to traditional methods of coercion and oppression to maintain the status quo. The lack of a broad platform was eventually recognised during the late 1930s when an attempt was made to ameliorate the vocal and persistent grievances of the Croats by giving the Croatian state semi-autonomous status within Yugoslavia. This agreement, which was signed in August 1939, only emphasised the weaknesses inherent in Yugoslavia as a state, and when war came the Croat nation quickly embraced the fascist alternative offered by its ally, Roman Catholic Italy.

Before the war, communism in Yugoslavia had enjoyed some support, particularly in Montenegro and Macedonia, but also to a limited extent in Serbia and Croatia. After the King's assumption of personal dictatorship in 1929, however, the communist party, along with the other opposition parties, had been banned. The Royalist Yugoslav Government had been wary of Bolshevisation from the outset: King Alexander had been a page at the Russian imperial court at St Petersburg, and since the revolution in 1917, Belgrade had provided a refuge for anti-communist émigré Russians. The Yugoslav Government had other reasons to fear the communists in this period: the Comintern's policy of overthrowing imperialism was at this time synonymous with a desire to establish a Balkan Federation, a policy which envisaged the dismemberment of Yugoslavia and her replacement by a federation which would also incorporate her immediate neighbours. In fact the Yugoslav communist party, under the leadership of the Serb, Sima Markovic, resisted the Comintern's line, a resistance which brought it into conflict with Stalin in 1925 and which was then abandoned. Thereafter, the Yugoslav Communist Party in constant co-operation with the 3rd International, and the International Anti-Fascist League, worked steadfastly towards a revision of the peace treaty. Dmiter Vlahov, a Macedonia and one of the leading figures in the struggle for Macedonian autonomy since 1908, published in Vienna from 1924–32 a bi-monthly review called *La Federation Balkanique* which carried articles by leading communists in the Balkans and elsewhere who advocated the establishment of a federated Balkan state, and waged a literary war against the imperialist governments in Albania, Macedonia, Greece, Yugoslavia and Bulgaria. Tito later incorporated Vlahov and many other members of this movement into his organisation and the policy of federation was to resurface at intervals until 1948.[2]

The election of Hitler to the German chancellery, and the resulting threat this posed to the Soviet Union, led quite quickly to a reversal of the Comintern policy towards Yugoslavia, the unity of which came to be promoted after 1934 as a bulwark against German expansionism. The new consensus about the dangers of the international situation was reflected in the signing on 25 June 1940 of the Soviet–Yugoslav agreement by which the signatories established diplomatic relations for the first time.

During the 1930s the Communist party had continued its activities from exile in Vienna and had sent many of its members to fight with the International Brigades in the Spanish Civil War. It was during this period that Josip Broz emerged as a prominent figure in the Yugoslav party and took over as Secretary General in 1939. Broz, known as Tito to the Yugoslavs, and Valter in Moscow, was of Croat peasant extraction from Kumrovec in the Croatian Zagora.[3] Described by contemporaries as somewhat under medium height, quiet in manner with a ready sense of humour, Tito had been conscripted into the Austro-Hungarian army during the First World War, but went over to the Russians during the Galician campaign of 1915. He acquired his first experience of Partisan warfare with the Red Army during the Russian civil war and joined the Communist Party in 1920. Returning to the new Yugoslavia in 1923, he engaged in political work and union leadership, activities which led to his imprisonment in Mitrovica gaol. He resumed his political activities and spent several periods in Moscow. By 1939, he was well regarded by the Comintern leaders, especially by its Secretary General, the Bulgarian Georgi Dimitrov, who maintained communications with the KPJ with the assistance of a team of émigré Yugoslavs headed by Veljko Vlahovic. During the eighteen months following the outbreak of war in Europe, the Soviet legation in Belgrade facilitated the establishment of several secure lines of communication between the KPJ and Moscow, which remained in place after Yugoslavia's collapse in April 1941.[4] When Germany invaded, Tito evaded capture, a fate which befell many Croatian communists. At a clandestine meeting in April, he had gathered together such members of the central committee as remained in Zagreb and spoke of the need to lay the foundations of an entirely new social order for the post-war period, one in which Yugoslav nationalism would form a central plank. In June, in the mountains of Serbia, Tito and his followers began to organise resistance.

Meanwhile, Britain had abandoned (in 1939) her inter-war policy of leaving the French to take the lead in Balkan questions and initiated a fresh attempt to persuade the south-east European countries to bury their disagreements and join together in a Balkan bloc aimed at withstanding German pressure.[5] This was to be based on the Balkan Entente between Rumania, Yugoslavia, Greece and Turkey of 1934 and was designed to give meaning to recent British guarantees to Greece and Rumania, a diplomatic initiative which the British Government had seen fit to make despite the lack of the military wherewithal to enforce it should the need arise. It also had the short-term tactical merit of being a means of discouraging the French from their apparent determination to repeat the First World War Salonika Front to which the British Chiefs of Staff and the Prime Minister, Neville Chamberlain, objected. The rifts between the Balkan states – and within them – made sure that this policy foundered. Just as in the mid-1930s, the Balkan Entente had been rendered ineffective by the revisionist aspirations of its various members against its supposed allies, so in 1939–40, Britain found it impossible to give practical effect to a policy of strengthening the Balkans against German expansionism through fostering a rapprochement between Yugoslavia, Bulgaria and the Turks. The Bulgarians, who determinedly held out for their territorial claims, particularly for the recovery of southern Dobruja from Rumania, were the principal source of difficulty, a policy which was encouraged by Hitler's successes in revising the terms of the peace treaty. Moreover, the Rumanian government, which had some inclination to compromise in order to secure Bulgaria's participation in a Balkan bloc, was nonetheless constrained by fear that territorial concessions to Bulgaria would encourage both Russia and Hungary to press their own claims. Any hopes of a neutral Balkan bloc ended with French capitulation in June 1940, followed as it was by Rumania's loss of large territories to Russia, Hungary and Bulgaria and its denunciation of the Balkan Entente and British guarantee. The alternative, short of invasion, which the British did not want to undertake for fear of upsetting Italian neutrality, was to seek a confederal solution for the Balkans.

Despite British encouragement to remain neutral, the Yugoslav regent, Prince Paul and his government under Cvetkovic finally bowed to the intense pressure placed on it by Germany and signed the Tripartite Pact on 25 March 1941. This action was out of step with the wishes of the Yugoslav people and the following day a bloodless coup was carried out by the military under the leadership of General Dusan Simovic and aided to some extent both by SOE and British air attachés in Belgrade. Prince Paul, was forced to abdicate and in his stead, the twenty-one year old King, Peter II, acceded to his throne.

This act of defiance infuriated Hitler whose policy towards the Balkans had been designed to secure the region prior to opening the invasion of the Soviet Union which he had been planning since the end of 1940. He responded by hastily launching an invasion of Yugoslavia in an operation aptly codenamed 'Punishment'.

While the King, his government and some of the armed forces fled, some members of the former Royal Army remained behind and took cover in the mountain villages. By 17 April 1941, Yugoslavia was overrun and forced to capitulate.

Hitler was able to exploit the fissures within the Yugoslav state for his own advantage, and in this he was assisted by Italian sponsorship of the Croatian fascist Ante Pavelic, as well as by Serb-Croat antagonisms. When Germany dismembered Yugoslavia she did so in a manner calculated to exacerbate existing tensions: Germany occupied the northern two-thirds of Slovenia and most of Serbia, giving her control of essential rail communications through the Balkans; Milan Nedic, the former Yugoslav Chief of Staff, was placed at the head of the quisling Serbian Government, but his position was nominal; Italy took possession of the southern third of Slovenia, the Dalmatian Littoral, a small part of Bosnia and the whole of Montenegro; she also acquired part of Kosovo-Metohija and the Sandjak of Novi-Pazar; a large part of Macedonia, and some of southern Serbia was annexed by Bulgaria while the remainder of Macedonia was awarded to greater Albania under Italian rule; Hungary acquired the territory to the west of the Danube; the remainder became the Independent State of Croatia under Pavelic.

There were some in Germany who argued that this division of Yugoslavia effectively weakened their hold on the region and facilitated the resistance. This may be so, but it was a situation

Map 1 The dismemberment of Yugoslavia by the Axis after Yugoslavia's capitulation in April 1941

in which a policy of *divide et impera* could arguably operate as effectively as a centralised police state. In practice this was what the Germans chose to do, playing on the perception held by many Yugoslavs that it was not the Germans, the Italians or even the Bulgarians who were their greatest enemy, but other Yugoslavs. The legacy of this period has endured to this day.

During 1939 and 1940, British intelligence agencies had established a network of contacts which were intended to prevent Yugoslav alignment with the Axis, but were also meant to form the foundation of Yugoslav resistance in the event of occupation. Yugoslavia would not be unimportant to either side given the rail communications from central Europe to Greece and the eastern Mediterranean which ran through Yugoslav river valleys. These contacts were predominantly Serb, and although they did not survive the German onslaught, there was, throughout the war in London a pro-Serb lobby in the secret service community which had close connections with the Yugoslav royal family and government, and which proved an additional stumbling block in the formation of policy towards the Yugoslav resistance.

Rivalry between SIS and SOE added to the complications in policy-making towards Yugoslav resistance.[6] This was compounded further by professional jealousies within SOE itself, particularly between SOE's London headquarters at Baker Street and its Cairo office, which was largely responsible under the supervision of the Middle East Defence Committee, for developing British contacts with Balkan resistance. SOE was placed under the wing of the War Office, emphasising its operational rather than political purposes. However, as Yugoslav resistance began to emerge as a political as well as military factor in British planning, so Foreign Office involvement increased. Intervention by the senior Deputy Under Secretary, Orme Sargent, was frequent from August 1942 onwards, and by the Permanent Under Secretary, Alexander Cadogan, less so, except where Yugoslav affairs impinged directly on issues affecting the Grand Alliance. More significant, though, was the personal involvement after 1942 of the Prime Minister, Winston Churchill, for whom the Balkan resistance movements combined two elements with which he had, over a long lifetime, been particularly fascinated: secret warfare and intelligence gathering.

First indications of active resistance in Yugoslavia reached Britain through clandestine contacts in August 1941. In the interim, since the collapse of Yugoslavia, Britain had herself become embroiled in the war on the northern Mediterranean shores, diverting troops from the campaign in North Africa to Greece, in a desperate attempt to halt the German advance. This campaign had ended in an ignominious and bloody retreat followed by withdrawal to Crete from whence the British forces were evacuated from Suvla Bay on 1 June. The general situation was desperate for Britain: Germany was in occupation of the European continent and since the launch of Barbarossa, her armies were advancing with ruthless efficiency across the Soviet Union. The Battle of the Atlantic – the struggle to maintain the British lifeline against the U-boat offensive – was a long way from turning decisively in Britain's favour. The possibility of war in the Far East was growing ever more likely and as yet the Americans remained firmly neutral. In London, the British government was host to a clutch of European governments and monarchs who had escaped into exile; to these were now added, at the British headquarters in Cairo, those of Yugoslavia and Greece. In the summer of 1941, German expansionism stood between Britain and her only ally still engaged in fighting, the Soviet Union, and it was far from clear Germany would meet there her defeat. News of resistance in the Balkans, however minor, was a glimmer of light in Europe which had fallen to darkness, and the British wasted little time in moving to investigate.

The first SOE mission sent to Yugoslavia, which was dropped on 6 September 1941, was composed of an SOE officer, Colonel D. T. 'Bill' Hudson, who had spent the inter-war years as a mining engineer in Yugoslavia and had extensive knowledge of the Serbo-Croat language and geography but little experience of politics. He was accompanied by two Yugoslav Air Force officers, Majors Ostojic and Lalatovic. The brief for Operation Bullseye was to make contact with all sources of resistance.[7] From the outset, however, there were 'Balkan problems' for his Yugoslav companions had separate, secret instructions from the Yugoslav Government at that time exiled in Cairo. The persistence of clandestine links between the Cetnik leader, Gervai Mihailovic and émigré Yugoslavs in Britain and the United States was to be a persistent hazard for the British in formulating policy towards the resistance.

Already, by the autumn of 1941, two distinct resistance movements had emerged. In Ravna Gora in the Serbian mountains, Draza Mihailovic, a Serbian army officer, with a chequered history, had organised a Serbian movement which adopted the name 'Cetniks' (cetnici) meaning armed bands which evoked the traditions of the irregulars who had fought for the Serb cause against the Turks in Macedonia during the nineteenth century and later in the Balkan Wars. Mihailovic had already shown himself to be an ambitious officer, frequently in opposition to his superiors. He had had close links with Bulgarian revolutionaries, particularly during his posting in Prague as military attaché; later he was transferred to Slovenia where he had taken a hostile attitude towards the Serb–Croat agreement of 1939 and acted as the exponent of pan Serb nationalism.[8] Mihailovic and the Cetniks were fighting for Serb domination of the region, probably through the monarchy, but possibly in the form of a military dictatorship. The Yugoslav army with its Serb officer corps had been the monarchy's principal source of power in the pre-war regime and their outlook was at once anti-communist and anti-Soviet, but at the same time, pan-Slav.

The Partisan bands which emerged under communist leadership in June 1941, were drawn from a much wider cross-section, particularly from among the ranks of disaffected peasantry and intellectuals, and were fighting for a Yugoslavia which would have a rather different political complexion. First and foremost, they were antithetical to the restoration of Serbian domination and sought to create a new federated republic. Their leader, Josip Broz Tito, lately the secretary general of the Yugoslav communist party, was himself to admit his intention to establish a communist regime in Yugoslavia to one British liaison officer in 1943.[9] Indeed, in the autumn of 1941, Tito attempted to proclaim a Soviet-style republic in western Serbia, but this failed to ignite the broader Yugoslav revolution for which he hoped, and resulted in the communists' expulsion from Serbia by the Germans. From the end of 1941, the Partisans, many of whose leaders had served in the International Brigades in the Spanish Civil War, (though not as has been popularly believed, Tito himself), began to put these experiences to effective use in mounting a guerrilla war whose purpose was continual harassment of the enemy. Theirs was truly a guerrilla war and it provoked savage German reprisals on the civilian population. By contrast, the Serbian guerrilla tactics adopted by the remnants of the Yugoslav Army were largely based on the 'Cetnik' tradition of resistance to Ottoman domination in which there was a closed season during the winter months when the guerrillas fraternised with the occupiers. Of course such habits encouraged collaboration, and this pattern was now to be repeated with far-reaching repercussions. Mihailovic's strategy was to lie low until an Allied landing provided the occasion and assistance for a mass rising. Until then, his objective remained that of avoiding drawing down on the Serb population reprisals such as Partisan activity had occasioned. In keeping with this policy, followers of Mihailovic were inclined to conceal their identity by enlisting in the Serb quisling forces of Milan Nedic and those of Dimitrije Ljotic, a notorious Fascist. Mihailovic maintained that his ruse was justified since such followers were pledged to come over to him when so-ordered with arms, equipment and even men. Added to this was Mihailovic's profound anti-communism, a factor that blinded him to any possibility of co-operation with the Partisan movement owing to its communist leadership.[10]

Of course this political conflict grated on and fuelled the ethnic conflict which had simmered during the inter-war years, and it gave focus and definition to the hatreds which had developed between the Serbs on the one hand and the Croats and Bosnian Muslims on the other. Indeed, Hudson's experiences in Yugoslavia during the autumn of 1941 encapsulated the difficulties this was to present to the British as they attempted to utilise Yugoslav resistance for Allied gain. Far from being warmly greeted as an emissary from an ally, Hudson was regarded by both the Partisans and Cetniks with suspicion and disdain. Deeply rooted in the minds of both leaderships was a fear that Britain would, through a campaign in the Balkans, seek to impose her will on the post-war settlement. Both sides had reason to resist such an outcome.

In strategic terms, which were Britain's primary concern in 1941, it was Mihailovic's policy that found favour with SOE and the Chiefs of Staff. Consequently, when the Russians, seeking any hope of relief from the heavy pressure the German army was exerting on their western flank, suggested in mid-October 1941 joint Russo–British–Yugoslav action in support of the partisan rising, the British Chiefs of Staff responded firmly that in their view such a rising was premature.[11] They wished, rather, to encourage all sources of resistance so as to embarrass the Axis and to discourage any reduction in the garrison. At the same time, they wanted the resistance movement to remain underground and avoid large-scale risings which might result in severe retaliation and possible destruction of the movement. How these seemingly mutually exclusive objectives were to be reconciled is not explained.[12]

During the autumn of 1941, it is likely that Tito would have accepted some form of compromise with the Cetniks; indeed, an agreement for joint action against the Germans was reached. However, Mihailovic's opposition to Tito's policy of liberating the country led to his refusal to agree to any form of joint command. Moreover, Mihailovic was already aware, as a result of a telegram from London despatched clandestinely from the London émigrés, that the British intended to send him supplies. He was convinced that it was his movement alone which was known outside Yugoslavia and he wanted this situation to continue. Although Mihailovic and Tito met again at Cacak between 27 and 28 November following an outbreak of fighting between the two movements, and produced a further agreement, this proved still-born.[13] Hudson's subsequent recommendations to London that air drops be suspended following the breach of the truce served only to damage his position with Mihailovic further and he found himself excommunicated until late March 1942 when their relationship was only superficially patched up.[14] On 3 December, Mihailovic made it clear that it was the Yugoslav civil war which interested him and instructed his followers to come out against the Partisans. This episode indicates that Mihailovic had a narrow and egocentric vision of the world which must be ascribed to the absence of any other than Balkan experience. This failure, at so early a stage, to recognise the political importance of cultivating the British through their intermediary was ill-judged. Tito, whose experience was wider and view of the world broader, was not to make the same mistake.[15]

Other factors bedevilled British attempts to implement a policy towards Yugoslav resistance. In addition to the secret Cetnik-émigré communications links mentioned earlier, British officials were also dimly aware of another source of clandestine interference which they were powerless to control. The Russians, whose attitude towards Yugoslav resistance might best be characterised as enigmatic, seem without doubt to have maintained some links with the Partisans from the outset, Russian denials of which were consistently regarded by the Foreign Office as disingenuous. This scepticism gained credence with the realisation in London in 1942 that the pro-Partisan Radio Free Yugoslavia was broadcasting its propaganda from the area of Kuibyshev, at that stage serving as the war-time capital of the Soviet Union.[16] In fact, as early as 1940, the Comintern had established a radio transmitter in Zagreb which continued to work throughout the war and was the only continuous outlet for Comintern liaison. Its position in Croatia was to confer on Tito additional influence.[17] Then, at the end of May 1940, as the Germans were turning the Red Army's attempted offensive at Kharkov into a rout, the Soviet Communist Party Central Committee established a 'Central Staff of the Partisan movements' as a co-ordinating body for East European resistance. The model they acclaimed was that of the Yugoslav partisan movement which hitherto the Comintern had been censuring for adventurism.[18]

It is a tragedy that policy, as pursued in London, aggravated the already considerable difficulties. The British were primarily concerned in 1941 that Mihailovic, as an officer in the Yugoslav Army, should be the recognised leader of the resistance. This was a tidy solution which officials in London, hard pressed with weightier and more immediate problems, were content to accept. Consequently, on receiving Hudson's reports in mid-November of Cetnik-Partisan fighting, the Russians were asked to use their influence with the 'communists' to urge them to join forces with Mihailovic unreservedly. Their realism in accepting Moscow's link with the Partisans was not, unfortunately, matched by similar understanding of the realities of the situation within Yugoslavia. When London received a message from Mihailovic vaguely reporting that the fighting had been settled, it was accepted by the Prime Minister, the Foreign Office and SOE without question.[19] Hugh Dalton, then in charge of SOE, was one notable enthusiast for Mihailovic who rejoiced that 'Juggery' had come to the 'top of the bill in view of the continuance of the revolt'. Foreign Secretary Eden somewhat ambitiously hoped that British support for Yugoslav resistance might convince the Russians that 'we are doing everything possible to create the second front in the Balkans which they desire'.[20] However, the direct, and damaging consequence of this was that Mihailovic was now encouraged in his belief that his importance for the Allies was somehow immutable. While King Peter gave him official recognition by creating him Minister of War in the new Government-in-Exile formed under Puric in January 1942, the BBC, under the direction of the Political Warfare Executive, (and despite the latter's own reservations) began to broadcast propaganda which in effect established Mihailovic as the hero of European resistance.[21]

2

Expedients of War: Tito or Mihailovic?

The first attempt to address the question of the comparative advantages of the two resistance movements from a British point of view occurred in early August 1942. During 1942, several further missions had been infiltrated into Yugoslavia, making contact with both groups, but the picture had merely become more confusing. The occasion for this reopening of the debate was created not by the Yugoslavs, but by the Russians, who presented in August the Yugoslav Government-in-Exile with a memorandum containing specific allegations against Mihailovic of inactivity and collaboration.[1] Since that autumn of 1941, the Russians had ignored Partisan claims of Cetnik collaboration and persisted with their efforts to negotiate a friendship treaty with the Yugoslav Government-in-Exile. However, when the negotiations broke down in July 1942, the Soviet Union began to allow some distance to build up in its relations with the émigré politicians and its agents in Yugoslavia, and began publicising their evidence of collaboration. The Partisans were praised with increasing use of the superlative, although Tito was not mentioned by name: for the time being the Russians continued to tell King Peter's representative, Gavrilovic, that they would send a mission to Mihailovic and supply arms, both of which were offers not extended to Tito.[2]

Already the British were aware that Mihailovic's strategy was not without compromise. Hudson's reports, in so far as these had reached London, had given evidence of this. The significance for British policy of this factor and of the Russian memorandum was discussed at a meeting at the Foreign Office on 8 August, chaired by Orme Sargent, then Deputy Under Secretary, and attended by representatives both of SOE and SIS. Following this Sargent argued on paper that although from the military perspective, the Partisans' policy was more beneficial to British interests, in the long term, and implicitly from the political perspective, Britain would be better served by continuing her existing policy of striving for unity under Mihailovic. However, the process of redefining British policy had begun and Hudson's response to SOE's request for his views on the Soviet allegations against Mihailovic was instrumental.[3] Hudson explained that Mihailovic was refusing to carry out further guerrilla activity against either the Germans or the Italians until a new front was opened in the Balkans. Moreover, he considered that a state of civil war existed between the two resistance movements and argued that this was so irreconcilable that the only solution was the arrangement of a division of spheres of activity while leaving Mihailovic as the recognised national leader. This idea, perhaps the only solution to the in-fighting, was inimical to British hopes of a unified post-war Yugoslavia since it would have strengthened the existing political separation of Serbia from the rest of the country. However, it was to be a recurring theme in Hudson's telegrams and those of his successors.[4]

Nevertheless, the Foreign Office had its own doubts about Mihailovic as a trustworthy ally, even for the long-term objectives as stated on 8 August: one official in Southern Department minuted that Mihailovic might eventually reach an open breach with his government 'whom he no doubt regards with small respect as having departed into distant security while he continues the fight in Yugoslavia. He clearly desires to free the country, but not in order to make it a safe place for Partisans and a refugee government.' The possibility that Mihailovic might seek to establish a military dictatorship had already occurred and was being sustained through evidence arriving from the field: Hudson's telegram to SOE on 22 October observed that the 'peasants everywhere [are] deeply conscious of having been let down by their former leader. Corruption and injustice of past years as the reasons for their present humiliation is keynote in appeal by both communists and D.M. while country looks forward to clean sweep after the war.'[5]

Another scenario, that of the revival of the notion of Serb–Bulgar accommodation under Mihailovic's leadership, also gave the Foreign Office cause for disquiet: 'Mihailovic's ideals are those of a Serb general', minuted Southern Department in October: 'Having been military attaché in Sofia, he has acquired a taste for Bulgarians and appears to favour a Serb–Bulgar understanding. It may not be long before his ideas crystallise into the conception of South Slav Federation. This conception is entirely irreconcilable with the idea of a Balkan Federation in which Croatia and Slovenia would have their places and it is moreover a conception which would best suit the Russian long-term ambitions in the Balkans.'[6] British policy was directed at the task of ensuring that the Balkans be neutralised and not, through disorder and civil strife, turned into a power vacuum into which Soviet Russia might expand. A Serb–Bulgarian alliance would threaten not only the chances of reunifying Yugoslavia, but also call into question the position of Macedonia which in turn could destabilise Greece. Although Mihailovic's worth seemed now to be at least questionable, the Partisans also remained an uncertain quantity. Their communist affiliations and links with the Russians were worrying, as was Russian disingenuity about them. The scenario carried the seeds not only of political instability in the shape of communist revolution, but also a divison in the alliance. Shrewdly, perhaps, Stalin remained content for the British to take the lead in Allied policy towards Yugoslav resistance. He may have been concerned to avoid any act which might encourage the British to think more constructively about leaving the Russians to fight the Germans alone – however, his bureaucratic mind with its preoccupation with hierarchy, was probably concerned not to give too much encouragement to the Yugoslav communists lest they become too bumptious. However, the hazards of attempting a compromise were also all too apparent: 'we all recognise,' wrote Douglas Howard, then head of Southern Department, 'that we may be faced with the awkward dilemma – Mihailovic or Partisans – but it would seem to me futile and fatal to try to back both horses at once!'[7] In the event, however, this is precisely what the Foreign Office attempted to do.

The strategic decisions taken during the British and American summit meeting held at Casablanca in January 1943 heightened the importance of Yugoslav resistance in Allied planning. A Combined Chiefs of Staff (CCS) background paper on 'American-British Strategy in 1943' recommended increased assistance to the insurgents in Yugoslavia and sabotage in Greece, since in both countries the garrisons were largely Italian. The planners believed that disorder in the Balkans would follow the collapse of Italy and that Germany would be unable to garrison both.[8] Before returning to London, Churchill travelled to Adana to probe the possibility of Turkey entering the war on the Allied side. Churchill was to some extent preoccupied with the possibility of a Balkan front which was driven partly by his fear of a recreation of the First World War stalemate on the western front, against which the Mediterranean seemed to offer a tempting alternative. The beginning of 1943 had brought allied military successes in North Africa and at Stalingrad, and consequently pressure was mounting from both the Americans and Russians for an early start on the reconquest of north-west Europe. Stalin had pointedly avoided any mention of the western Allies in his 'Order for the Day' for the Red Army's anniversary on 23 February, presenting the war as a Russian–German conflict. Furthermore, he warned Churchill several weeks later of the danger of further delaying the opening of the second front in Europe.[9] There was also undoubtedly a sense in which the Prime Minister's predisposition to an interest in intelligence and irregular warfare gave a certain predictability to his interest in the struggle in the Balkans. At the end of January he made the first of his personal interventions in policy making towards Yugoslav resistance.

En route to Adana, Churchill stopped off in Cairo and while there he sent for Bill Deakin, a history don from Wadham College, Oxford who had assisted him during the writing of his life of Marlborough in the 1930s and, who since November 1942, had been serving in the Yugoslav section of SOE Cairo. This visit was intended to be social rather than official but proved to be of some significance. The Prime Minister wanted a view on the Yugoslav front and was advised by Deakin to send for the Chief of Staff at SOE Cairo, Brigadier C. M. Keble. Keble, whom one contemporary mischievously described as 'a small and rather bouncy man of most conservative opinions' was by accident rather than design especially well informed on the situation in the Balkans. His source was Ultra intelligence to which he had access as a consequence of his previous post at GHQ Middle East (MI 14, Germany Army). Following his transfer, no one in Whitehall had remembered to strike his name from the access list and the official historian of SOE, M. R. D. Foot, records that such was the forcefulness of his personality that probably no one in Cairo dared.[10] The point is important. Keble met Churchill on 30 January and later had delivered to him via a member of his private office a note of the same day, but founded on a paper which was due to go to the Commander-in-Chief Middle East for consideration.

This paper, written by Keble but based on the result of the combined efforts of Bill Deakin and Basil Davidson, was founded on the latest reports from SOE officers at Mihailovic's headquarters and, as a consequence of Keble's access to Ultra, on Cairo's decrypts of German medium-grade and low-grade hand cyphers, chiefly those used by the Abwehr and the police.[11] While Keble argued that aid to Mihailovic was as necessary as ever to strengthen and extend the resistance in the vital strategic area of Balkan communications, it contended that consideration should also be given to the possibility of strengthening resistance in areas outside Serbia, thereby implying that British officers should also be attached to Partisan headquarters. But the justification for this was political as well as military: if Britain did not act, so the paper argued, then the Russians or Americans would take a practical interest and effectively weaken Britain's position. More immediately perhaps, the question of Russian involvement on the Partisan side raised the possibility of two members of the United Nations backing mutually antagonist groups with obvious consequences, not just for Yugoslavia, but for Allied co-operation. The British were already aware of the growing strength of their two major allies, now that the fortunes in the war were beginning to turn in the Alliance's favour. At a political level, British policy makers were concerned that Britain's world role would be protected, as far as possible, and the determination to provide an active leading role in the Balkans was closely related by early 1943 to this policy.

The second issue raised in Keble's paper was that of collaboration. Ultra decrypts indicated that Cetnik links with the Italians could now be accepted as fact, but as yet there was no suggestion of any Cetnik–German contact. Churchill asked the Government Code and Cypher School (GC&CS) at Bletchley for a detailed report and this inclined him to agree with Keble; his agreement with the report's recommendations in general terms was minuted on his return to London; the Foreign Office, spurred by the recent recognition of the Partisans by the Russians, endorsed the report within a week.[12]

On Christmas Day 1942, Hudson had been joined at Mihailovic's headquarters by a more senior officer, Colonel S. W. 'Bill' Bailey. Bailey was an SIS officer who had been in Istanbul on the outbreak of war from where he had been able to establish early links with the Yugoslav resistance. To an extent, Hudson had come in for increasing criticism during the previous autumn, partly because his reports had placed some emphasis on Cetnik collaboration with the Italians which had inclined the SOE Cairo chief, Lord Glenconner, to inform London on 8 Dec. that contact between Mihailovic and Djutic was 'regular' and 'intimate': 'This does not mean,' Hudson, observed, 'that Mihailovic is actually negotiating with the Italians but simply that his lines are well laid.'[13] This was politically unwelcome in the pro-Mihailovic atmosphere of SOE London, and steps were taken not unsuccessfully to discredit Hudson as a witness.

However, far from undermining Hudson's reports, as some in London may have hoped, Bailey had within a month arrived at much the same conclusions which he set forth in his own report which reached the Foreign Office on 3 February.[14] He was convinced that Mihailovic and the Partisans could not be reconciled so long as they were simultaneously in occupation of territory in which both considered themselves vitally interested, since they were 'direct competitors for the leadership of the people and Mihailovic, for his part, is determined to eliminate all rivals before attacking the armies of occupation'. According to Bailey, Mihailovic was unshakeably convinced that guerrilla elements in Croatia not under his command were one hundred per cent Communist and under complete Soviet control: 'For this reason,' he explained, 'he is set on their extermination.' He added that it would help if SOE could provide him with information suggesting that the guerrillas in Croatia were not exclusively Communist and that it would be necessary to establish capable British observers with the Vojvoda, Bircanin and the Croatian guerrillas. This, of course, tied in with the recommendations of Keble's memorandum of 30 January. Bailey's solution was to restate Hudson's notion of dividing the country into spheres of activity, but he was not sanguine about the chances of success and warned London that, 'Mihailovic would even risk losing British support in order to pursue his policy of exterminating communists in Serbia'. Bailey's ensuing reports were even more declaratory: evoking the Spanish precedent he ventured that unless Anglo-Russian plans were prepared in advance with both resistance movements on an equal footing, and implemented without delay, Soviet forces would enter Yugoslavia on the communists' side, facing Britain with the burden of a decision as to whether or not she should intervene on behalf of the King. He need hardly have added that should anarchy be allowed to take hold in Yugoslavia it would spread rapidly throughout the Balkans and Hungary.[15]

During January, the Germans had launched a fresh offensive, Operation Weiss, in Banija and Kordun in the mountains of Bosnia, which was designed to eradicate Tito's forces: the Germans sought to contain the guerrilla war not simply in order to maintain their dominance of an area which was a source of vital raw materials, but also against the day when the Allies might attempt a landing in the region. This is not to undervalue, however, the importance the German High Command attached to Mihailovic as a potential source of trouble and until the Italian surrender in September 1943, it is clear that Berlin perceived the greater threat as coming from the Cetniks, partly because of the appeal of the Cetnik movement in Serbia, and also as a result of Mihailovic's relationship with the Italians in Croatia and the dangers this held for Axis unity in the Balkans. What concerned the Germans most, however, was the possibility of a reconciliation between the Cetniks and the communist leaders which was perhaps the only circumstance in which the Yugoslav resistance could provide a significant challenge to the German occupation. While their efforts, through military operations, to exacerbate Cetnik–Partisan conflict were successful in heightening the division there was never any realistic possibility of the two factions uniting: they would rather destroy each other than bury their differences for the common cause.[16] It is a measure of the discouragement Bailey already felt that he concluded in late February that Britain's best hope lay in the destruction of the Partisans in the present German offensive.

The question of damping down the Yugoslav civil war was discussed at length within the Foreign Office during February and March, but Bailey's proposal of spheres of activity, although logical, was not seen in London as a realistic option but rather one which might in fact intensify the struggle. As Douglas Howard, then head of the Foreign Office's Southern Department, observed, 'Mihailovic is becoming increasingly Pan-Serb, anti-Croat and anti-Partisan and is willing to co-operate with anyone except the Germans in order to crush Tito.' He continued that while the need for a united Yugoslavia was pressing, 'it might also be very embarrassing for us to face a hostile Partisan force should we decide to carry out operations on the Dalmatian coast or in Croatia'. In summing up, Howard now expatiated the policy of attempted compromise to which the Foreign Office in general and Anthony Eden in particular were to cling for the following twelve months. Britain, he wrote, could not afford to be on bad terms with either side; being on merely good terms with both would be an improvement on the present situation; it was therefore time to adopt a policy of supporting both sides. This proposal was endorsed by Orme Sargent who added a note urging early support of the Partisans, while continuing the present scale of help for Mihailovic.[17]

The Foreign Office now discussed ways and means of contacting the Partisans with SOE and SIS on 18 February.[18] SOE and the Foreign Office were at loggerheads, as the Foreign Office summary reveals: 'quite naturally SOE had put all their money on Mihailovic. That policy coincided with our own up to a point. But when it came to our suggesting getting in touch with the Partisans they raised endless difficulties, due of course to their displeasure at the prospect of doing anything to upset Mihailovic or make Bailey's position more difficult than it already was'.[19] Grudgingly, SOE appeared to accept the new Foreign Office policy of contacting the Partisans, but simultaneously attempted to throw a spanner in the works by raising logistical problems – specifically the shortage of transport planes – as a further reason for taking no action.[20] Indeed, revisionist accounts of the development of British policy towards Yugoslavia often overlook the fact that despite the enthusiasm of Keble's staff in Cairo for this new adventure, Cairo too was sceptical about the Partisans' worth: in early March Glenconner had sent a cautionary telegram to London warning that although the Partisan's immediate aim was to rid the country of the Axis, their principal object in so doing was to establish a Yugoslav Socialist Republic: 'This is the explanation of their impetuous policy, based on belief in early Russian victory . . . It is unlikely that they can be deterred from this fanatical course and these are tactics which do not suit us.'[21] The Partisans, once their power had increased, would be difficult to control, particularly as they would be likely to call on Soviet solidarity, and they were not, in any case, well supported in Serbia. The Chiefs of Staff were of the same opinion: at their meeting on 4 March they concluded that 'on balance, taking the long view', the better military alternative was to continue to back Mihailovic: 'he would provide some organisation and control, whereas under the Partisans, chaos would probably ensue when the Axis forces were defeated'.[22] During the next three months, their perception was to change dramatically, which was due partly to the accumulation of evidence from Yugoslavia itself, and partly to developments in Allied strategic planning.

In fact there seems to have been a growing rift between SOE Cairo and its Baker Street headquarters. The Foreign Office convened a further meeting on 21 April, this time to discuss what with hindsight seems a particularly important series of telegrams from Hudson concerning his experiences in Yugoslavia since 1941. These telegrams, often neglected, had been transmitted to London at intervals during the early part of 1943 and the reason why they were concealed from the Foreign Office until the second week of April is unclear.[23] It is perhaps the case that the less than favourable account of Cetnik activities and qualified pro-Partisan bias might provide at least some explanation of Baker Street's coyness. In fact, Glenconner had mentioned their existence in a telegram to London at the end of February, reflecting on the point made therein that Britain's inability to send material support might lead Mihailovic to feel that there was no alternative to collaboration with the Italians.[24] Briefly, Hudson concluded that the communists and not Mihailovic had united the Serbs and that 'Mihailovic's job is to change this unity against the communists to unity against the Axis. Mihailovic and Co have done precisely nothing themselves in their line in Italian-occupied territory'. Hudson described the Cetnik leader as 'merely a mouthpiece chosen by the British', completely influenced by conservatives who, as a result of the BBC's supportive propaganda, had not been made to decide between Mihailovic and Nedic. It was the very threat of communist ascendancy over the peasants which Hudson felt should now force 'the conservatives to split into traitors who co-operate with Nedic and patriots who do not'.[25]

Consideration of these telegrams coincided with a demand from the Chiefs of Staff for the tuning up of guerrilla warfare in the Balkans, which was presumably connected with decisions on wider strategy and in particular, the planned invasion of Sicily to be launched from North Africa in July. Indeed, the Foreign Office summary of the meeting on 21 April reveals that Charles Hambro now went so far as to hint that if Mihailovic did not change his ways SOE would be prepared to switch their support to some other resistance group. 'This,' Howard minuted, 'was an innovation, since SOE had never previously deviated one inch from their blind support of Mihailovic.'[26] But Mihailovic had done little to help his cause: on 28 February he had made a speech in which he stated his chief enemies to be the Partisans, the Ustase and the Moslems, and that the Italians remained his sole means of support. At SOE's recommendation Mihailovic was sent instructions on 9 May via the Yugoslav Government, which stated that continued British support depended on a cessation of collaboration with the Italians, and making no contact with Nedic, while attempting to co-operate with other guerrillas against whom all operations should be suspended, except in self-defence.[27]

When deciding to contact the Partisans in mid-February, the Foreign Office had also recommended that one further attempt should be made to secure Moscow's assistance in uniting the resistance. This only drew from the Russians renewed denials of contact with the Partisans accompanied by the increasingly familiar mimicking of the American chant that Cetnik–Partisan conflict was a matter of internal Yugoslav affairs. The Russians were to transgress this edict before the year's end. But SOE contacts in Moscow indicated that the Russians were perplexed by the British determination to maintain links with Mihailovic. Indeed, the British Ambassador in Moscow, Sir Archibald Clark Kerr, always among the first to think positively about Anglo-Soviet relations, now echoed Bailey in wondering if the British were not being unduly scared by the 'Bolshevik Bogey' who 'as shown by accumulating evidence are likely to become the group that is going to build up the future of their country. In short are we not perhaps boosting another General Franco against the people.'[28]

The role of the Balkan theatre in Allied strategy was raised again at the Washington conference (Trident) in mid-May as part of the strategic debate about the best way to exploit the collapse of Italy. A series of British planning papers, the conclusions of which were endorsed by the Combined Chiefs of Staff, proposed limited action at Durazzo and the Dodecanese, to be followed up if the Germans started to withdraw from the Balkans, to reinforce the Italian front, and also in the event that Turkey entered the war. Churchill's imagination had been caught by the possibility of seizing a foothold on the Eastern Adriatic and on 2 April he minuted to the Chief of Staff, General Sir Hastings Ismay, 'It must be considered a most important objective to get a footing on the Dalmatian coast, so that we can forward the insurgents of Albania and Yugoslavia by weapons and possibly commandos.' But he was not wholly out of sympathy with Mihailovic's policy and recorded for posterity his belief that 'in spite of his present foxy attitude, Mihailovic will throw his whole weight against the Italians the moment we are able to give any effective help. Evidently great possibilities are open in this theatre.'[29] In the event, the decisions taken at Washington laid to rest any notion of a Balkan front. Despite the fact that Roosevelt was prepared to acknowledge the value of breaking German communication lines in the Balkans, he was concerned about the drain on Allied resources of any further Mediterranean diversion and mindful of the pressure now being exerted by the American Joint Chiefs to agree an invasion of north-west Europe or switch American priority to the Pacific theatre.[30] Furthermore, from a military standpoint, Yugoslav resistance was no longer a matter of seeking an ally that could co-operate with Britain in action, only in aiding the most effective disrupters of Italo-German lines.

Following the decision of 18 February, three SOE missions were sent to the Partisans briefed to make clear that British policy was to support all those in Yugoslavia prepared to take arms against the Axis.[31] The most important of these was dropped into Yugoslavia on the night of 26/27 May led by Bill Stuart (an intelligence officer) and Bill Deakin and codenamed 'Typical'. The Germans had launched a fresh offensive against the Cetniks and in their efforts to annihilate them had shrewdly driven them up against the Partisans, forcing the latter to break through Cetnik lines in order to escape.[32] The British officers found themselves plunged immediately into fierce fighting and their initial reports gave substance to the existing impression that the Partisans had real worth as a fighting force.[33]

Little time was wasted by SOE Cairo in communicating the conclusions drawn from these reports to the Prime Minister's office in London. In early June, the British Minister at Cairo, Richard Casey, weighed into the debate, advancing the view that the Partisans represented 'the most formidable anti-Axis element in Yugoslavia' and that 'resistance to the Axis must be the paramount consideration': the arrival of his telegrams in London now provoked something of a crisis.[34] The Middle East Defence Committee (MEDC), which had overall responsibility for co-ordination of intelligence and military planning in this theatre, was of the opinion that, following recent German activity, Mihailovic was a spent force, even in Serbia. Bailey was now informed by SOE Cairo that unless Mihailovic broke with the Axis and withdrew to Serbia, British aid would cease.[35] This action, as is clear, was well ahead of the cautious position which had been adopted in Whitehall, and Sargent recorded his view in a letter to Churchill's intelligence liaison officer, Desmond Morton, that the current situation papers emerging from Cairo appeared from the Foreign Office perspective, to be based on factual errors.[36]

The military machine had now taken over and was at this point the deciding force in policy towards the resistance. The Chiefs of Staff, in a paper presented at a meeting on 17 June, argued that insufficient weight was being given by the Foreign Office to the Partisans as a fighting force and that 'most secret sources' showed that the Cetniks were 'hopelessly compromised in their relations with the Axis in Hercegovina and Montenegro'. With the exclusion of Serbia, the Partisans were considered 'the most formidable anti-Axis element and deserve the strongest support SOE are able to give them'.[37] The Foreign Office and SOE London, alarmed by the political implications of such a policy, were now united by their determination to place a brake on the military, and sent a joint appreciation to the Cabinet Office on 21 June which demanded continuing support for Mihailovic, suspension of the threat of abandonment communicated to Mihailovic via Bailey, and argued that supplies to the Partisans should be of medical and sabotage material only, with war material to follow if and when they attempted to collaborate in operations with the Cetniks.[38] Mihailovic had reacted violently to the latest ultimatum, and although the Foreign Office–SOE paper succeeded in obtaining the withdrawal of the offending telegram, the Chiefs of Staff had secured approval for supplies to be sent to the Partisans. A minute to this effect was addressed to the Prime Minister on 23 June. In fact they were approving a *fait accompli*: the first supply drop to Deakin had aleady been made.[39] This development was critical in political terms. The only bargaining counter Britain had in dealing with Tito, and this a very weak one, was the promise of supplies. This had now been handed over in a manner which also gave the Partisans formal allied recognition.[40]

While contact was being established with the Partisans, a series of missions was also despatched to Serbia in order to obtain a more comprehensive picture of the value of the Cetnik movement in Serb territory. These missions had radio links with Cairo separate from the mission with Mihailovic. This was partly for security, but was also designed to help the missions in their objective of persuading the local commanders to act independently of Mihailovic or at least to provide a safe base for British officers to carry out operations.[41] However, British efforts to persuade Mihailovic to join the fray were clearly futile while the latter failed to grasp that the British were coming to believe that the Partisans were a viable alternative. This point was made by Bailey to SOE Cairo at the end of August, and reiterated by the American liaison officer, Walter Mansfield, who had arrived at Mihailovic's headquarters earlier that month. Mansfield's critique of British policy was recorded in a series of telegrams despatched at the beginning of September, which explained that Bailey's efforts to persuade Mihailovic to fight the Germans in Serbia were being undermined by 'Churchill praising Mihailovic' which was leading Mihailovic to sit back and fight the Partisans 'because Churchill backs his government against the

Partisans'.[42] While there may have been an element of truth in this, it was naive and simplistic and indicated a lack of understanding of the nature of the Mihailovic–Partisan struggle.

A much clearer understanding of the complexities emerges from the report submitted by Bailey and Charles Armstrong. The latter had been sent to Mihailovic's headquarters on 24 September as part of a general upgrading of representation to the Balkan resistance movements initiated by Keble. Armstrong was a regular soldier of twenty-five years' experience, but had little political experience. He arrived in Yugoslavia several weeks after the Italian capitulation and faced the difficult task of encouraging Mihailovic to demonstrate the Cetniks' worth in operational terms at a time when the Partisans as a fighting unit were at their zenith. Although the vacuum created by the Italian collapse and surrender earlier in the month had given both movements the opportunity and room to expand separately from one another, it was not long before they were pressing up against one another's territory again. Initially, boosted by an influx of supplies, which prior to September 1943 had been negligible, the Cetniks moved into action. However, some of these triumphs were erroneously attributed by the BBC to the Partisans. This was almost certainly an unfortunate mistake rather than a deliberate slight since the BBC similarly miss-attributed Partisan achievements to the Cetniks.[43] Nevertheless, its effect was detrimental. Following Partisan incursions into Cetnik territories won from the Axis, Cetnik activity lapsed. This was instrumental in causing opinion in SIS (which had remained not unfavourably disposed to Mihailovic) and the Foreign Office to harden. Enigma decrypts supported reports of the decisive advances made by Tito in Cetnik–Partisan fighting while Mihailovic had suffered a severe psychological defeat. They also indicated that since the Italian surrender, German attention had been focused on Partisan rather than Cetnik endeavours. Furthermore, SIS concluded that Mihailovic had failed in the crucial matter of persuading Serbs and Croats to fight side by side.[44]

The Armstrong–Bailey report, submitted to Cairo at the end of November, argued that Mihailovic had great political influence in Serbia, especially among the peasants who were anti-communist at heart. These attitudes were personified in Mihailovic who was characterised as 'a career officer, narrow minded and stubborn, very pan-Serb, wily and a master of evasion and procrastination'; he would not co-operate unless he was convinced that Britain would support him politically. This, they suggested, might be achieved through an agreement promising the restoration of the pre-1941 status quo and guaranteeing free elections to determine the future form of government. In return, the Yugoslav Government would be asked to recognise that all military operations came under the direct command of the Allied military authorities. The report also revived the idea, consistently rejected by the Foreign Office as inimical to long-term interests, that secret (and separate) protocols be agreed with Tito and Mihailovic by which specific areas be allotted to each with a neutral buffer zone.[45]

The Armstrong–Bailey report coincided with intelligence reports revealing that since mid-October the Germans had moved the 1st Panzer Division from Greece to Roumania over railways passing through Mihailovic-held territory.[46] There was also now some evidence in the form of an enigma decrypt of Mihailovic's alleged collaboration with Nedic and tacitly, thereby, with the Germans. On this last point, Bailey sent to Cairo a spirited defence: 'Mihailovic has not yet received sufficient provocation from the British to justify such action before the Serb people after the war', he claimed, but added that the Partisans were also attacking the Cetniks and were employing equally ruthless measures.[47] But Foreign Office exasperation with Mihailovic was already so great that Howard had minuted on 22 November that this latest evidence of collaboration 'could mean a radical alteration in our whole policy and make it impossible to continue to support Mihailovic in any form whatever, whether military, political or moral'.[48]

Armstrong's own frustrations at Mihailovic's policy are evident from his communication to the Cetnik leader on 30 November in which he complained that 'never since I have been attached to your staff have I had from you one voluntary suggestion or plan to carry out military operations to the east in Serbia'.[49] Indeed, throughout 1943, Britain had persistently attempted to persuade Mihailovic to recognise that his policy was out of step with the prevailing climate. At the end of the year there were some eleven missions with the Cetniks (as against eight with the Partisans), but all attempts to gain a measure of influence over the local commanders had failed: as Bailey later reflected, Mihailovic had determined that they should.[50]

Britain's political and military policies were, in the autumn of 1943, contradictory. This was pointed out to Churchill by Casey in a telegram of 3 October, requesting his 'personal views' on the future policy towards Greek and Yugoslav resistance. Since Allied troops would not be available for the region except on a very minor scale, it would be necessary, he observed, to rely on stimulating guerrilla activities which meant arming left-wing guerrilla forces in both countries to an extent that would enable them to dominate their respective countries militarily and so politically as soon as the Germans were driven out.[51] The solution Casey put forward, was to maintain existing pressure on the enemy without any formidable building up of the left-wing guerrillas; at the same time 'we should endeavour to build up Right-wing elements by all means in our power'.[52] Churchill asked Eden for his comments but was pre-empted by the arrival of the views of the Chiefs of Staff which were quite clear that every effort should be made to maintain pressure on the Germans with the object of forcing withdrawal which in their view would greatly outweigh any political troubles thereby created.[53] Churchill initialed this without comment, but Eden argued against Casey's solution as it applied to Yugoslavia because the communist-led army was now recognised to be of operational importance. He added that he was going to discuss the matter in Cairo and Churchill agreed to await the outcome. Bill Donovan, director of the American OSS, meanwhile, had attempted to insert himself into this debate in the role of mediator, but was rebuffed by Churchill for this interference.[54]

At the same time as Armstrong was being despatched to Mihailovic's headquarters, so a Brigadier was also sent in to liaise with Tito. Fitzroy Maclean was Conservative MP for Lancaster, a seat he had sought on the outbreak of war in order to escape from his desk at the Foreign Office and join the armed services. By nature a maverick and adventurer, and an excellent linguist, Maclean had been an unusual diplomat, having taken the unauthodox step in 1936 of requesting a transfer from the opulence of the Paris Embassy, a jewel in the Foreign Service crown, for a post in the much drabber and less prestigious Moscow mission. This he was granted and he availed himself of the opportunity to travel widely in the Soviet Union during which time he gathered much local information about a country which for even the most well-informed Britons was a dark and often threatening mystery. Maclean's posting to Moscow also coincided with one of the most brutal episodes of the Stalinist period and he witnessed the persecutions and show trials of the late 1930s which decimated the officer and intellectual circles as well as the political sections of the Soviet society. It also drastically altered the leadership of the Comintern. Tito was instantly an object of fascination for Maclean partly because he was a survivor of this period.

Maclean was not an SOE man – an organisation he despised and distrusted as much as many of its staff resented him. He had served in the western desert as a founding member of the SAS Regiment and in 1943 had been hoping for an assignment to Greece. But his mission was to the Partisans and following his appointment, he registered his contempt for SOE by demanding – and getting – his own direct communications link with the Prime Minister. And so, in September 1943, British liaison with Tito passed out of the hands of SOE and the Middle East Defence Committee and into those of the supreme British political authority. In this lies one of the principal explanations for later controversy.

The arrival at Tito's Bosnia headquarters of Churchill's personal representative was undoubtedly a turning point and it coincided, as had Deakin's arrival three months previously, with a moment when the Partisans were amply able to demonstrate to the British officers their fighting strength. Maclean's observations of communists in Moscow had left him with the impression that the one thing all had in common was a reluctance to think for themselves, a terror of responsibility combined with a blind unquestioning obedience to the party line dictated by higher authority. It is unsurprising therefore that he was immediately impressed when on meeting Tito he found a rather different kind of man, 'a principal', he later recorded, 'not a subordinate', who was accustomed to the decision-making and responsibilities of leadership.[55]

Maclean fulfilled his brief well. He established an instant rapport with Tito and a friendship developed which was to endure for the remainder of Tito's lifetime and which was to be of significance in the development of western relations with Tito's Yugoslavia in the immediate post-war years. The conclusions of Maclean's report of 6 November are well known: Maclean was very clear in stating that the communist party had already established a tight hold on Yugoslavia and that at the end of the war the Yugoslav people would have to do as they were told and elect some form of communist regime. No one reading his report could be in any doubt of the political implications of supplying the Partisans with military aid. As for Partisan strength, Maclean estimated a total of 220,000 troops with 30,000 in Serbia and Macedonia. These figures were probably somewhat exaggerated, as critics of British policy have been quick to point out, but in their efforts to establish the existence of communist conspiracy, they generally fail to note that both the Foreign Office and SIS recorded their view that Maclean's figures were 'way out', particularly for the predominantly Cetnik-controlled areas, which attracted considerable scepticism precisely because they had been garnered from Partisan sources.[56] A situation report in June had shown Mihailovic with 20,000 men under arms in Serbia with 150,000 mobilisable while the JIC figure for the Partisans in Croatia, Hercegovina, Bosnia and Montenegro was 65,000.[57] These criticisms were reflected in the Chiefs of Staff paper produced in the light of the Maclean report on 26 November. Nevertheless, this report argued that on *military* grounds there 'was every reason to discontinue supplies' to Mihailovic.[58] This conclusion was supported by OSS officers who were in Yugoslavia as part of the British missions and who were equally convinced that the Partisans were the only signficant fighting force. Indeed, the reports of Linn Farish, the chief OSS agent attached to Partisan headquarters, were instrumental in persuading Roosevelt to accept the arguments for exclusive support for Tito which Churchill ventured at the Tehran summit meeting held at the end of November.[59]

Acceptance of Tito's military value raised, however, the major political difficulty in all this: what to do about the King whose Cabinet still included Mihailovic. Eden had already given his views on Maclean's report when he met the MEDC in Cairo on 7 November. While the Foreign Secretary did not disagree that aid to the Partisans should now be stepped up, he was adamant that King Peter and Tito be brought together so that short-term military interests should not be permitted to outweigh long-term political considerations. In an effort to secure absolute proof of Mihailovic's refusal to co-operate, Eden proposed that Mihailovic be ordered to carry out a test operation, failure of which would occasion the cessation of aid.

Although Yugoslavia was not given much attention at the Tehran Conference, German successes in their drive to recapture ground lost by the Italian capitulation caused the Big Three to agree to increase support for Tito as a matter of urgency. Roosevelt went along with the joint British–Russian statement that made no mention of Mihailovic, while declaring that the Allies would provide extensive aid to Tito.[60] The Foreign Office, at last convinced that Mihailovic could not be used as a unifying element, now began to promote the idea of monarchy as the great unifier in Yugoslavia.

This was an exaggerated perception and Maclean had already indicated that the question would be a thorny one in the Partisan context. Nevertheless, if Britain were not to adopt a policy of wholesale abandonment of the Yugoslav Government-in-Exile, to which they were allied, and effectively abdicate British interests in the region, promotion of the monarchy was the only policy remaining.[61]

When Churchill discussed the Tito–Mihailovic problem with Deakin, Maclean and Ralph Stevenson the British Ambassodor while in Cairo in the second week of December, he would have had some knowledge of the Partisan–Axis parleys which had also occurred since 1941 and only became generally known long after the war.[62] Ostensibly these were motivated by Partisan wishes for a truce and exchange of prisoners such as they had negotiated with the Ustase in the previous September 1942.[63] German sources indicate that such a meeting took place on 11 March 1943 when a Partisan delegation, headed by Vlatko Velebit, stressed they wanted only to fight the Cetniks, that they were orientated towards Soviet policy because they were anti-British, and they would fight Britain should the latter enter Yugoslavia. A further meeting was held in Zagreb on 25 March but the Partisan proposals were unacceptable to the Germans and Berlin was in any case utterly opposed to any accommodation with them: Hitler reportedly said that 'one does not negotiate with rebels – rebels must be shot'.[64]

Hitler's distaste for the Partisan rebels was matched by his contempt for the Serbs who were in his eyes 'perpetual conspirators'.[65] The Serbs had been responsible for the coup d'état which had necessitated the German invasion of 1941. Accommodations between the Cetniks and the puppet government of Milan Nedic were aimed essentially at preservation of the Serbian state. Nonetheless, the view was taken by the British officers and Stevenson, that Mihailovic was irredeemably compromised and that relations with him should be broken off. At the same time, they were convinced the weapons given to the Partisans would be used against the Germans and this was the point on which the debate turned.[66] If King Peter were to have any chance of returning then he must dismiss Mihailovic and lend his support to the Partisans.[67] There was, of course, a paradox in this since Maclean impressed on Churchill that the communists were already well on the way to securing political power and would set up a regime after the war closely allied to the Soviet Union. Communist dogma did not, of course, admit of monarchies.

Whether these factors were discussed at this meeting is a moot point. No official record of the meeting exists apart from the accounts of some of the participants. But Churchill was left with the impression that a decision to abandon Mihailovic had been arrived at on this occasion. In fact the military had made up its own mind on this and supplies to Mihailovic, such as they had been, virtually ceased during November. But in London there seems to have been no awareness of this and on 11 December Orme Sargent minuted his concern that this debate was still dragging on and being overtaken by events which were going to make the present situation 'increasingly acrimonious and indefensible'. Britain had to 'put herself right' by freeing herself from the commitments in connection with Mihailovic 'for which we cannot possibly find any justification which we could put to the British public'.

At the end of 1943, the Grand Alliance was divided about Yugoslav resistance. The British had taken the lead in policy making and were in consequence in a more advanced and exposed position. The military authorities in the eastern Mediterranean had acted on military expedients and with customary pragmatism diverted assistance to the most profitable benefactors from their point of view. From the political angle, all those sufficiently well informed to make any judgement were agreed that partition into spheres of influence was the only real solution, and this was rejected as impracticable for other, equally political reasons. Apart from the fact that dividing Yugoslavia into spheres of responsibility for the separate resistance movements would have been difficult – if not impossible – to enforce, it was open to objections as interference in the internal politics with possible prejudice to the post-war settlement. Moreover, the British showed no interest in considering any form of dismemberment of Yugoslavia after the war – their policies were firmly rooted in the assumption that Yugoslavia should continue to exist and Foreign Office policy was consistent at least in being directed towards this goal.

What 1943 had revealed above all was the impotence of the major allies when it came to imposing any shape on Balkan politics. By the end of the year, Tito was firmly in the ascendant and this really owed little to the morsels of military aid received from the Allies. The task which now confronted Churchill, who had agreed in principle with the abandonment of the Mihailovic, a decision which he may later have regretted,[68] was to somehow discharge his responsibilities towards the exile government, to which his country was playing host, by bringing at least some part of the King's Cabinet into active dialogue – and agreement – with the Partisans.

3

Expedients for Peace: the Politics of Yugoslav Unity

While the Allies were defining their own position in regard to Yugoslav resistance, the Partisans were taking steps to lay the foundations of a political revolution. At Bihac in November 1942, delegates from the four principal regions of Yugoslavia met and formed an Anti-Fascist Council for the National Liberation of Yugoslavia (AVNOJ), which in turn elected its own executive, the National Liberation Committee. From now on Tito began to speak and behave in a manner which indicated that he believed he had both an army and a state. The second meeting of AVNOJ was held the following year at Jajce on 29–30 November and coincided with the meeting of Churchill, Roosevelt and Stalin at Tehran. Tito had reported to Moscow his intention of holding this meeting but had not disclosed the details of the resolutions to be put before the Council. However, the Allies had been informed indirectly through a statement sent to the Foreign Ministers' meeting held in Moscow at the end of October, when he stated clearly that the Partisans would not permit the King's return.[1] Through the Resolutions ensuing from this conference, Tito took his political revolution a stage further: included among them was a declaration prohibiting the King's return until a referendum had been held on the future of the monarchy, and depriving the exiled government of its right to represent the interests of the country abroad.

The process of making an official break with Mihailovic was already under way in London where, following the 'meeting' between Churchill and his agents with Tito, the Foreign Office, had drafted a telegram to Cairo instructing Stevenson to persuade King Peter to dismiss Mihailovic was drafted but held so that Eden could seek Cabinet approval.[2] However, receipt of the text of the

Jajce Resolutions on 18 December brought the political process abruptly to a standstill. There could be no question now of the King dismissing Mihailovic in the face of this Partisan power play.[3] The Russians, who had sent to London a memorandum expressing for the first time a willingness to assist the British in the search for a compromise, had also only learned of the full text of the Jajce Resolutions after the event and available evidence suggests that they were also very annoyed. Indeed, Tito had confided to his intimates that he did not intend to give Moscow advance knowledge of his plans to declare AVNOJ the provisional government precisely because he feared that they would seek to prevent him from fulfilling his plans.[4] An article in *Pravda* records that Vletko Vlahovic was sent for by Dimitri Manuilsky, formerly Stalin's chief liaison officer in the Comintern, and told that 'the Boss is very angry. He says that this is a stab in the back for the Soviet Union and the Tehran decisions'.[5] Tito was already showing a disturbing tendency to pursue his own interest independently of Moscow, which given the control which Stalin sought to exercise over the international communist movement could only have been regarded as unwelcome. Moreover, this was not the first occasion that Tito had demonstrated to Moscow his assertiveness, as the Yugoslav leadership, in a flurry of self-justification following Yugoslavia's expulsion from the Cominform in 1948, were quick to record.[6]

At the beginning of 1944, Yugoslavia had two fundamentally estranged groups claiming to be the representative government and the Allies were in the anomalous position of being committed to both: to the King's Government, the 'government of clerks', as Milovan Djilas later described it,[7] they gave political recognition, though the British and Russians had specifically rejected his Minister of War and thus the Royal Government's only concrete link with its country. Military aid was now being directed instead to the Partisans and Churchill, through his personal envoy, Fitzroy Maclean, was in contact with their leader, and head of the self-appointed provisional government, the self-styled Marshal Tito. Churchill, who had gone to Marrakech to recuperate from pneumonia, believing the question of British policy towards the resistance settled, was persuaded by Eden to write to Tito explaining British obligations to the King, while reaffirming that no further aid would go to Mihailovic. The rearguard action fought by Eden with the backing of his senior officials delayed an announcement of British withdrawal of aid to Mihailovic but made no difference to the outcome. The decision was announced by Winston Churchill in the House of Commons on 22 February and communicated to Tito in a personal letter from the Prime Minister three days later.[8] The Mihailovic question, like British aid, had been a *quid pro quo* of dubious value since it was then, and remains now, difficult to see how either might have been used effectively to bring Tito into line with British wishes. At the end of May 1944, the British missions with the Cetniks were finally withdrawn.

The search for political union was continued at Britain's initiative throughout 1944 and into 1945, with Churchill's direct and personal involvement. In this he was motivated in part by a sense of obligation to the Yugoslav Government-in-Exile, and more particularly to the King who, by severing his links with Mihailovic, would lose his only link with the resistance. However, there were British interests at stake too. Uppermost in Churchill's mind was Greece which, he feared, would be destabilised if Yugoslavia were permitted to descend into disorder and civil war following the liberation. Tito appeared to be a force for unity and stability, if not necessarily of western-style democracy and regardless of his motives, which during the debate about recognition and supplies had been kept firmly secondary, he was bent on fighting Germans. Given the evidence available it is difficult to see how any other decision than support for Tito was possible. However, no sooner had this decision been made, than the political questions surfaced with great force.

It is necessary at this point to say something about the American attitude towards the question. Franklin Roosevelt and his senior commanders had remained steadfast in resisting Churchill's attempts to open a front in the southern Mediterranean. The Americans were deeply imbued with the suspicion that Churchill and maybe the Russians were playing a traditional spheres of influence game in the Balkan playground and it was a wariness of this which above all determined American policy in the region. These concerns had been set out for the President in a State Department memorandum by Edward Stettinius, the Under Secretary of State, in which he argued 'the important factor in the Yugoslav situation today is not so much the Tito–Mihailovic–Cairo conflict as the interplay between British and Soviet policies on the question.[9] While the imposition of some restraint on Churchill's enthusiasms was possibly beneficial, the Americans' persistent equivocation throughout 1944 exacerbated the pervasive atmosphere of Balkan intrigue which characterised these negotiations.

In general, the Americans tended to regard the Balkans as peripheral to the central issues in Europe. The American missions in Yugoslavia had been regarded as sufficiently minor for OSS to have permitted hitherto all communications to be handled by SOE. As the British missions had taken on a more political importance, which became so in September with the desptach of Maclean and Armstrong, so Bill Donovan had taken the question more earnestly. He objected, he told his superiors in Washington, to the placing of OSS officers under Maclean, whom he believed to be with some reason, essentially a political agent of the Foreign Office, and whom he did not like for personal reasons. At a meeting with British military and civilian authorities in Algiers on 17 January, Donovan persuaded the British, with some difficulty, to permit the Americans to send an independent mission to Tito. Meanwhile, a conservative faction within OSS continued to argue for a deal with Mihailovic, long after the British had withdrawn. This was reflected at the political level: during the spring of 1944, Americans watched with growing unease, fearing that British manoeuvres might implicate the United States in actions that would violate the 'no interference in internal affairs of Allied nations' clause of the Atlantic Charter. However, the United States did not share in the British abandonment of Mihailovic. Nevertheless, the OSS, the State Department and the American Joint Chiefs of Staff accepted their British counterparts' view of the high fighting potential of the Partisans in 1944 and made great efforts to get supplies to Tito and keep as many OSS missions as possible in Partisan territory.[10]

The OSS believed that while the Partisan army was waging guerrilla war against the Axis and Mihailovic, they were also organising under Russian leadership all the Balkan countries into an underground federation. There was some evidence of this in so far as Tito had sent Generals Apostolski and 'Tempo' to Macedonia and there kept in touch with EAM–ELAS leaders in Athens through George Siantos and others.[11] The OSS had also infiltrated officers into Yugoslavia, but until the autumn of 1943 these had shared SOE communications links, and to an extent this is reflected in the reporting. Nevertheless, the reports of American officers taken across the period reveal a similar pattern of confusing, contradictory allegiances as those reflected in the SOE records; common to all is the summation that Yugoslavia was in open civil war, that Mihailovic was saving his efforts for D-Day, and that he was deeply distrustful of the British. The Partisans, on the other hand, were all out for a communist post-war Yugoslav republic.[12] An American mission under the leadership of Robert McDowell, was dropped to Cetnik headquarters as late as August 1944 and remained there until November and McDowell's subsequent reports were inclined to criticism of British policy as a result of the relentless persecution of the Cetniks by the Partisans which he had witnessed.[13] But given the framework of Allied relations and the dictates of strategy, in the formulation of which the Americans had of course played a major role, McDowell's solutions were no more practical than those advanced by Hudson, Bailey and Armstrong.

In fact, Churchill had proceeded in his correspondence with Tito during January and February 1944 without keeping the Americans closely informed of these exchanges in deference to the delay and possible resistance that might be incurred thereby. However, the substance of the letters was being given Ralph Stevenson, apparently on his own initiative, to the State Department through the medium of the United States envoy to the allied governments exiled in Cairo, Lincoln MacVeagh – presumably on Eden's instruction. At the same time, Stevenson had let it be known to MacVeagh that the Foreign Office did not concur with Churchill on this matter. British officials (and Eden himself) felt that by making a direct approach to Tito, Churchill was increasing Tito's stature without making a solution to the King–Cetnik–Partisan conflict any easier. In short, the State Department was unwilling to be associated with the Prime Minister's initiative and informed MacVeagh to that effect on 5 February.

The British had the opportunity to discuss Yugoslav affairs with their American counterparts in April when Stettinius and the Deputy Director of the Office of European Affairs, H. Freeman Matthews, were in London. During the course of a long conversation, Stevenson and Sargent informed the Americans that Britain had lost all hope of bringing about a reconciliation between the King and Tito in as much as Tito clearly did not want the King to return to Yugoslavia.[14] Since the end of March, Eden had been pressing the King to form a new government, 'not as part of a bargain with Tito but in order to improve his own position during the next phase'. The Foreign Office largely shared the American view that Serbia, at least, remained both loyal to the monarchy (if not to King Peter personally), and pro-Mihailovic, whilst also being passionately anti-communist. A further American memorandum, this one produced by Cavendish Cannon, then Assistant Chief of the

Division of Southern European Affairs, on 19 May, contains perhaps the best statement of US policy and preoccupations with regard to Balkan affairs. This reaffirmed that the United States did not intend to intervene in the political question, but that it did wish, however, to strengthen all forces of resistance and emphasised a desire to see all leaders within Yugoslavia concentrating on the military tasks in hand. The American view was that neither of the leading resistance groups could lay solid claim to representing, in the political sense, the sentiments of the whole country. The Memorandum then turned to Allied policy, stating that the British and Russians had interests in the region which the United States would prefer not to support. Finally, it stressed the need to avoid becoming involved in the political 'transaction purporting to be on a joint basis, in which the undoubted American prestige in Yugoslavia would be exploited and American responsibility engaged, unless we know what is going on'.[15] This was all very fine and principled but was not especially helpful.

Churchill was meanwhile becoming ever more deeply involved. At the same time, the problem of determining Soviet motives and objectives was becoming increasingly his major preoccupation. At the beginning of April he wrote to Eden, reminding him of the arrival at Tito's headquarters in February of a 'grandiose Russian mission' under General Korneyev: 'There is little doubt,' he wrote, 'that the Russians will drive straight ahead for a communist, Tito-governed Yugoslavia, and will denounce everything done to the contrary as undemocratic.'[16] These views were reinforced in a secret memorandum to the War Cabinet in June which observed that in Yugoslavia, Tito 'by his own efforts and our support, will probably emerge as the governing force, whether or not as the result of civil war against Serbia. The probability is that the Red Army will eventually gain contact with the Partisans and this will ensure Tito's position.'[17] Churchill used these arguments on the King, explaining that a rapid Russian advance would bring the Red Army into Yugoslavia, provoke resistance from Mihailovic, thereby leaving King Peter in the position of being, through the actions of his Minister of War, on 'the wrong side'. King Peter weakly responded that there were simply not enough uncompromised politicians with which to form a new government.

Much diplomatic effort was now expended on persuading the young king to accept as a new Prime Minister, Ivan Subasic. The latter had been agreed by the British and Americans in April as a suitable choice since he had both Royal links, having formerly been adviser to King Alexander, and his confidant on all Croat questions, while also having been the former Governor of Croatia and a close associate of the Croat Peasant Party leader, Vladko Macek. During the 1930s, he had actively worked to heal the Serb–Croat breach and escaped to the United States shortly after the outbreak of war from whence he had maintained a distance from the Yugoslav Government-in-Exile and continued to represent and work for Serb–Croat unity. He had also been one of the first Yugoslav politicians in exile to express some sympathy for the Partisans. Subasic – a sincere, patient and courageous man – was perfect for the role the British and Americans envisaged, except for the fact that he was totally lacking in political sense. Nevertheless, he remained, as all parties agreed, the best available.

Within two weeks of being appointed, Subasic met Tito on the British-held island of Vis to which Tito had escaped, narrowly, following a well organised German operation to eradicate him and his movement. Here, they drew up an agreement for 'closer co-operation between the Royal Yugoslav Government and Tito's National Liberation Committee'. The objective of national unity was declared and Tito gave a verbal assurance that he would not introduce a communist system after the war. The future of the monarchy was, however, to depend on a referendum.[18] Tito had now placed himself firmly in a commanding position, neatly wriggling out of a meeting with the King, a point which the British and Americans had been pressing since February. Furthermore, the Tito–Subasic Agreement made no provision for those who were willing to fight the Germans but who would not accept Communism, particularly the non-collaborators among the Cetniks. Since it was British policy to avoid a forcible subjection of the Cetniks, if at all possible, the absence of a working arrangement between Tito and Subasic on this was viewed as yet another unwelcome and ominous complication.[19]

The position was unchanged when Churchill met Tito and Subasic in Naples in the middle of August. Churchill did extract from Tito on this occasion a verbal declaration reaffirming his statement to Subasic in June regarding communism, but this did nothing to quell Churchill's growing sense of disquiet. On the 31st he reflected in a letter to Eden that a great responsibility would rest on Great Britain after the war when all the armies in Yugoslavia, supplied by the west, would be in the hands of Tito and could be used by him to subjugate the country. In response, Eden observed that British policy had been determined on the ground of short term military expediency rather than long-term political interests.[20] This was true, up to a point, but as we have seen, the political debate had simmered – and occasionally surfaced – since the German invasion of the Balkans in 1941.

Despite Roosevelt's formal congratulations, the State Department, which was by now receiving the first of McDowell's reports that American arms were being used by Tito's forces to 'kill the Serbs', informed their political representative at AFHQ, Robert Murphy, that the United States could not approve of any plan to build up Tito's forces at the expense of the Serbs. Eden expressed a similar concern, since Subasic had publicly endorsed Tito's claim that the Partisans had the allegiance of the Serbian population. Writing to Ralph Stevenson, Eden said that he could not help feeling that Subasic as a Croat 'is underestimating the Serb problem in his efforts to come to an understanding with Tito. There may be a large number of Serbs among the Partisans, but there is a much larger number who are opposed to the Partisans, not merely those who follow Mihailovic or Nedic.'[21] In any case, all agreed that Tito was dragging his heels in putting the agreement with Subasic into effect. When, at the end of August, Subasic suggested to Tito that the time had come to form the Government of National Unity, Tito used the moral superiority of being actively engaged in resistance activities to dodge the issue, claiming that it was unimportant while the Partisans were engaged in an exceptionally hard battle with the Germans. Angered by Tito's evasive behaviour, Eden took this up with him directly: far from being unimportant, he argued, this matter was of utmost importance. He then instructed Clark Kerr in Moscow to raise the question with Molotov with a view to persuading the Soviet Government to exert some pressure to secure Tito's co-operation.[22] With or without Russian pressure, Tito agreed to meet Subasic at the end of September. In fact, Tito had already been summoned to Moscow, a visit which the Partisans organised in great secret, spiriting Tito out from under the noses of the British who were still providing him with a safe haven from German assault on Vis. Tito was accompanied on his visit to Moscow by General Korneyev and Ivan Milutinovic and while there negotiated an agreement regarding the operation of Soviet troops on Yugoslav territories bordering Hungary. This agreement also called for the withdrawal of Soviet forces after these operations were complete. Stalin took the opportunity to encourage Tito to be co-operative.

The urgency now felt by the British was occasioned by King Michael's coup d'état in Rumania on 23 August which, by breaking his country's association with the Axis had opened the way for the Red Army to move against both Bulgaria and Hungary. The British were concerned that this would not also lead to a move into Greek Thrace in line with territorial promises made by the Soviet envoy to Bucharest in November 1940, Sobolev. Eden indicated this concern that Soviet manoeuvres might be intended to threaten Greece in a series of telegrams despatched to the Foreign Office during the Quebec Conference in August. Churchill, accordingly, was now preparing to protect British interests in Greece by making concessions to the Russians over Bulgaria. As for Yugoslavia, Eden said: 'we should require the Soviet government to agree that . . . there should be close consultation between us and that it is our common interest that Yugoslavia should be in a strong, ultimately independent and democratic state'.[23]

There has been much debate as to Churchill's objectives when proposing in Moscow to Stalin during his visit of 10–12 October, a division by percentages of influence in the Balkans and Hungary between the Soviet Union and the 'others'. The facts of the matter have proven illusive because neither the British nor the Soviet minutes of the meeting mention the deal.[24] Churchill was eager to strike a bargain, his anxiety about Soviet intentions having increased steadily since the spring. He seems to have been optimistic in October 1944 about the chances of persuading Stalin to acknowledge British interests: 'Uncle Joe had shown himself more forthcoming than ever before', he wrote, though he added that no time should be lost in capitalising on this atmosphere.[25] It is a clear indication that Churchill saw one solution to the problem of a power vacuum in Europe following the defeat of the Axis powers to be found in a traditional spheres of influence arrangement, the ground rules of which he seemed inclined to attempt to set before the war's end.[26] What might Churchill have hoped to achieve, or pre-empt, when he proposed a 50–50 share of post-war influence with the Soviet Union in Yugoslavia? Stalin himself did not enquire and ticked the piece of paper on which Churchill had scribbled his proposal, without further discussion. Molotov subsequently tried to get the percentage revised to sixty–forty in discussion with Eden, an indication that the exchange with Stalin did hold some serious significance for the Russians: Molotov tried to explain to Eden that the revised percentages were intended to indicate no Soviet interference along the Adriatic coast, but a right to assert her influence in the interior, particularly in Serbia.[27] Elisabeth Barker, in her search for an understanding of this agreement, identified through an examination of Churchill's dealings with Tito before and immediately after the Moscow visit, four possible objectives, two political and two military.[28] Firstly he was hoping for Stalin's co-operation in his effort to sponsor the United Yugoslav Government which would relieve Britain of its obligations to King Peter and might possibly allow the establishment of a compromise government in which non-communists would also be represented. Churchill probably also wanted Stalin's support in preventing Tito from doing anything which would threaten Britain's protégé, Greece, particularly any links with Bulgaria which might undermine Greek Macedonia. On the operational side, he wanted to retain a degree of influence in post-war Yugoslavia through an arrangement whereby the British would train and equip the Yugoslav navy and armed forces. Finally, he probably wanted immediate assistance from Stalin in encouraging close Anglo-Yugoslav co-operation in the joint operations in the Adriatic over which Tito's commanders were at that time being especially difficult. However, it is the political question which is of concern here.

Stalin certainly appears to have played his part in assisting the British in bringing the Tito–Subasic Agreement to fruition, an arrangement which probably suited his purposes. He had already warned Tito during the latter's visit to Moscow in September that it was necessary for him to take King Peter back, at least 'temporarily', although Yugoslav witnesses, if these are to be believed, claim that Stalin also added that they could dispose of the king 'at a suitable moment'.[29] This done, Stalin then welcomed Subasic warmly in Moscow in November. Tito was also invited to this meeting but declined and sent Kardelj in his place. Kardelj recorded his impression that generally speaking the talks had seemed designed to get Allied policy across to Subasic in the best possible light, and that Stalin even chastised the Partisans for being 'too narrow minded' in not permitting the return of King Peter.[30] Stalin also took the occasion to reveal to Edverd Kardelj the 50–50 agreement, and probably hoped to impress the Yugoslavs, for his own purposes, that he was taking British interest in the region seriously. Stalin probably hoped that British influence would have a restraining effect on the

Partisan leadership: in any event, tension between Britain and Tito would place Stalin in the advantageous position of arbiter.[31] In practical terms, his support of British efforts was largely that of the bystander, content in the knowledge that the Yugoslav communists 'would never sacrifice to foreign interests what had been won in the war'.

In the letter, at least, the Tito–Subasic agreement, which was initialled on 1 November, fulfilled Allied objectives in so far as it facilitated the union of AVNOJ and the Royal Yugoslav Government. Accordingly, Tito's Anti-fascist Council was to be the supreme legislative body while the United Government would be made up of twelve members from the National Liberation Committee and six from the Royal Yugoslav Government. The United Government, so formed, would hold elections in due course but in the meantime, Yugoslavia, on paper at least, would continue to be a monarchy, the King remaining abroad and being represented in Belgrade by three regents. The fact that Tito, by virtue of being in Yugoslavia and backed by a substantial battle-hardened army, held all the cards in his hands, is only too evident. There was no acknowledgement of constitutional monarchy except by implication through the Regency, and the government would, in any case, be weighted heavily in favour of the Partisans; conversely, Subasic would be swamped. Moreover, the regents would have no authority over the Government since members of the latter would be taking their oath to the people and not to the King.[32]

Hitherto, a fundamental assumption underlying British policy had been that a genuine plebiscite could be held which would determine the popular will regarding the monarchy. However, the Tito–Subasic Agreement raised the question which was to occur again and again during 1945: how realistic was it to assume that genuinely free elections could be held in the Soviet sphere? During the war, the British had chosen to disregard the possibility that Nazi dictatorship would be replaced by an equally authoritarian communist dictatorship in areas liberated by the Red Army. At a practical level it was doubtful whether the Americans and Russians would be prepared to provide personnel for supervision: Yugoslavia was after all an ally. Even if the elections were to be supervised, the precedent would have to be observed in Italy when the same question was submitted to the popular vote. The British and Americans were careful to avoid any action which might precipitate such a demand from their Soviet ally. No one in London seriously believed that the Tito–Subasic Agreement would ever be put into effect. But there was nothing more to be done. Tito was in possession and he was now backed by the active presence of the Red Army which by the end of October had liberated Belgrade.[33] In the absence of Subasic, who had angered all parties in London by going directly to Moscow without consulting the King and Cabinet, Churchill was faced with the task of securing King Peter's acquiescence. Churchill, who had just received a letter from Stalin observing that the agreement could be useful to Yugoslavia and that its implementation should not be put off, attempted to advise the King that the agreement should be accepted because it did at least preserve his constitutional position. Young though the King may have been, he was not deceived as to the reality and complained to Churchill that the Agreement was a means of getting rid of him 'more or less painlessly'.[34]

The United States remained unhelpfully uncommitted, despite increasingly alarming reporting from its Ambassador in Moscow, Averell Harriman, regarding Soviet intervention throughout eastern Europe.[35] Colonel Charles Thayer, head of the American Military Mission in Belgrade, had received strict instructions not to become involved in Yugoslav internal affairs in general, and the Tito–Subasic Agreement in particular.[36] This must have been a difficult brief to fulfil since the attention of most in Belgrade was now focused on the political problems. Stettinius had reaffirmed American policy in the region in a memorandum to Roosevelt of 8 November in which he argued that the United States should be wary of identifying its interests in eastern and south-eastern Europe and the near east with those of Britain and the Soviet Union. Instead, it should follow a course of independent interest in favour of equitable arrangements designed to attain general peace and security as the basis of good neighbourly relations. In short, the Americans were without a coherent policy towards Yugoslavia at the end of 1944. As regards the Tito–Subasic Agreement, they took the line that it was acceptable in principle but the question, which was not unreasonable, was whether effective and legal implementation of the principles it contained, would be achieved. If the King accepted the Agreement, then the question of American 'recognition' did not arise. If the King rejected it, however, and Tito repudiated the Royal Government then the entire issue would require, in their view, reconsideration.[37]

American ambivalence almost certainly encouraged the King's

persistence in withholding his approval of the Agreement. In two letters to Churchill he set forth his objections, but succeeded only in provoking Churchill to respond with a warning that the Great Powers would not 'lift one finger nor sacrifice one man to put any King back on any throne in Europe'. If the King persisted in his refusal to accept the agreement he would simply be bypassed. The advice went unheeded. On 11 January, without consulting Subasic, the King issued a statement to the press in which he rejected the agreement.[38] Churchill had now lost all patience and wrote immediately to Stalin that the Agreement be put into effect and the King's objections overlooked, but on the 14th, in a cooler moment, he wrote to both Roosevelt and Stalin that he was now trying to see if the agreement could be saved and the title of Royal Yugoslav government preserved until the peoples of Yugoslavia had the chance of going to poll. Balkan stubbornness, combined with endemic American equivocation was probably in large measure responsible for the King's attempt to hold out against this development. Certainly, the Foreign Office thought so, and seized the occasion to instruct Halifax to tell the State Department that while 'it was all very well and good for them to stall on the Yugoslav situation', the crisis was being contained on British shores and that the British Government could not afford the same 'waffling' line, and that further procrastination on the part of the King would provide the Russians with an excuse to back unilateral action by Tito, who was reported by both Thayer and Maclean to be increasingly impatient about the delay.[39]

The Foreign Office was still awaiting a reply when news arrived that the King had compounded the crisis by dismissing Subasic for concluding an agreement without his consent. Several weeks passed as Subasic, who had refused to resign, worked at producing a face-saving compromise. The Allies meanwhile reinforced their demand for immediate implementation of the Agreement, and this time effectively tied the Americans down to supporting the position in the form of a communiqué issued as a tripartite declaration from the Yalta Conference.[40] Correspondingly, when the nominations agreed upon by Tito and Subasic were presented to King Peter for his approval, the British ensured that he was discouraged from raising further objections. Churchill had informed Eden that more delay at King Peter's behest would result in a British request that he leave the country. But in the event, the King gave his assent and on 7 March the Regency Council appointed a United Yugoslav Government under Tito's premiership which received allied recognition.[41]

The Partisans had achieved their political objectives for their war-time strategy, and had secured for themselves a dominating position in the post-war government. They were successful within Yugoslavia because they stole the thunder from Mihailovic and the Yugoslav government by hoisting the flag of Yugoslav national unity at a time when the common people of Yugoslavia had grown tired of the Serb–Croat antagonisms which had been expressed during the war through mass murder. Moreover, they had guaranteed to respect and protect the Croatian nationality in a future Yugoslavia.[42] At the same time, the Partisans were successful in gaining allied support because they promised a solution to the Yugoslav problem, or at least an alternative to the resumption of Serbo–Croat rivalry of the 1920s and 1930s.

Just how difficult it would be to accomplish national unity for Yugoslavia, and the methods that would be employed to achieve this end, were understood only by those for whom the Balkans were home. The nature of the problem is exemplified, and in a sense explained in the report of one OSS officer on leaving Yugoslavia. George Wuchinich was a second-generation American of Serbian parents, but despite this Americanisation, Wuchinich explained that he had been taught by his parents 'the superiority of the Serb in war and also that nothing was impossible for a Serb to do, whether in war or peace. Fundamentally,' he continued, 'I was taught to hate Croats and brand them as the greatest traitors the world had known.' Similar sentiments were expressed by the Croats about the Serbs.[43] The communists were the first national party in Yugoslav history and it was this supra-nationalist ideology which the Partisan leadership evoked to unite Yugoslavia in the war's wake.

4

Yugoslavia between the Allies: Trieste and the Emergence of Cold War Europe, 1945–1946

Although the Allies had brought the opposing parties to unite in a single government, securing any meaningful implementation of the spirit of continued co-operation implied in the Tito–Subasic agreement was quickly shown to be impossible. In any case, neither the British nor the Americans showed much enthusiasm for further interference in Yugoslav internal affairs, while Stalin was content to allow Tito to lay the foundations of a communist dictatorship and inevitably resisted any suggestion that either the Tito–Subasic Agreement or the Yalta declaration on Liberated Europe, which had been published following the Big Three Conference held at Yalta between 4 and 11 February 1945, were not being carried out.[1] At the same time it was clear that Yugoslavia was developing a close relationship with the Russians; commenting on the announcement of the Soviet–Yugoslav Treaty of Friendship and Mutual Assistance, Churchill observed that this was yet 'another proof of how vain it is to throw away our substance in Titoland'. As his correspondence with Eden during March and April shows, Churchill had written off British interests in Yugoslavia and was in favour of devoting his energies towards ensuring Italian stability as a west European bulwark instead.[2]

Shortly before the German capitulation in early May 1945, the practical consequences of British and American promotion of the Italian cause were worked out in a small province at the head of the Adriatic, where the western allies and the Yugoslav partisan forces now vied with each other for occupation of Trieste. The question of the post-war disposition of the region, referred to as Venezia Giulia, a term first adopted in the mid-nineteenth century to indicate all Austrian controlled territories claimed by the Italians, and which encompassed the valuable Adriatic port of Trieste, had an enduring effect on Yugoslavia's relations with all three great powers. At an early date, Tito had made clear his intention to claim the region for Yugoslavia in the post-war settlement.[3]

The interests of Yugoslavia and Italy in Trieste were founded on a mixture of ethnic and political factors which had surfaced during the First World War peace settlement and had contributed to the regional unease and inter-state jealousies of the inter-war period. Both had good claims on ethnic grounds, and both obviously had strong political motivations. Indeed, the occupation of Trieste was to be the first trial of strength between the communist world and the western powers, and was to give perspective to the British concern for the Balkans. It also brought the new Yugoslav government up against all three allies simultaneously,[4] since the Great Powers each had reasons for opposing Yugoslav ambitions. In the spring of 1945, the British military and political authorities had defined both long-term and short-term objectives in Venezia Giulia. Operational considerations required that SACMED, Harold Alexander, should secure his lines of communication through Trieste to link his forces in northern Italy with those of southern Austria. British intervention in Athens in the civil war, which had broken out in December 1944, had revealed the hazards of Allied forces becoming entangled with communist guerrilla bands.[5] Political considerations, essentially the stability of the western-style democratic government of Marshal Badoglio in Rome, would require that Italy receive some share in the further administration of Trieste, and that it would be prevented at least from becoming an additional Yugoslav province. Noel Charles, the British Representative in Rome warned the Foreign Office in late March 1945 that if an Allied Military Government were not established as promised, and if the Italians lost Trieste, 'the present government would probably disintegrate and no one from any party, with the possible exception of the communists, would undertake to form a government'.[6]

For most of the war there had been a marked ambivalence in the attitude of the western allies towards Italy. They tended to regard the Italian people with a mixture of pity, condescension and affection, and a great effort was made by Roosevelt and, with more reservation, by Churchill, to distinguish between them and their fascist government which had led them astray under the more sinister influence of their Nazi ally. Although the principle of unconditional surrender technically applied as much to Italy as to Germany and Japan, Anglo-American propaganda implied that Italy would be forgiven if she turned against Germany.[7] On 25 July 1943, shortly after the beginning of the Anglo-American invasion of Sicily, Mussolini was overthrown and the Badoglio government began secret negotiations with the western allies for an armistice. Despite his attempts to persuade the British and Americans to accept Italy as an ally against Germany rather than a victim of a surrender, the western powers insisted that their right to decide Italy's fate should be unprejudiced. The Italians found they had little choice, and duly signed the armistice on 8 September. Just over a month later, Italy was accepted as a co-belligerent following her declaration of war on Germany.

Although this arrangement had been conditioned primarily by military considerations, political factors, too, had weighed heavily in Allied calculations. The Russians had not been included in the negotiations, nor were they invited to participate in the subsequent management of Italian affairs. This had been largely in deference to American wishes, the British having shown some preference for a tripartite approach in Italy, probably in the hope that this would set a precedent which might be extended to Germany's allies in eastern Europe. American concern for Italy stemmed from the existence of some six million Italian-Americans, many of whom lived in Roosevelt's home state, New York. The result of this was that the American government was particularly susceptible to popular pressure at home for leniency in the treatment of Italy. The tortuous policy-making – and at times circuitous diplomacy – which was conducted in both Washington and London with regard to the Trieste question can not be understood except with close reference to their attitudes towards Italy.

Trieste's significance for the major powers lay in the fact that its position at the head of the Adriatic made it a useful, if not vital centre for central European trade and a gateway which linked the Balkans with western Europe. The renewal of central European trade would, so the British and Americans believed, be critically restricted should the port not function as an open trading outlet as it had done previously. Politically its value was measured in terms of its relative importance in the minds of the Italian and Yugoslav people and the value each ally placed on these relative terms. The loss of Trieste to Yugoslavia was seen in London and

Washington as likely to damage Badoglio's government because the city was 85 per cent Italian and the Italian people had been imbued with propaganda propounding Italy's right to govern Trieste since that country's unification in 1870. Nevertheless, the surrounding hinterland of Venezia Giulia, without which Trieste could not function effectively as a port, was largely Slovene which in turn gave much strength to the Yugoslav case, already inflated by the fact that Yugoslavia could claim to have fought consistently on the Allied side during the war and had, moreover, endured a harsh Italian occupation. Eager to avenge themselves, the new government in Belgrade, which wanted, of course, to be seen as a successful negotiator on behalf of the Yugoslav peoples, could now demand that they had a right to some territorial concession from their neighbour as just recompense. Of course, Trieste also formed the southern most tip of the division in western and Soviet spheres of influence and as such it was the first real cold war challenge.

The Americans adopted a position roughly analogous to the British, although they were persistent at this stage in paying formal homage to the maxim laid down by State Department planners for the peace as early as 1941 that Yugoslavia's frontiers should not be negotiated until the peace conference. The Russians, however, were compromised. The port could be economically useful for the Soviet sphere and there would be the fillip in the negotiation of its acquisition by Yugoslavia of a political victory over the western powers. But it is unlikely that Stalin's assessments of their interests would permit him to be so naive as to believe that they would give in readily to Tito's blusterings; while he may have seen an advantage in not discouraging Tito's aggression as a means of testing western resolve, Stalin's ambitions were probably more speculative than pre-determined. Moreover, there was the question of the Italian communist party (PCI) which could also make political capital if Trieste were indeed to revert to Italian sovereignty. In one sense, then, Stalin could not lose in Trieste and, given his predisposition towards opportunistic policy-making, it is likely that he formulated Soviet policy accordingly.[8]

Against this background the drama which ensued on the liberation of Trieste began to unfold. Possession being ultimately nine-tenths of the law, a race for the occupation of the city and its hinterland was, with hindsight, perhaps inevitable, despite the various attempts on the parts of the key players to establish their claims beforehand. Tito had made clear his intention regarding the occupation of Trieste during his visit to British headquarters at Caserta in August 1944. At this meeting Alexander agreed that he would maintain close liaison with the Yugoslav authorities and that they would co-operate in ensuring communication lines through Ljubljana and Maribor to Graz. The matter was discussed again when Alexander travelled to Belgrade at the end of February 1945 to inform Tito formally of Allied requirements regarding liberation and occupation of the region either side of the pre-war Italo-Yugoslav frontier. During his talks with Tito, he stated that Trieste must fall under his jurisdiction, which would involve occupation of all territory to the west of the 1939 frontier and the establishment there of Allied Military Government (AMG). Tito apparently accepted the proposal on the condition that he would be able to retain the civil administration which he had already set up in the areas under Yugoslav occupation. He agreed nevertheless that such civil authorities should be responsible to AMG.[9]

The lines of occupation were also negotiated at this meeting although there appears to be no written record of the precise details of the demarcation line. In theory, the Yugoslav army was expected to occupy the area of Venezia Giulia that fell to the east of the so-called 'Robertson Line', which had been discussed by the great powers at the Yalta conference two weeks earlier.[10] It is a moot point, however, whether or not Tito was actually shown on a map where Alexander envisaged the line would fall.

Two months of drift followed. By the time Alexander received instructions from the Combined Chiefs of Staff on 28 April to establish AMG throughout Venezia Giulia, and request the Yugoslavs to withdraw from the position they had already taken up, the latter had entered Trieste and other key points, all of which were well to the west of the Robertson Line supposedly accepted by Tito in February. In the meantime, Tito had made his own intentions clearer. During his visit to Moscow in April to sign the Soviet–Yugoslav Treaty, he had given an interview to *Red Star* in which he stated that, not only would Yugoslavia build a strong army after the war, but that he was certain that Istria and Trieste would become part of Yugoslavia; he then added, 'We have no intention of laying down our arms after liberating Trieste.'[11] This was conveyed to Churchill in a telegram from Eden who was then in Washington attending the funeral of President Roosevelt who had finally succumbed to illness on 12 April. The telegram provoked Churchill's often quoted reply that he had ceased to trust Tito after he had levanted on a secret visit to Moscow from under British protection on the island of Vis during the third week of September, 1944.[12] He then continued that the submergence of central and western Europe in the Russian sphere had to be prevented: Tito's claims should be used, in his view, 'as a means of splitting the Italian Communist Party; the United States Government', he added, 'are very fond of Italy and would, I should say, certainly support them, especially on account of the strong Italian vote which the new President would surely be glad of.' To Harry Truman, Roosevelt's successor in the White House, Churchill urged that positive action be taken. Truman had little experience of foreign affairs – in 1941, he had glibly stated that the Nazis and Bolsheviks should best be left to kill one another off – and his elevation to the White House introduced a new element of uncertainty. Mindful of the new President's lack of familiarity with foreign affairs, Churchill wrote to remind him of the importance Roosevelt had attached to Trieste 'which he thought should be an international port forming an outlet into the Adriatic from all the regions of the Danubian basin'. The immediate concern, however, was to be in Trieste 'before Tito's guerrillas are in occupation . . . the actual status of Trieste can be determined at our leisure'.[13]

In the event there was a scramble for the occupation: Tito's National Liberation Army entered the city on 20 April; the following day they made their first contact with the advance guard of the 2nd New Zealand Division just west of Monfalcone. On 2 May, General Freyberg entered Trieste taking the surrender of the German garrison and occupying the port. A large troop presence was now maintained under Freyberg's command in order to discourage Tito, with or without Moscow's support, from seeking to advance any further. In the meantime, Alexander sent Tito a message on 4 May which challenged on military grounds the Yugoslav action and their failure to honour the agreement he believed had been struck in Belgrade in February.[14]

Reports from the British Embassy in Belgrade suggest that the position of the Yugoslav Government itself might not have been entirely straightforward: there was ignorance among senior government representatives as to the situation there and Yugoslav officials were reported to be 'sheepish' in their contacts with British diplomats. Stevenson took the view that the present crisis was largely the result of the machinations of Tito's General Staff and of the two hard-liners, Generals Jovanovic and Terzic in particular.[15]

Orme Sargent was unconvinced. Far from being led by the nose by the military, Tito was more likely, in his view, to be counting on Stalin's support in a matter which he had long considered to be Yugoslavia's legitimate interest.[16] This latter was confirmed in Tito's reply to Alexander in which he explained that not only did Yugoslavia have just cause against Italy for her aggression, but the territories had been 'unjustly annexed by Italy' as a result of the 1919 peace treaties.

The question was the extent to which Tito enjoyed Moscow's backing. Noel Charles, then Ambassador in Rome, was in no doubt that the issue was being regarded by the Soviet Union as a test of the western allies will to stand up to Russian political domination and that Tito had probably been promised 'moral, though probably no concrete support' and that Stalin would be hoping to use Trieste to persuade Italy to lean further in their direction and away from the British position. He concluded that unless the western Allies came up with a solution quickly, the Russians would propose one which would be just about acceptable all round and they thereby would gain favour with the Mediterranean countries.[17] The complication in this situation lay in the danger that Tito was indeed being sponsored by the Russians, which if true would render the act of using force to push his forces out of Trieste a direct challenge to the Russians. American support was critical to the British and initially had appeared by no means certain. However, on 12 May, Truman sent a telegram to Churchill expressing his anxiety about Belgrade's unyielding posture and his conviction that the only solution now open to the western allies was to 'throw them out'. This line had also been recommended by Stevenson who warned London that Belgrade's confidence was growing with every hour that Alexander's original demands remained unsatisfied.[18]

British and American Notes handed to the Yugoslav Government on 15 May stated that they expected the Yugoslav government immediately to accept Alexander's control of the territory specified earlier, including Pola, Trieste, Monfalcone, Gorizia and the lines of communication through Tarvis to Austria as well as an area sufficiently to the east of that line to permit proper administrative control. Audaciously, Tito rejected these demands and put forward counter-proposals which, as he quite possibly knew all along, were completely unacceptable to the western allies, but which were probably intended to buy some time while he appealed to Moscow for support.[19] However, as the western powers underlined their intention to act by making obvious military preparations, the Yugoslav Government conceded, accepting the terms of the recent Note and signing an agreement to this effect with the allied command. This set a line on the map which came to be referred to as the Morgan Line, dividing Venezia Giulia into Allied and Yugoslav zones of occupation, A and B respectively. This was concluded on 9 June and was a purely military agreement specifically without prejudice to the ultimate disposition of the territory.[20]

The Russian position during this crisis had doubtless been the critical factor. Stalin had been made aware of Anglo-American intentions regarding Trieste, firstly by Eden during the Yalta Conference, and later via Molotov who had received from the American Ambassador in Moscow, Averell Harriman, in March, a telegram explaining American determination to ensure that this disputed region be placed under AMG until the peace settlement. When the crisis occurred, the Western Allies did not notify Stalin officially of their position and request his understanding of it until after Tito's initial rejection of their demarche of 15 May. This Note, which also asked Stalin to exercise his influence with Tito, was not delivered until 21 May, the day on which Tito gave in. Although Stalin subsequently wrote to Truman, defending Yugoslav rights, he also expressed himself satisfied with the solution.[21] If Tito had requested support from Moscow, it seems clear that he did not get it. Tito nurtured his anger at what was interpreted in Belgrade as a betrayal on the part of the Russians, sentiments which he revealed publicly in a speech in Ljubljana at the end of May.[22] The Russians promptly informed him in what, as we have already seen was not the first rebuff for independent policy-making, that his comments were regarded in Moscow as offensive and unacceptable.[23] Yugoslav territorial ambitions were not something for which the Russians were prepared to risk war with the west.

The Yugoslavs had found themselves similarly lacking in support in their attempts to seize and occupy southern Carinthia where Tito sought to occupy Villach and Klagenfurt, so presenting the western Allies with a *fait accompli*. The west demanded a withdrawal – they had recognised the agreed demarcation line in Germany, and required similar recognition where their allies had overrun the Anglo-American zones. Stalin moved to stop the Yugoslav advance, so permitting the British to take control of southern Carinthia; Yugoslav units in territory designated for Soviet occupation were also ordered out.[24] Stalin had been devoting some energy towards his objective of ensuring the Social Democrat, Karl Renner, succeeded in establishing himself in Vienna. Renner had placed himself at Moscow's disposal and Stalin hoped that through him he could gradually impose Russian dominance over Austria.[25]

Nonetheless, the Trieste episode confirmed for the British their current view of the closeness of the relationship between the Tito Government and the Soviet Union. During the third week of March, Eden had minuted a balanced appraisal of British policy towards Yugoslavia which assessed the relative value of the country in terms of Britain's long-term interests.[26] The present policy, he thought, was 'realistic and not over-ambitious', recognising that Yugoslavia did not have the same long-term strategic and political importance for Britain as Greece and Italy and that she lay on the edge of major British interests. He explained that British policy continued to be based on '50–50 Agreement, the principle of which is in effect that Yugoslavia should be a sort of neutral buffer area between the British and Russian zones of influence'. As to the future, he ventured that since Yugoslavia would be likely to develop into the most powerful and influential of the Balkan countries, 'if we abandon all claim to advise or express our views on the conduct of Yugoslav policies, we shall lose one principal means of influencing Balkan affairs as a whole'.

The succeeding months had indicated just how unlikely was the scenario that Yugoslavia would be a neutral area, but the general thrust of this policy remained valid. Despite the Trieste crisis, which indicated that Anglo-Yugoslav relations would remain stressful for some time, Cadogan argued in a minute to Eden that Britain should not pull out of Yugoslavia altogether. Britain's interests, he suggested, would be best served by the avoidance of too much contact with 'reactionary forces' such as King Peter now that the new regime as constituted under the Tito–Subasic Agreement was established.[27] The Yugoslav issue was discussed briefly at British instigation by the Great Powers during their last war-time summit conference held at Potsdam between 17 July and 2 August. In the middle of the proceedings, Churchill and Eden returned home to receive the results of the General Election; to the surprise of many it was the Labour leader Clement Attlee and not Churchill who returned to the final days of the conference as the British prime minister. Attlee, whom one official subsequently described as 'an outstanding manager of an often difficult team', a man lacking even the slightest trace of 'personal vanity or conceit',[28] was unlike his predecessor in having a relative disinterest in foreign affairs. He returned from Potsdam with a jaundiced view of the Russians whom he dismissed as 'ideological imperialists',[29] but tended to leave the making of foreign policy to his highly capable, if idiosyncratic, Foreign Secretary. Although there were significant ideological differences between conservative and labour politicians in general, Attlee's views on foreign affairs and those of his Foreign Secretary, Ernest Bevin, were remarkably consistent with those of their predecessors. Bevin believed that, as a matter of principle, British foreign policy should not be determined by ideological sympathies or socialist solidarity. Rather, he saw foreign policy as a matter of national interests which he considered were unchanged by the change of government. He also resisted pressure from the left wing of the Labour Party to alter greatly the personnel in the most senior posts in the foreign office and diplomatic service. He came to office with few illusions: shortly after the Potsdam conference he commented that the Russians, having carried out two five-year plans and won the war, were returning to their 'original Lenin idea' and 'any hope of a new style diplomacy of "cards on the table, face upwards, was inconceivable"'.[30]

Bevin's concern for continuity was underlined by retention of Alexander Cadogan, who had been the Permanent Under Secretary at the Foreign Office since 1938, an unusually lengthy tenure by any standards. Cadogan, who had served in neither the Soviet Union nor the United States, showed himself nonetheless very conscious of the ideological threat posed by Moscow in east and central Europe and of the danger of leaving this region 'open to the peculiar methods of cultivation employed by the Soviet Government'.[31] Orme Sargent, his war-time deputy, succeeded him in January. Sargent, whose career had been marked by a reluctance to accept overseas postings, was among those who in the late 1930s had emerged as an opponent of appeasement. In 1945, he took a similar attitude towards growing Soviet bellicosity: in his paper 'Stocktaking after VE Day', which received wide circulation within government in July 1945, he argued that 'Britain should take the offensive in challenging communist penetration . . . in Eastern Europe'.[32] Aware of Britain's relative weakness, he also urged co-ordination of Anglo-American policy in the region, and the joint avoidance of 'promises, express or implied, to the peoples of these areas which it might be found could not be carried out'.[33]

Policy towards the Balkans was implemented within the Foreign

Office largely by the Southern Department consulting the Northern Department, which among other things took the lead in Soviet policy, and certain specialist departments, most notably those dealing with economic issues (Economic Relations Department) and refugees. Head of the Southern Department during the latter half of 1945 was William Hayter who had just returned from a war-time posting in Washington. Within Southern Department, Yugoslav affairs were handled by John Colville who returned to the Foreign Office in October 1945 after serving since 1943 as Churchill's Private Secretary. It was, he later wrote, part of his job to 'compose in flowery prose indignant despatches to our Ambassador in Belgrade instructing him to complain, in the name of His Majesty's Government, of the tyrant's behaviour. As exercises in composition,' he recalled, 'they were enjoyable; as protests they were ineffective.'

In Belgrade, Ralph Stevenson had been accredited to the United Provisional Government in March 1945. Halifax's PPS during 1940, Stevenson had enjoyed a spell as Ambassador to Montevideo before his posting to Cairo in August 1943. He never displayed excessive sympathy for the Royalist politicians and when the elections of November 1945 confirmed Tito's provisional government in power, he would argue firmly that the Yugoslavs had probably got the government the majority of the population wanted.[34] In the embassy, he was supported initially by Bill Deakin as first secretary, but Deakin returned to London in January 1946, and was succeeded by George Clutton whose crisp and often perceptive reporting forms one of the principal official records of Yugoslavia's political development in this period.

Bevin placed some weight on the possibility that increased trade might be used to secure a relaxation of many of the restrictions on movement in the Russian sphere. The exploration of economics as a weapon of diplomacy in this regard was conducted primarily by John Coulson, then head of ERD. During the autumn of 1945 and spring of 1946, Coulson produced a series of thoughtful papers on the subject, which are notable for the emphasis they place on the constraints on the British Government in its attempts to pursue a forward policy in eastern Europe, both in terms of the Soviet occupation and as a result of its own economic weakness. Much of the burden of handling the highly sensitive issues surrounding the refugees in the British occupied zones of central and southern Europe fell to George Rendel in his capacity as UK Representative on the European Regional Commission of UNRRA, as well as the

Superintending Under Secretary of the Refugee, Prisoners of War and Supply and Relief departments. His earlier posting included a spell as Ambassador to the Yugoslav Government-in-Exile, as well as being Minister in Sofia between 1938 and 1941 when he narrowly escaped being killed by a bomb placed in his staff's luggage at an Istanbul hotel.[35]

Without exception postings to eastern Europe in the summer of 1945 obliged British diplomats to work under very trying circumstances. This was nowhere more true than in Tito's Yugoslavia where the zealous communists among the leaders seemed only too anxious to demonstrate their loyalty and subservience to the new hard, anti-western rhetoric of post-war Soviet diplomacy. Diplomatic business was hampered by difficulties in transportation and communications, and information gathering was severely restricted since discussion with individuals opposed to the existing regime was hazardous at best. The facilities for disseminating information were equally great, a matter of particular concern to the Foreign Office since cultural relations were regarded as 'one, if not the most powerful, of the means at our disposal for countering Russian influence'. At the end of August 1945, Orme Sargent reflected: 'It now looks as though the communists will take concerted measures in these countries to thwart our efforts and those of the Americans in this direction, unless we act vigorously and promptly.'[36]

These problems greatly enhanced the value of such information as diplomats were able to glean. They also encouraged conjecture and speculation when it came to assessing Soviet policies and intentions. With only limited access to emerging political elites and with few opportunities to engage in negotiation, Britain's representatives in eastern Europe could in the end do little more than monitor the imposition of Soviet authority upon the region and reflect upon the irrelevance of the principles enunciated at Yalta and Potsdam.

The Trieste crisis was instrumental in shaping British perceptions of Soviet policy at a time when allied relations in the aftermath of the defeat of Germany were very fluid. Indeed, with the collapse of German power, and France too weak to be a leading player in European affairs for some time to come, Britain and the Soviet Union were, in effect, contesting the right to dominate the region. As early as 1942 the Foreign Office had identified the Soviet Union as Britain's chief rival in Europe and the Middle East after the war.[37] Although British policy following the Anglo-Soviet Treaty in 1942 was characterised by a sincere determination to make the Anglo-Soviet partnership work, the doubts about Moscow's intentions remained. These resurfaced in the spring of 1944 when they were given expression by Churchill in a minute to Anthony Eden of 4 May regarding 'the brute issues between us and the Soviet Government which are developing in Italy, in Rumania, in Bulgaria, in Yugoslavia and above all in Greece', and concluding that the western powers were evidently 'approaching a show down with the Russians'.[38] The Chiefs of Staff were of the same opinion, and cautioned that the best policy would be to remain on good terms with Moscow. On the basis of this recommendation, the Post-Hostilities Planning Sub-Committee (on which the Foreign Office was represented) prepared an analysis which concluded that Britain must avoid obstructing Soviet demands where these did not conflict with vital British interests. Vital interests, as defined by the Chiefs of Staff, did not include eastern Europe. A Joint Intelligence Sub-Committee (JIC) paper of December 1944 elaborated on this, predicting that the Soviet Union would seek to use this region as a buffer zone.[39] The so-called Percentages Agreement of October 1944, in which Churchill appeared to recognise Soviet predominance in Romania in return for a similar recognition of the British position in Greece suggests that, although the Prime Minister accepted Soviet interest in the region, he was, by reserving a percentage share, signalling British intentions to maintain a foothold.[40]

During the following nine months, however, the British recognised that Stalin had either interpreted this claim as merely a token, or else had ignored it altogether. In late August, Bevin wrote to James Balfour, Minister in Washington, that it was time to consider whether Britain was going to acquiesce in Soviet domination of eastern Europe. But the Foreign Office position had already been outlined by Sargent in his 'Stocktaking' memorandum, and argued that Britain must take a stand in Europe 'in the immediate future if the situation were to be prevented from 'crystallising to our permanent detriment', as British military power declined.[41] In practical terms this meant 'keeping our foot firmly in Finland, Poland, Czechoslovakia, Austria, Yugoslavia and Bulgaria', challenging the Russians in these six countries, instead of waiting until the Soviet Government, threatens us further west and south in Germany, Italy, in Greece and in Turkey'. Sargent added that such a challenge would be inevitable 'if we let Stalin pocket for good these six countries. This statement indicates not only a sense that Stalin's foreign policy was incrementally expansionist, but also a preoccupation with asserting Britain's right to protect, through diplomacy, her pre-war world status.[42]

However, Britain was severely hampered in pursuing such an offensive. In the first place, they had been denied a physical presence in the area by virtue of the disposition of the Red Army at the end of the war. Conversely the Soviet presence gave Moscow the ability to exercise a stranglehold over those liberated territories. The second handicap arose from British economic weakness and the third centred largely on the relationship with the United States. The Americans were highly suspicious of British motives: the thesis that Britain was indulging in traditional great power rivalry for spheres of influence in Europe continued to hold much currency in Washington where policy makers were not only disapproving but determined that they should not allow the United States to appear to be accomplices in British machinations.

In the Foreign Affairs debate of 20 August, Bevin gave public expression to his misgivings when he told the House of Commons that the British Government had gained the impression that 'one kind of totalitarianism [was] being replaced by another'.[43] In Yugoslavia, where, as we have seen, Britain had been instrumental in organising the Tito–Subasic Agreement which had united Tito's provisional government and the Government-in-Exile, the process of excluding the latter and all other moderate influences was well under way. The lack of American support at the Potsdam conference in July for the British suggestion of a three-power protest at conditions in Belgrade had led the British to retreat from their earlier attempts to exercise some influence on these developments. Moreover, the bitterness of the Trieste crisis, and the massacre by Tito's forces of the Croats and Slovenes mistakenly repatriated to Yugoslavia by the British in May, had been alarming demonstrations of the impossibility of collaboration with the Tito government now that the war was over.[44]

During preparations for the London Council of Foreign Ministers and in anticipation of his preliminary meeting with the new Secretary of State, James Byrnes, Bevin had written to Balfour that Britain ought now to consider 'what inducements, economic or cultural, we can offer these countries to look West rather than East.[45] Britain's ability, in the immediate post-war years, to manipulate foreign economic policy to achieve diplomatic ends was severely limited. As Winston Churchill had so aptly remarked at Potsdam, Britain, in the summer of 1945, was indeed 'the world's greatest debtor'. The Foreign Office had discussed the likely effect of Britain's finances on foreign policy in the broadest terms during March when an Economic Relations Department paper pointed out that British post-war policy would have to be commensurate with Britain's economic strength in a world where effective post-war diplomacy would depend on economic power.[46] This caveat notwithstanding, it was a generally accepted maxim within British official circles that resumption of trade with eastern Europe was vital to the economic recovery of Europe as a whole and that British policy should be directed at achieving this end.

As the Foreign Secretary contemplated, on his return from Potsdam, the difficulties presented by the Soviet presence in eastern Europe, he conveyed to his officials his belief that an increase of trade might be used to secure a relaxation of many of the restrictions on movement in the Russian sphere. By 23 August, John Coulson had responded to this suggestion in a paper which discussed with enthusiasm, if little optimism, the practicalities of such a policy.[47] Coulson argued that while the assumptions of Bevin's suggestion were eminently sound, the prospects for a substantial resumption of trade were far from encouraging. Not only were the restrictions on movement and publicity proving formidable handicaps but Soviet policy was to denude these countries of all materials which could be used for Soviet reconstruction, leaving eastern Europe without the wherewithal to conduct trade on anything approaching a reciprocal basis. That they were in need of British goods was not disputed; but it was questionable that they could pay for them in money or in kind. And Britain had to be paid. The earlier than expected end to the fighting in the Far East had brought an abrupt cessation of Lend-Lease. British policy was determined above all by the need to pay off the external debt as rapidly as possible and to renegotiate with the Americans for a renewed loan. Nevertheless, Coulson argued, 'this is not to say we should throw in our hand' and he recommended continued defiance, while noting that greater freedom of publicity must be pressed for before the possibilities of trade could be assessed: 'That this freedom should itself derive from increased trade does not seem at the present time practical politics.'

The prospects for trade with Yugoslavia were not promising. Yugoslavia was seen as the economic as well as the political vassal of Moscow, arguably the most effectively sovietised by the end of

1945. A status report produced by Southern Department in August stated that it was unlikely that commercial relations would give Britain much influence over Yugoslav affairs, not least of all because Britain herself had no commodities to spare for Yugoslavia. 'The general problem is that in the long term Yugoslavia will be largely outside the area of our economic sphere of influence.'[48] This theme was repeated in the Northern Department paper of November 1945 which argued that as long as 'the present regime lasts in Yugoslavia, it is to be expected that Yugoslavia will dispense with trading with the West unless in any given instance it is seriously embarrassing for her to do so'.[49] Little was done to make advances in this direction prior to the Yugoslav elections in November. But owing to the British decision to acquiesce in the new regime, and Bevin's belief in the need to establish a foothold in Yugoslavia for strategic reasons, John Colville, in his capacity as Yugoslav desk officer, wrote to the Board of Trade on 27 November stating that in order to get relations with Yugoslavia onto a more friendly footing, primary efforts were to be devoted to getting trade restarted: 'Tito apparently welcomes the prospect and there is now some hope of getting the essential preliminaries settled.'[50]

Successful exploitation of economic policy was closely linked, as Coulson pointed out in his memorandum in August, to the extent to which Britain could establish greater freedom of publicity within the Soviet sphere. Although the machinery for overseas information, which became established under Foreign Office auspices during Bevin's tenure as Foreign Secretary, did not begin to develop until 1946, Bevin and his officials were already alive to the importance of exploiting publicity and cultural contacts to British advantage throughout eastern Europe. During the inter-war years, the Foreign Office had increasingly, if reluctantly, channelled resources into 'projecting' Britain overseas in order to counter the propaganda of totalitarian regimes and their experience of such methods had been greatly increased by the recent war. But the 'tendentious and one-sided' treatment by the Polish press of Bevin's speech in the Foreign Affairs debate in August foreshadowed the difficulties the western powers were to encounter in making their voices heard in the Soviet sphere.[51]

Nevertheless, British officials in east European posts were convinced that publicity and renewed cultural contacts would prove one of the best means of exerting British influence in the region. In publicising British views in eastern Europe, several means were available of which the most potent was probably the World Service of the BBC. British officials based in the region were strongly in favour of publicising the misdoings of the local regimes as a way of boosting the morale of the local populace while also providing a counter-balance to anti-western propaganda. The increasingly vocal denunciation of BBC transmissions was considered, moreover, the best possible proof of the effectiveness of such criticisms.[52] But direction of these broadcasts for political ends was also a double-edged weapon for while it was undoubtedly an excellent method of getting the British view across, not least of all because of the credibility ascribed by east Europeans for the BBC news service, this propaganda could also inadvertently undermine British policy in that it was inclined to raise false hopes and encourage the local populace in resistance in the belief that the British would back their words with actions. This, of course, was never an option.[53] Aside from providing English papers in east European languages, Britain also sought to keep communications open through promotion of cultural contacts. But, as with the local press, the local regimes had a firm grip on all forms of exchanges with the west: in Yugoslavia, where the press had been tightly controlled by Tito's faction since the liberation, the British Embassy suffered the indignity of seeing the British Reading Room closed as a consequence of the Yugoslav Government's accusations against the staff of espionage activities.[54]

The Potsdam Conference had revealed more clearly than before the disparities in British and American policies with regard to eastern Europe and the abrupt cessation of Lend Lease following the earlier than expected Japanese capitulation, had brought a new tension to the relationship. There was little attempt made in the interim between Potsdam and the London CFM to co-ordinate the approach, nor is there evidence that such an attempt was thought necessary. American confidence had certainly been boosted by the successful use of the atomic bomb in bringing the war against Japan to an abrupt halt, and the evidence suggests that Truman and Byrnes probably believed that possession of this would give an advantage in diplomatic negotiations with the Russians.[55] This confidence, combined with a victor's euphoria, inclined them to behave in a bullish and egoistic manner which seemed to take little account of the perceptions and concerns of their allies. As one British official tartly commented, 'The Americans seem moved at present by enthusiastic and self congratulatory emotions and they are probably in one of their more irritating cockahoop moods.'[56]

As regards the Balkans, a preliminary meeting between Balfour and American Secretary of State James Byrnes had served only to give the British the impression that Byrnes was 'out of his depth' in south-east European affairs. Be that as it may, Byrnes came to London in September determined to make a stand over Roumania and Bulgaria and was faced with equal determination on the part of Molotov to use the occasion to secure an end to western influence in the region. Consequently, the sessions on the Balkan peace treaties were characterised by increasing acrimony as British and American representatives refused to recognise these regimes until they had been broadened.[57]

From the British point of view, the London CFM was instrumental in another respect: it seems that it was during the course of these proceedings that Bevin and his officials came to the unshakable conclusion that the Soviet Union was not concerned simply with securing its western frontier by establishing friendly regimes in the Balkans but was actively seeking to challenge the British position of dominance in the Mediterranean. Bevin's Private Secretary, Pierson Dixon, wrote in his diary of 24 September, 'The main objective of the Russians is access to a base in the Mediterranean. The Mediterranean is therefore the real Russian challenge at this conference.'[58] And again on 2 October, 'a new point which seems to me to emerge . . . is the intensity of Russian jealousy of our position in the Mediterranean now that France and Italy have ceased to be first class powers'.[59]

It may have been that this is what the British came to believe because of the traditional Russian policy of seeking a warm water port and of equally traditional British fears for their position in the Mediterranean. Lord Bullock, Bevin's biographer, concludes that the Foreign Secretary was almost certainly wrong in his analysis and cites Molotov's continued insistence that Roumania and Bulgaria were the cause of the difficulties at London. This may be so, but the essential point here is that not only Bevin but the Foreign Office who was becoming increasingly convinced that Soviet policy directly threatened vital British interests and this altered British policy in respect to the Balkans. Moreover, the British were not the only ones to draw this inference from Molotov's behaviour in London. In his memoir of the occasion, Byrnes recalled that one of the principal concerns for the American delegation was 'the unmistakable evidence of Russian expansionism . . . her determination to dominate the Balkan states had become apparent'.[60]

The British experiences at the London Conference occasioned fresh debate about the motives of the Soviet Union; these perceptions of Soviet power and intentions inevitably conditioned Britain's relations with the east European states. There was already a tendency within the Office to regard much of the area as having fallen within what Thomas Brimelow, then attached to Northern Department, referred to as the 'Soviet sphere of influence'.[61] A few days before the London Council of Foreign Ministers opened, Britain's ever-optimistic Ambassador in Moscow, Archibald Clark Kerr, wrote that he considered Russia to be on the defensive in Europe and that he perceived a 'certain relaxation in the Soviet grasp over Eastern and Central Europe' to the advantage of 'Western democratic influence'. He attributed this in part to Soviet involvement in the Far East, election of a Labour Government in Britain, and Soviet appreciation of a change in the balance of power brought about by the West's possession of the atomic bomb.[62] But the proceedings at the London Council of Foreign Ministers seemed to suggest otherwise and, on 18 October, the JIC produced a report which put a slightly different interpretation on Soviet actions.[63] It attributed the deterioration in relations with Moscow to Soviet 'insistence . . . on treating Eastern Europe as their exclusive sphere of influence regardless of the interests of their Allies'; to disagreements over the interpretation of the Yalta and Potsdam Agreements and the Soviet sense of inferiority engendered by Anglo-American development of the atomic bomb; and to resentment at co-ordination of policy between Britain and the United States in matters of dispute with the Soviet Union and Soviet failure to secure long-term credits from the West. The JIC's recommendation that Britain should proceed by showing clearly where she stood and that there were limits to her forbearance was supported by the British Minister in Moscow, Frank Roberts, who suggested that through this action London might hope to create 'a more solid foundation' for Anglo-Soviet relations.[64]

But this tougher stance was not universally subscribed to in British official circles.[65] Indeed an awareness of Western weakness despite possession of the atomic bomb was apparent in the JIC Report of 18 October, and alluded to in a speculative minute by Thomas Brimelow of 27 October in which he contended that the

Russians did not appear to believe that the West would use the atomic bomb since 'far from making them modify the aims of Russian foreign policy' it had actually made them 'more obdurate in pursuit of their aims'.[66] At the same time there was a growing tendency among British officials to emphasise the ideological aspect of Soviet policy; Clark Kerr remarked in November 1945 that communist ideology and Soviet nationalism both seemed 'essential elements in Soviet foreign policy and therefore in the activities of communist parties abroad'.[67] During September, Bevin requested assessments from posts worldwide of the relationship between local communist parties and the Soviet Union.[68] This question had already arisen in response to initiatives by the Yugoslav Government which had already raised a succession of territorial claims not just against Italy but also in respect to Austria and Greece, all of which were being seen increasingly in London as the demarcation line at which the Soviet advance had to be halted if British (and implicitly Western) interests were to be defended. Although it is now thought that Stalin did not support Tito's ambitions in these directions, British officials were fairly convinced in 1945 that Tito was being used as the catspaw of Moscow's foreign policy.[69]

The shift in thinking about Soviet ambitions was soon reflected in communications with British representatives in the Balkans. Writing in November to Houstoun–Boswall, Orme Sargent stated that it was Britain's policy to put a limit on Russian expansion in the Middle East.[70] Accordingly Sargent wrote to Stevenson following the Yugoslav elections in mid-November:

> Yugoslavia is strategically too important to our position in the Mediterranean, and Greece and Italy for us to adopt a policy of sulking towards her. Our object must be, therefore . . . to re-establish our influence in Yugoslavia and thus to challenge and even undermine that of the Soviet Union.[71]

Bevin went to the Moscow foreign ministers' conference in December determined to demonstrate firmness because this seemed the only means left to the West to counter the Soviet presence. Three months later, John Coulson's summing up of the options left to Britain in pursuit of her objectives in eastern Europe reflected a greater realism of Britain's position: 'The best we can do,' he wrote 'is to hold the door open – or to hold enough doors open – for the Eastern Europeans to catch frequent glimpses of a more attractive

Map 2 The federal units of Yugoslavia, 1945–1991

and prosperous world in the West and be encouraged, when the occasion offers, to pass through.'[72]

The Yugoslav Republic had been proclaimed on 23 November 1945 following elections to the Constituent Assembly on 16 November. The proclamation marked the official exclusion of all 'democratic elements' including the three regents appointed in March, and Ivan Subasic, who now retreated into retirement. The government was dominated by four men in addition to Tito: Aleksander Rankovic, head of State Security, Edvard Kardelj, the new foreign minister, Milovan Djilas who was in charge of propaganda and Boris Kidric, responsible for economic planning. These five men held dictatorial powers. The new constitution was modelled on that of the Soviet Union of 1936 and adopted on 31 January 1946.[73] Yugoslavia was now a multinational federation of eight units, created on both ethnic and historical criteria and intended to establish a balance between them to avoid division of territory with mixed communities and provide special status for the two regions associated with Serbia, Kosovo and the Vojvodina. Indeed, the central thrust of the 1946 Constitution was that Serbia be kept relatively weak, to which end she was denied Bosnia, which had been a key element in Serbia's national expansion programme since the middle of the nineteenth century and which the Axis powers had included in Croatia. Serbia was also obliged to abandon Macedonia, 'Old Serbia' in pre-war Yugoslavia, and thus forsake her version of *Drang nach Salonika*. The regions of Vojvodina and Kosovo were given semi-autonomous status within Serbia to achieve the reduction of Serbia while simultaneously appeasing her sensibilities. At the same time, the Serbs were permitted to resume their inter-war prominence in both the Army and the civil service.

The central government gained its legitimacy through monolithic communist dictatorship, personified in Tito, bolstered by Marxist–Leninism and a national mythology which elaborated heavily on the romanticism of war-time resistance. Opposition, as in the pre-war state, was ruthlessly stamped out. Examples were made of those who would challenge the new regime. The most notable of these was Draza Mihailovic, who had been rounded up, with the remnants of his supporters, and imprisoned. Extermination of the Cetniks as a military but more importantly political force was an early objective of the Tito government. Mihailovic was subjected to a show trial in May 1946 and subsequently executed as a traitor and collaborator. These events attracted little more than token protest from the west: war-weariness, combined with the not unreasonable belief that a similar fate would have been meted out to Tito and his followers had circumstances been reversed, inclined the British to leave well alone.[74] During this period, the Catholic Church also came in for fierce repression: its traditional association with Croat nationalism made it a source of possible resistance to the new constitutional arrangements, while its connections with the Ustase, and role in protecting known war criminals among the Croat population,[75] made it an easy target for government censure. After a long trial, the Archbishop Stepinac, Primate of Zagreb, for many the living symbol of the Catholic Church in Croatia, was imprisoned in October 1946.

These were just particularly public manifestations of the ruthlessness of the Tito regime in stamping out opposition; this policy extended to the effective extermination of the Volksdeutsche population which inhabited Slovenia, and the massacre of disaffected Cetniks mistakenly repatriated by the British forces of General Freyburg in the spring of 1945.[76] At the same time a new economic policy sought to destroy the propertied classes; the bourgeoisie had largely been destroyed during the war and the peasantry problem was tackled with care. Collectivisation was not immediately imposed.

Following the Yugoslav elections of 16 November, the Foreign Office had briefly re-examined current policy. The Americans were determined to mark their disapproval of undemocratic electoral methods and issued Richard Patterson, their Ambassador in Belgrade, with instructions that formal diplomatic relations did not signify American approval of the policies or methods of the current regime, implying that economic aid would not be forthcoming from the United States until changes had been made.[77] In London, however, there was little inclination to protest further, and Orme Sargent recorded in his letter to Stevenson of 24 November that there seemed 'little doubt that the Yugoslavs have the Government which the majority in fact want' and that, 'having made no protest about the Tito–Subasic Agreement we really have no alternative but to acquiesce in the new regime'.[78]

Acquiescence did not mean disdain, however. The Yugoslav government was prompt in indicating its interest in trade and property agreements and in resolving outsanding questions relating to Yugoslav war criminals, many of whom were believed to be hiding in British and American administered refugee camps in Italy and Austria. The Yugoslavs also wished to press their claims against Italy andAustria for revision of Yugoslavia's frontiers. In December 1945, following formal recognition of the Tito Government, Bevin directed the Foreign Office to respond to Belgrade's initiatives and work at putting Anglo-Yugoslav relations onto a sound footing.[79]

5

Limited Objectives: Seeking a Balkan Foothold, 1946–1947

'Seeking a foothold', 'establishing Anglo-Yugoslav relations on a firm footing', 'putting Britain right with Yugoslavia': these were phrases which occurred regularly in Ernest Bevin's spasmodic forays into Yugoslav affairs during 1946 and 1947. The sentiment is understandable, but what did it mean in practice and what were its objectives? Yugoslavia was to all intents and purposes on the eastern side of the 'Iron Curtain' which Winston Churchill so graphically identified in his speech at Fulton, Missouri on 5 March 1946:[1] she was, as one Foreign Office official observed, 'the economic as well as political vassal of Moscow'.[2] However, Britain did retain some tangible interests – through ownership of property, through her responsibility in handling Yugoslav refugees and as a result of her 'great power' responsibilities which emerged particularly forcibly over the Italian and Austrian peace treaties with both of which Yugoslavia was deeply concerned.

Aid, Trade and British Property

The British were convinced that trade with eastern Europe was essential to the recovery of Europe as a whole and that the following two years would be vital for establishing trade patterns. The Foreign Office addressed the problem in a paper entitled 'The effect of Russian influence in East Europe and on the European economy', which was circulated within the Office and interested departments at the end of November 1945, and discussed at some length the prospects of Anglo-Yugoslav commerce. The paper argued that 'for political, ideological and racial reasons, the new Yugoslavia looks to the Soviet Union in economic as in other matters and chooses to make herself the economic as well as the political satellite of Russia'. So long as the new regime lasts, it continued, 'it is to be expected that Yugoslavia will dispense with trading with the west unless in any given instance it is seriously embarrassing for her to do so'.[3] However, this perception was closely bound up with the more general long-term question of the shape of eastern Europe in the post-war period. In May 1945, the Department of Trade had produced a paper which reviewed the economic prospects for the region and argued that the real point of principle which had to be considered in formulating policy was whether the British government was 'to acquiesce *sub silentio* in the apparent extension to Yugoslavia of a closed system of economy which may ultimately extend over a substantial part of Europe'.[4]

This was the real issue in Yugoslavia as elsewhere: war-time policy towards the Balkans had been directed, from the political point of view, towards the end of securing a foothold with the post-war regime and, despite the Trieste crisis in May and the sham that had been made of the Tito–Subasic agreement, Bevin was unwilling in 1946 to abandon this objective. During the autumn of 1945 Foreign Office officials, in consultation with their opposite numbers in the Board of Trade and Treasury, began preparing the ground for restarting Anglo-Yugoslav trade. In early 1946, as part of the process of evolving a strategy for dealing with the Soviet Union, the Foreign Office undertook two major studies of the uses to which economic policy could be put in furthering political objectives, the products of which formed the basis of British thinking concerning economic relations with Yugoslavia until the autumn of 1948. The first of these was produced by John Coulson during March 1946 and incorporated much of the Economic Relations Department paper of the previous autumn.[5] While acknowledging that pre-war trade with the region was small and that the British-owned capital assets there, valued then at some £200 million, were not significant, Coulson argued that should imports from these countries not be resumed on any considerable scale, Britain would have little chance of recovering the money owed on commercial debts and interest on Government loans; potentially, the greatest loss however, would be that of the political import of renewed economic links. He recommended that in Yugoslavia, Czechoslovakia, Austria and Poland, Britain should do whatever she could to keep up every kind of trade connection, 'partly as an encouragement to these countries, as soon as they feel able to exert themselves more strongly', and also because it would be easier through them to penetrate once more the Balkan countries if and when the British position became stronger. Nonetheless, the policy recommended was cautious: trade had to be conducted on a strictly economic basis; loans, credits and financial inducements of any kind were considered out of the question. Robert Hankey, then Chargé d'Affaires in Warsaw, was immediately critical. He could see no advantage in pouring resources into these countries so long as they were under the influence of communist or crypto communist governments: 'That would only redound to the credit and great advantage of those who are welding these countries into a bloc aimed at the British Empire. It would just be financing the Soviet Five Year Plan.'[6]

The inescapable fact was that Britain would be severely hampered in her commercial policy towards Yugoslavia, and indeed the region as a whole, firstly by the Russians who had cornered the market for anything worth buying, thereby making a nonsense of east–west trade in terms of an exchange of goods, and secondly by the United States. The Foreign Office had produced a brief for the British delegation to the Moscow Conference of Foreign Ministers in December 1945, which had made a detailed analysis of this latter problem. The paper stated the Foreign Office view that the field of economics would pose the severest test to the transatlantic relationship during the short and medium term. Two stumbling blocks were identified: the first was thought to be largely superficial and arose from the fact that Britain and America wanted to pursue the same ends by somewhat different means. Thus, while the United States was committed to a system of free private enterprise which affected and abhorred controls, restrictive practices and state ownership, Britain was committed to a policy of socialisation, to a policy of controls (at least temporary and within well-defined limits) by reason of her economic difficulties. Such differences, it was nevertheless argued, were not as great as might appear.[7] The second obstacle, and this the more fundamental, arose from the fact that each country laboured under a serious and separate handicap in its efforts to implement a parallel policy, and the nature of that handicap in each case was so alien to the experience of the other that it constituted a perpetual barrier to the realisation of joint aims. The two handicaps were, of course, the American political system and the British financial position.[8] In the former, a system in which policy making was slowed down by the rigid separation of the executive from the legislature was quite different to the British experience, as was the more pervasive influence public opinion was able to exert on the business of the United States government. Britain, on the other hand, having mortgaged her future to pay for the war, had seen her international status drastically eroded; Britain was, in the early post-war years, inescapably dependent upon her American ally for economic assistance, an ally to whom she was already greatly in debt as a result of the recent conflict.

During the spring of 1946 there had been much discussion within the Foreign Office of the possibility of a joint Anglo-American initiative with respect to east European trade. Bevin got as far as sounding out the Americans in May about an agreed Anglo-American commercial policy towards the Soviet sphere, but pressed the issue no further when Byrnes failed to reply to his enquiry.[9] Moreover, there were the constraints of the American Loan to consider: Britain was required to confine herself to buying in the cheapest markets and adopting minimum regulations of imports and so on. Bevin might ideally wish for an aggressive forward policy towards eastern Europe, but in practice Britain did not have the resources to implement it. Even if the United States could be persuaded to pursue a parallel policy, this would clearly be impolitic since the necessity for long-term credits would mean that the American Treasury would have to bear the main burden. Moreover, the Treasury believed that a separate and quite different system of trade with these countries would be required and that the current American expectation that these states would join the International Trade Organisation was naive.

While this discussion of the international means for pursuing east–west trade was in progress, there was also a general awareness that the present machinery for monitoring and analysing Soviet activity in Europe and around the world, was in need of revision. The spring of 1946 had seen a steady worsening in the Soviet–western relationship: the crisis in Iran, occasioned by the refusal of the Russians to withdraw their troops from their zone of occupation by the agreed date of 2 March, combined with the deadlock which resulted when the Iranian government referred the problem to the United Nations Security Council, compounded by the growing virulence of the Soviet propaganda campaign being waged through the press and radio and aimed, so it seemed in London at British interests, had led to earnest consideration of what might be behind Soviet policy. Among the most significant contributions to this debate were a series of despatches received from Frank Roberts, then Chargé d'Affairs in Moscow. Roberts had been posted to Moscow in 1945 and although he was inclined initially to accept the view of Archibald Clark Kerr that Stalin wanted above all to retain Big Three co-operation, he also cautioned his colleagues in London that the Russians were genuinely afraid of Britain and the United States. In his detailed assessment of the meaning and implications of Soviet policies and propaganda, transmitted to London during March 1946 in a series of despatches which have since been compared with George Kennan's celebrated 'Long Telegram', he argued that the manner of the Soviet Union's attack on Britain indicated a profound fear of Britain's inherent strength.[10] Roberts emphasised the role of ideology in the making of Soviet foreign policy, leading him to speculate whether it might 'even be asked whether the world is not now faced with the danger of a modern equivalent of the religious wars of the 16th century, in which Soviet communism will struggle with western social democracy and the American version of capitalism for domination of the world'. These despatches were evaluated in London in conjunction with assessments being prepared by the Joint Intelligence Sub-committee and the Chiefs of Staff. Both of these bodies concluded that Soviet policy appeared at present to be to extend her influence further by all means short of war, and that for 'diplomatic reasons' such efforts would be directed towards areas where Moscow calculated that the resistance would be weakest in terms of combined British and United States pressure. Such areas included the Mediterranean, Turkey and Iran, all of which remained within Britain's sphere of primary responsibility.[11]

An indication of the sense of persecution current within the Foreign Office in the spring of 1946 can be found in a memorandum by Christopher Warner. This paper, which was given Cabinet circulation, explicitly addressed the question of the perceived 'Soviet campaign against this country and our response to it', the terms of reference themselves an indication of mounting British paranoia, and argued that 'Russian aggressiveness threatens British interests all over the world. The Soviet government are carrying out an intensive campaign to weaken, depreciate and harry this country in every possible way.' Perceiving a direct threat to British social democracy, Warner argued that Britain must now address herself primarily, if not exclusively, to its own defence.[12]

Among the recommendations contained in Frank Roberts's

despatches was a proposal that a committee be set up for close co-ordination and study of Soviet actions.[13] Although the Foreign Office rejected his suggestion that this body should be under Cabinet auspices, doubtless wanting to keep control over this sensitive and vital issue within its own purview, the Foreign Office took steps to strengthen and develop its planning machinery. For this purpose an inter-departmental body, which came to be known as the Russia Committee, was created within the Foreign Office and held its first meeting on 2 April 1946. Though arguably not as influential in policy making as some scholars have suggested, its composition of deputy and assistant under secretaries and counsellors of the Foreign Office, and the level of material placed before it, meant that it was centrally involved in British interpretations of and reactions to the onset of the Cold War.[14] It was an economic spin-off of the Russia Committee which produced, in June 1946, the second of the two major economic policy papers pertaining to east and south east Europe.[15] This report pointed out that the disappearance of Germany as a market and source of supply opened up certain opportunities to Britain to expand her trade with eastern Europe and despite the difficulties, recommended that these be exploited. British businessmen were, however, reluctant to trade with this region and the working party advocated that the present policy of withholding credit guarantees in order to facilitate activity be abandoned. In Yugoslavia in this period the principal British flagships were Unilever, Trepca, Shell and Coates and, in line with the general policy, John Colville recommended these firms at least should be encouraged to keep going, even if the smaller firms were discouraged from trying to keep up 'the uneven struggle'.[16]

Meanwhile, the delicate balance between political and economic considerations was being worked out in practice as the British attempted to negotiate with the Yugoslav government, a short-term trade agreement. Inevitably, preliminary discussions were beset by inter-departmental dissension as the political and economic departments in Whitehall worked out the balance of interests. Thus, while the Foreign Office had repeatedly stressed the political importance of these negotiations and the urgency of embarking upon them, the Board of Trade, supported by the Ministries of Supply and Food, were more constrained by the prosaic, but tangible, discipline imposed by economic realities. Pre-war trade with Yugoslavia had been very small and her use now as a trading partner could only be relatively minor: she could supply foodstuffs such as maize and dried fruit, as well as timber and a few minerals, but these commodities could be obtained quite easily elsewhere. In any case, so the argument went, it was questionable that Britain would be able to provide exports in return: British traders would be faced, for some years, with a seller's market, and would be inclined to seek more profitable markets with long-term prospects. The greatest obstacle, however, was the Treasury's objections to the extension by the British Government of favourable financial arrangements without which any trade agreement would be still-born.[17]

The Yugoslav trade delegation which had arrived in London in January had already made it clear that Yugoslavia could not afford to pay off war debts owed to the British, valued by the Treasury at £2.5 million and the Treasury was pessimistic about the chances of ever regaining these monies. There was also the question of trading mechanisms.

Given the autonomy of British traders, the Government could not enter into a binding commitment with a foreign country to deliver given quantities of specified commodities at fixed prices within fixed periods. The solution was to set up a centralised trading organisation in Britain under general auspices, but the British were not prepared to undertake such an arrangement. The only alternative would be to offer the Yugoslavs a Monetary Agreement by which the Bank of England would hold an agreed amount of dinars and the National Bank of Yugoslavia an equivalent sum in sterling. This was precisely what the Yugoslavs wanted, not least because such an agreement had been put together with the Czechs and they wanted comparable prestige.[18] The suggestion was being firmly opposed in Threadneedle Street: the Yugoslav government already held £3 million in gold in the UK and, moreover, the dinar was considered in the City to be greatly overvalued. Under Foreign Office pressure, the Bank agreed, however, not to oppose conclusion of a Monetary Agreement, provided that official recognition of the present rate of exchange was avoided, and that the amount of Sterling held by the Yugoslav National Bank was limited to the minimum of working capital. In order to get the negotiations started, the Treasury, on the grounds of showing goodwill, agreed to hold £250,000 in dinars, but was adamant that this would be the highest offer.[19]

By mid-May 1946, a small agreement of £1.5 million had been drawn up. That it was reached at all was due to British endeavour, motivated by the political will to demonstrate goodwill towards

Tito's government, and had little basis in commercial considerations. But there was a more serious purpose underpinning British negotiations: the Foreign Office intended that this agreement would act as an inducement to the Yugoslav government to agree a satisfactory settlement of the question of British-owned property in Yugoslavia, much of which was being affected by Yugoslav nationalisation laws. British held property in Yugoslavia in 1946 was worth £12 million and, like pre-war trade, was of little importance in economic terms. Its significance to British diplomats was derived from its perceived value as a means of influence. At the end of 1944, the Provisional Government had drafted the nationalisation proposals and despite the assurances Tito had given to Maclean in the spring of 1945 to the effect that British property would be restored to its owners, it was soon clear that these were platitudinous: the confiscation of the American-owned Socony–Vacuum oil concession in the spring of 1945 was the first indication of the new government's intentions, and this was followed on 20 August 1945 by the publication of a draft nationalisation law with respect to Yugoslav mineral wealth. In the meantime, British businessmen seeking to return to Yugoslavia to inspect their properties after the war's end, found themselves up against a wall of bureaucratic difficulties.[20]

Since the British government was itself engaged upon a programme of nationalisation of the nation's resources, it could hardly object if the Yugoslav government chose to do the same. Initially there was optimism on the part of British officials about the chances of obtaining the return of property which did not fall within these laws, but they were soon to be disillusioned. The Yugoslav government now introduced the question of collaboration to suit its economic programme, and made it clear that foreign owned property would only be returned where there was no suspicion of collaboration on behalf of the owners or operators. Most British property-holders in the region could be charged to varying degrees with compromises with the war-time occupation authorities and quisling regimes. Nonetheless, the Yugoslav Government agreed to negotiate and took the initiative in proposing the setting up of an Anglo-Yugoslav Mixed Commission in Belgrade in order to discuss conditions under which British-owned property might be returned. The optimism surrounding these negotiations among British officials when they began in London in April 1946 was not receiving much encouragement from the British Embassy in Belgrade. From there, George Clutton sent a series of cautionary telegrams saying that it was most unlikely that the Yugoslav Government would restore British property without what it regarded as very favourable terms for payments, property and trade agreements.

The trade agreements were by the beginning of May virtually complete, and the Foreign Office called an interdepartmental meeting to review the position. Although some of the companies' representatives had been given permission to inspect their properties they arrived in Yugoslavia to be confronted by hampering supervision. Trepca's emissaries were not permitted to freely consult former employees and given only limited access to their companies records; representatives of J P Coates had been prevented from visiting their properties in Zagreb which had been confiscated on not unsubstantiated charges of collaboration.[21] When six weeks into the Mixed Commissions' deliberations, it was clear in London that the question would not be settled, the negation of the trade agreements became inevitable. The political import of any concession was constantly weighed in the balance throughout these negotiations and by June 1946, the Foreign Office concluded that the limit had been reached. Although a fresh attempt was made during the summer of 1947 to re-activate these negotiations, in practice the difficulties proved insurmountable until Yugoslavia's expulsion from the Cominform in 1948 opened up new possibilities and necessities in her relations with the west.

During the summer of 1946, relations between Yugoslavia and the western powers were severely strained by a series of incidents which originated with the Tito government's determination to assert its rights, aggressively if need be, in the international community. The first of these involved the loss of two unarmed American transport planes which strayed into Yugoslav air space over northern Slovenia in August. The first was forced down by the Yugoslav air force, but the second, which occurred a few days later, provoked the Yugoslavs to use open force, shooting the plane down with the loss of five American airmen.[22] After this second incident, Truman ordered American troops along the Morgan Line augmented and the reinforcement of the air forces in northern Italy. Naval forces were also assembled and moved into Greek waters. Dean Acheson pithily records that 'Tito quickly got the point and backed down'.[23] The second episode was occasioned by mining of the Corfu Channel to the detriment of two British destroyers which consequently foundered there in October. This latter action, although it occurred in Albanian waters, was widely believed to have been inspired and aided by the Yugoslavs, who at that time were fostering close links with Albania, with the help of Greek communists.[24]

These essentially parochial concerns did nothing to improve the atmosphere of Yugoslav–western relations, but were aggavations which formed the background to the negotiations then in progress in Paris regarding the Italo–Yugoslav frontier.

Yugoslav Revisionism: the Paris Peace Conference and Beyond

At Potsdam, the Soviet Delegation had circulated a memorandum concerning Trieste and Istria and re-stating the arguments of Tito and Subasic concerning the Yugoslav claims in the region which had been put to the major allies during the Trieste crisis in May. Stalin now added to this by requesting the holding of democratic elections in the AMG areas of Venezia Giulia in order to establish a civil administration. The question had arisen owing to Alexander's request to the Combined Chiefs of Staff (CCS) for authority to abolish the Yugoslav committee system of local government in areas which had earlier been under Yugoslav occupation, and to reinstate in its place the Italian prefectorial system throughout the whole area. Deadlock was immediately created by the refusal on the part of either the British or the Russians to compromise, and consideration of the question was deferred. Truman, whose position on this question would determine whether or not British objections were given a hearing, had taken a detached view which had surprised even State Department officials and probably indicates uninterest on Truman's part. The United States remained mindful of the dangers perceived by the State Department of being drawn into British–Soviet rivalry in Europe and may, for this reason, also have been seeking to take a neutral stance in Anglo-rivalries in Europe.

Negotiation of the peace treaties with Italy and Germany's former allies in central and southern Europe began in September 1945 and continued until the signing of the final texts in February 1947. The machinery adopted for these negotiations worked against Yugoslavia and the smaller powers by awarding to the Big Four, which now included France, the responsibility for producing draft treaties. These drafts were then to be submitted to a larger conference for comment and recommendation after which the major powers would meet again to agree the final texts. This meant that the smaller powers at the peace conference were in a position which differed very marginally from that of their former enemies. Their only power of veto was that of refusing to sign the treaties, a power that the Yugoslav delegation often threatened to invoke, but never actually used. The consequence of this arrangement was that the small powers were vitally dependent on the Great Powers to protect their interests and listen to their demands. Given the ideological solidarity of the Soviet camp, this meant that Yugoslav interests would be represented to the degree to which she enjoyed Soviet backing.

The main clauses of the Italian Peace Treaty were drawn up after long and exhaustive bargaining between Britain and the United States on one hand and the Soviet Union on the other. France generally supported the former, but often served as a moderating influence through the mechanism of being the chief advocate of compromise. The French, whose policy was dominated by their obsession with the danger of German revival, saw good relations with the Soviet Union as a means of controlling this problem. Their greater inclination to accommodate Russian sensibilities on this and other questions must be seen in this light.[25] The basis for Italian and Yugoslav claims for sovereignty over Trieste were well known by the Great Powers and neither claimant could introduce anything during the course of negotiations which would alter their preconceived positions. Italy had acquired the Istrian peninsula by the Treaty of St. Germain in 1919. This territory, which juts out south from the head of the east side of the Adriatic, almost opposite Venice, had Trieste as its chief city and the former Austro-Hungarian naval base of Pola (Pula) at its southernmost tip. Its acquisition by Italy had meant the transfer to Italian nationality of some half million Slovenes who had felt the full weight of oppression under the fascist regime. In 1945 both Italy and Yugoslavia claimed the whole area of the Istrian peninsula. As far as the Great Powers were concerned, the Soviet Union supported the Yugoslav claim and even favoured the addition of further territory to it. The western powers, meanwhile, wanted the disputed region to be partitioned with the largest part being assigned to Yugoslavia, but leaving the city and port of Trieste to Italy.

When negotiations began at the London Council of Foreign Ministers in September 1945, the Morgan Line had placed Trieste, together with a narrow corridor which included the railway running between Gorizia and Carinthia, under AMG which also assumed authority over Pola and anchorages south of Trieste. The remainder of Venezia Giulia was under Yugoslav occupation. World opinion considered Trieste a test case in East–West relations: as the American Under Secretary of State, Dean Acheson observed, the future of Italy's north eastern frontier had really become a 'prestige battle between the Russian and Anglo-American position'.[26] Throughout, the Yugoslavs were more aggressive in defending their position than the Italians. On 3 September, shortly after the Council had convened in London, the head of the Yugoslav delegation, Ljubo Leontic, presented a memorandum outlining Yugoslav claims to Trieste and Venezia Giulia which encompassed all the areas acquired by Italy at the end of the first world war. The British were firmly opposed to such a revision on ethnic grounds and regarded the Yugoslav argument that the territory was required for economic reasons as similarly spurious: in the British view, Trieste's value as a port to either Italy or Yugoslavia was of minor importance compared with the use likely to be made of it by the central European states. It was the revival of central European trade which, as we have seen, was of particular importance in British calculations.[27]

After listening to the Yugoslav and Italian presentations, the Council concluded in October, that the new frontier should follow 'in the main' the ethnic line, 'leaving a minimum under alien rule'. But quite how this was to be achieved was left unclear. Furthermore, the major powers did not enter into detailed discussion of precisely where they understood the ethnic line to be, but adopted the suggestion advanced by Byrnes that deputies representing the four major powers should undertake a detailed study of the problem and report at the next conference.[28]

Attention now turned for the time being to the local arrangements in the province which had brought the Yugoslavs into dispute with the British and Americans authorities on the spot. During August 1945, the Anglo-American administration had persuaded the Yugoslavs, after much discussion, to agree to the establishment in Zone A of the Italian prefectorial system of government in return for a promise from Britain and the western powers that elections would be held to determine a local government. Although AFHQ initially agreed to this, by early January 1946 the local military authorities were making it clear to their superiors that they were not well disposed towards the holding of such elections in principles:

Harding explained the reasons in a letter to General William Morgan who had recently replaced Harold Alexander as SACMED.[29] His principal concern was that such elections would be open to interpretation as a plebiscite on the long-term political future of the area and would stimulate civil disorder with which AMG lacked the military resources to deal. Furthermore, if local government officials were popularly elected, and in the rural areas these would inevitably be Slovene, AMG would be unable to remove them in the event they proved disruptive. The military's reluctance to hold elections raised a diplomatic difficulty, since both Britain and the United States had given pledges that the elections would be held, and those which had been accepted in Belgrade in lieu of the restoration of the Slovene system of government. By way of a compromise, the Foreign Office proposed that preparation of the electoral lists should go ahead, which would at least serve to forestall Yugoslav protests and, it was to be hoped, that by the time these had been drawn up, the future settlement of the whole region would be much nearer completion, making elections a more attractive option.[30]

Internationalisation still offered a possible way out of the impasse. This solution had the obvious advantage of removing the hazards inherent in awarding sovereignty over the city and its port to either claimant, but the serious disadvantage of being, through its artificiality, intrinsically easier to upset than some form of formal partition. Other possibilities were also discussed in London, including the holding of a plebiscite in the city to determine the popular will, but this too had a major drawback in so far as the majority of informed Yugoslav opinion already accepted that Trieste itself was largely peopled by Italians. The Yugoslav claim to the city was based essentially on economic considerations, and their status as a war-time ally, rather than on the ethnic question. A plebiscite in Trieste would certainly go in Italy's favour and would be dismissed accordingly in Belgrade as an irrelevance.[31]

When the Foreign Office prepared its briefs for Bevin for the Paris Peace Conference in the spring of 1946, British policy was less than clear. Christopher Warner was among those who advocated the internationalisation of the port while giving sovereignty over the city to Italy.[32] This would be in keeping with the decision at the London CFM the previous September to ensure that the smallest possible minorities only would be left under alien rule. The status quo would be safeguarded additionally by the fact that should Yugoslavia wish to upset the international regime, she would first have to violate Italian sovereignty. In early March, the Four Power Boundary Commission appointed by the CFM began its work in investigating the ethnic situation in Venezia Giulia. The Commission arrived in the province to be greeted by a virulent pro-Slav propaganda campaign and civil unrest in Trieste. As if to emphasise their determination to secure their reparations at the peace conference, the Yugoslavs had significantly reinforced their garrison in Zone B, while bombarding the British and American Embassies in Belgrade with a series of Notes containing strong criticism of AMG's administration of Zone A. Tito himself was particularly aggressive when addressing the question in a speech in the Skupstina on 1 April.[33]

In London, the Foreign Office elected to orchestrate a similarly aggressive, though rather more subtle diplomatic, riposte. The British feared that failure to assume the offensive might encourage the Italians, the Yugoslavs, and for that matter, the rest of the world, to think that they and the Americans were prepared to let the case go by default. In the context of the growing belief in London and Washington that Soviet policy was intrinsically expansionist and revolutionary, which could be curtailed only by a show western determination to stand firm, the significance of this demonstration in Trieste assumed considerable importance. Trieste, like Iran, had become a symbol of western determination to meet the Russian challenge in Europe and elsewhere.[34] Given this highly charged atmosphere of the spring of 1946, any joint Anglo-American statement on the future of Trieste would be likely to receive coverage in the press and radio which would redound to the west's credit: the Americans now joined in a joint reply to the most recent of the Yugoslav communications, taking into account all of Yugoslavia's complaints about Venezia Giulia, and reproaching the Belgrade government for its encouragement of the unco-operative attitude of the Slovene population. This was delivered to the Yugoslav government on 25 April, although the details were in the event withheld from the press so as not to prejudice discussions due to be held at the preparatory foreign ministers' meeting just opening in Paris. At the same time Morgan was authorised to publish a statement protesting at Yugoslav troop reinforcements with the intention of arresting the growing tension among the local populace.[35]

The Four Power Boundary Commission duly reported on the ethnic and economic aspects of the Italian and Yugoslav claims at the Preparatory meeting for the Paris Peace conference on 3 May. Such was their indecision, and so great were the complexities they observed, that their report contained four separate recommendations as to the possible location of the Italo–Yugoslav frontier.[36] It is true that the British, French and Americans were more or less agreed on a line, but the Russian recommendation, perhaps not surprisingly, was at considerable variance with the other three. Their report initially solved very little and confirmed the state of deadlock since neither side was prepared to make substantial enough concessions for a compromise solution to be reached. The Russians now attempted to introduce the idea that Trieste and its hinterland be declared an autonomous state under Yugoslav sovereignty and controlled by international statute dafted by the Four Powers. Molotov approached Byrnes directly in the first instance, but the American responded that this would create an impossible situation: 'with Yugoslav sovereignty and a Yugoslav governor there would be little for the representatives of the Four Powers to do and there would be no connection with the UN'.[37] Nonetheless, he also acknowledged to Molotov that the Soviet Union was similarly unable to accept Italian sovereignty. Molotov now attempted to barter with the Americans: perhaps, he suggested, they might be prepared to exchange concessions on reparations and the peace treaty with Bulgaria if the Soviet Union were to acquiesce in their solution for Trieste. Byrnes was having none of this and turned instead to consideration of the possibility of internationalisation, which seemed increasingly to hold the only hope of breaking the impasse. The British and French had reached much the same conclusion and officials in London and Paris were separately reconsidering the framing of such a proposal which in essence would seek to internationalise the whole city, and so create a Free Territory in addition to the Free Port which had by now been discussed at Paris and agreed in principle. Indeed, Bidault suggested such a solution very tentatively in mid-June, providing for United Nations administration and a governor appointed by the UN. Byrnes did not like the Free Territory idea, but accepted that 'since this was the only way out of the dilemma', it would have to be tried and he was now determined to set it up so that it 'had a chance to work'. The peace conference agreed to adopt this solution on 3 July.[38]

Few believed in the summer of 1946 that internationalisation would work since the essential component of trust between the factions was non-existent. The talk in the conference halls at Paris had been of the likelihood of a Yugoslav coup in the city.[39] The Americans, in particular, were of the opinion that the Yugoslavs, with Russian help, would take military action when the opportunity came, or at the very least would do everything possible to subvert the Free Territory's government and seize control from the inside. Indeed, the Yugoslavs had already demonstrated their hostility to the solution by demanding that all real power should go to a popular assembly, an arrangement they sought, clearly because it would be the easier institution to control or at least subvert. The powers of the governor, who would be an international appointment, should in their view be severely limited. This position was effectively reinforced by the Russians who made a parallel demand for the establishment of a Free Port Commission. It was unfortunate from a western point of view that the Americans should respond to this with a counter proposal that extraordinary powers be given to the Governor to maintain the independence and integrity of the Free Territory. Byrnes recorded in his memoirs that precedent played some part in the thinking of the western powers: the unhappy experience of the League of Nations and the free city of Danzig threw its shadow across these negotiations: the High Commission appointed by the League had proved powerless to protect the city after a well organised Nazi minority had captured control of the local assembly.[40] However, the suggestion proved ill-judged for it gave all propaganda advantage to the Soviet camp, making it possible for them to present themselves to the world as champions of democracy against an apparent advocacy of dictatorship on the part of the west.[41]

British and American proposals for the Provisional Regime of the Free Territory were substantially similar but differed in one important respect: whereas the Foreign Office had drawn up a proposal which provided for elections to the Provisional Assembly as soon as possible after the regime came into force, the State Department wanted the democratic element in the regime to be provided by a governor's Council of Five who would be elected as soon as 33,000 persons had registered themselves on the electoral rolls. The American draft also gave the Governor's council the right of appeal to the Security Council over the Governor's head.[42] The British proposals had a number of advantages over the American ones. In the first place the Governor's hands, which the British felt should be absolutely free during the provisional regime, would be tied by the council's right of appeal to the Security Council; secondly it was only to be expected that Yugoslavia would use the not inconsiderable resources available to her to ensure that there was a pro-Slav majority among the first 30,000 electors enrolled. Finally, under the British system the western allies would be able to reject any Russian and/or Yugoslav criticism that the draft did not provide for participation of the inhabitants in the regime by pointing out that the Governor would, at the outset, be making the necessary preparations for the elections. The British then, were satisfied when the State Department expressed its willingness to negotiate at the CFM on the British draft.[43]

Perhaps the greatest problem for the west, however, was that of disentangling Soviet and Yugoslav policies, as the comments of British officials at the time reveal. Although the predominant view at this stage was that Yugoslavia was the political and economic vassal of Moscow, there was a second interpretation of Yugoslav policy which argued that it was just possible that Yugoslavia's foreign policy might be tailored rather to Belgrade's interests and be evolving separately from the official communist line expounded from the Kremlin. The notion that Tito was a Yugoslav first and a communist second had been advanced by Fitzroy Maclean, Bill Deakin and others during the war, following which it had retained some currency with the Foreign Office among those who were generally reluctant to accept the thesis that the Soviet sphere was a monolith. There had already been some fragmentary evidence during the Trieste crisis the previous year, and subsequently, that Yugoslavia might be resistant to merely accepting her place as an extension of the Soviet empire. George Clutton neatly encapsulated the dilemma when writing to Bevin in July that the difficulty he experienced in assessing the situation in Belgrade was 'that Yugoslavia is not a free agent, and that her actions are a reflection not of Yugoslav policy, but of Soviet policy'. He added that he felt he could never be sure 'how far any given Yugoslav action is of someone else's game of bluff'.[44]

The major powers each permitted their doubts about the viability – or acceptability – of the Trieste solution to surface. The continued uncertainty about Trieste's future was causing unrest, particularly increased incidence of racial animosity, in the region itself: in London, Clement Attlee gave an assurance during his speech in the Foreign Affairs debate in the House of Commons on 23 October that Anglo-American troops would remain on the Morgan Line until an agreement had been reached and implemented.[45] There was a contradiction here, however, since SACMED's proposals for dealing the Yugoslav aggression were based on the notion that the Morgan Line and Trieste itself would be abandoned. The British originators of the scheme for internationalisation, under pressure by the mounting crisis created by civil unrest, reopened the debate as to whether the internationalisation was at all viable. Reports from Italy and Trieste itself gave substance to the concern of British military officials that the Yugoslavs were not only determined to secure Trieste, despite the peace conference decision, but would go to great lengths, including strong-arm tactics, to achieve this end. By August 1946, the Americans also acknowledged that it might be necessary for Allied forces to remain in Zone A indefinitely since civil war was being prevented only by the presence of AMG and Anglo-American troops.[46]

The political and social instability of the Free Territory was compounded by the fact that it was intrinsically an unnatural economic unit. Before the war, it had been subsidised by Italy and its separation from the Italian economy, which had largely absorbed its produce hitherto, would now create currency and financial difficulties. Not only would the Free Territory be inherently unstable, then, but Yugoslav and Russian machinations would combine to prevent the creation of a truly international, neutralised territory, and to make it at almost any cost an appendage of Yugoslavia. The British adopted the position that the only sensible course was to proceed for the time being with the negotiations to establish the Free Territory, while seeking in parallel an alternative course in case this solution should founder irretrievably. In practice this meant that British policy in the autumn of 1946 had acknowledged that the peace conference solution was not practical and sought to revise the terms by returning to the policy of awarding Trieste to Italy with the boundary fixed at the French line. Secret negotiations with the Americans and French revealed that both were in substantial agreement.[47]

When the Paris Peace Conference ended in September 1946, the major powers were still unsure as to whether they had the makings of a settlement for Trieste. Many of the issues were still awaiting agreement, the draft Statute being among them. The draft, as voted by the conference, remained unacceptable to the Soviet Union and Yugoslavia: indeed, the decision had been achieved because the voting system, which had given the western powers automatic majorities in the ratio of fourteen or fifteen to six, meant that Soviet and Yugoslav proposals were perpetually voted down. The Yugoslav delegation had responded by refusing to be bound by the majority recommendation and declined to sign the treaty. While recognising that this was the only mechanism by which the Yugoslav government could save face, the British would similarly refuse to sign if Yugoslavia carried out this threat since the absence of Yugoslav co-operation would render the situation impossible. Unsure as to whether or not the Yugoslavs were bluffing, but nevertheless convinced that the ultimate attitude of the Yugoslav government would depend on that of the Soviet Union, the British and American delegations recorded their intention to reconsider their position towards the Council's decision of 3 July if there was failure to reach a satisfactory agreement on the Statute.

The foreign ministers met again in New York between 4 November and 12 December. The Yugoslav representatives came before the Council and presented again their case for control of the city. The British position was summed up by Orme Sargent who minuted that the present firm British attitude regarding the French Line should not perhaps be made the breaking point at New York, unless the present rundown of the Trieste garrison were to be reversed and the military strengthened. In the event, the final session of the CFM for 1946 proved to be the most constructive of all, although not before several further weeks had been taken up with inconclusive discussion. The difficulties encountered over Trieste at New York were largely the product of renewed attempts by the Russians to secure a statute which would leave both the provisional regime and the governor fundamentally weak. In the first place, they returned to the charge with their earlier demand that power be concentrated in the elected assembly and in the council of government to be chosen by it, to the detriment of the role of the Security Council or its agent, the Governor. Moreover, they clearly hoped to make the CFM rather than the Security Council responsible during the provisional Regime and to restrict the Governor's economic powers, giving the Council of Government the lion's share of authority in these and other matters such as the control of policy. Inevitably, the Soviet delegation pressed hard for withdrawal of British and American troops from the region within a fixed time limit, as well as to secure the maximum economic footing for Yugoslavia in the Free Territory.[48]

At this point, Byrnes, who had again wearied of the Soviet

stubbornness and prevarication, decided that the time had come to draw the line. On 5 December, he informed Molotov that the treaties would either be completed in the current session or they would not be completed at all. The United States, he said, had made all concessions possible.[49] Shortly after this stormy encounter, Byrnes received a visit from the Yugoslav delegate, Stanoje Simic. The latter made a further attempt to urge modification of the Yugoslav boundary, but Byrnes, believing that Molotov had put the Yugoslavs up to this as a test stood firm.[50]

This seemed to impress Molotov, who returned to the Council with some significant concessions from Moscow, including Russian acceptance of the proposed statute for the Free Territory which was largely based on the Peace Conference recommendation of 3 July. This embodied the French Line for the Italo–Yugoslav frontier, with the Free Territory of Trieste within it. This latter covered an area delineated by Duino in the north and Novigrad in the south, and included a hinterland to a maximum depth of ten miles. The integrity of the Free Territory was to be guaranteed by the United Nations Security Council, whose role was defined in the broadest possible terms. The governor would be appointed by the Security Council, with the concurrence of the four powers and, largely due to British persistence, his power to intervene wherever his responsibilities were affected, had been maintained. Ultimate responsibility for organising the elections was vested in his office, and in case it proved technically impossible to hold them within the stipulated four weeks of his coming into office, the Governor was empowered to report to the Security Council in the interim. In the meantime, the withdrawal of Anglo-American troops, though possible within the required four and a half months of the Governor's assumption of office, would in practice be dependent upon conditions in the Territory and would therefore be left to the decision of the Governor. With the exceptions of the railway and, critically, the interim currency arrangements, the Free Territory was to be entirely independent of both Yugoslavia and Italy. Special provision had been inserted in the statute to ensure freedom of transit without discrimination and without customs or fiscal duties of goods transported by rail between the Free Port and the states which it served. Until the Governor had been appointed, the Free Territory was to be temporarily divided into two zones, A and B, on the same principle as the division made by the Morgan Line. The northern zone (A) was placed under the joint administration of

Britain and the United States; zone B, to the east of the Free Territory, was to be left to Yugoslavia in keeping with the ethnic principle. This arrangement was intended to be a temporary expedient only, but in practice it remained in force for a further seven years.[51]

When the Council of Foreign Ministers broke up at the end of December, three points were still left outstanding; firstly approval of the Provisional Regime and the Free Port by the Security Council, the decision on which had been requested by 15 January 1947 at the latest. Secondly, the question of finance: this was to be investigated by a four power commission which would report later in the year. Finally, there was the problem of what action should be taken in the event that Yugoslavia carried out her threat of refusing to sign the Treaty. This latter concern was soon allayed, however, as the Yugoslav Government (presumably responding to Soviet pressure) was persuaded to retract its objections. The Italian Peace Treaty was duly signed on 10 February 1947.[52]

Bled Agreement, 1947

Progress with the Italian peace treaty had brought to the fore a particularly sensitive and difficult aspect of Anglo-Yugoslav relations which was concerned the rounding up and repatriation of Yugoslav war criminals from among the displaced persons camps in Italy, Austria and Germany.[53] The debate about the Yugoslav Displaced Persons (DPs) is essentially one about collaboration. The return to Yugoslavia in May 1945 by General Keightley's forces in Klagenfurt of over 9,000 Croats, who were massacred on arrival by the Partisans, has been the subject of extensive academic, journalistic and eventually legal debate.[54] The archival evidence indicates that it was an error of judgement under pressure, combined with a communications failure, following which pains were taken to avoid a repetition of the error. This notwithstanding, the British and Americans recognised that there was genuinely a question of war criminality which had to be addressed in respect to the Yugoslav DP camps since these were believed to contain many known quislings and war criminals who had escaped, along with genuine dissidents and refugees from the fighting, the former hiding under the auspices of the western Allies in the hope of escaping prosecution.

Yugoslav government requests for repatriation of war criminals and quislings had been made first in June 1945. The official British position had been set out some months earlier in a statement to all twenty-one Allied governments, in which HMG promised to surrender anyone resident in British territory or territory under British control against whom a *prima facie* case could be made.[55] Shortly after receipt of the Yugoslav note, a joint Anglo-American policy emerged regarding the Yugoslavs which reiterated the essence of Britain's earlier statement while elaborating the requirements for a *prime facie* case to be adequately established by British and American authorities before an individual could be surrendered.[56] By the end of 1946, however, little progress had been made in locating even the most notorious individuals known to be hiding in British and American held refugee camps.

The Foreign Office had taken the view, from the end of 1945, that the Yugoslavs had just cause for grievance: thus, in January 1946, Orme Sargent wrote that he could not agree with those who argued that the Yugoslav government was using the quisling issue as a pretext for attacks against Britain: the issue, he thought, 'is one to which the Yugoslav Government genuinely attaches great importance and which they look upon as a test of good faith'. He added that since Bevin had decided 'to do his utmost to establish friendly relations with the Yugoslav government', every effort had to be made to resolve the question since it was 'one of the major obstacles in the way'.[57]

Public opinion was at considerable variance with this view: the bias against Tito, which had been engendered initially by the clash over Trieste in May 1945, had been given substance by the public hostility of the Yugoslav government towards Britain. The execution of Draza Mihailovic in June 1946, who rightly or wrongly was held in public esteem by the British people, not least as a result of his connections with the deposed Serbian royal family, had contributed much to British antipathy. The contiguous persecution by the godless communists of the Roman Catholic Church had further alienated the British – if that were possible. However, much though Attlee and Bevin were cognizant of public opinion, there was a tacit recognition among the most senior members of the government and Foreign Office officials that this picture, born of prejudice and emerging cold war rhetoric, represented something of a distortion of the facts and that, on the contrary, the grievances of the Yugoslavs regarding war-time activities of both the Cetniks (if not necessarily Mihailovic himself) and the Roman Catholic Church were not without genuine foundation.[58] In a minute to Bevin of 29 March 1946, commenting on the Mihailovic trial which had been under way in Belgrade since February, Attlee wrote: 'I do not see that we are called upon to intervene. Mihailovic did nothing against the Germans for a long time. He then was a party to the attacks on Tito's forces.'[59] Integral to this was the assumption generally held in official circles that this was a Yugoslav internal matter and that Mihailovic's fate, and those of similar personalities, was no different to that which they would have meted out to Tito and the Partisans had the balance of power in Yugoslavia been tilted the other way by the war's end. Furthermore, the war criminals question was bound up with the Italian and Austrian peace settlements and policy was being formulated on a more practical basis than sentiment and conservative political bias.

The Italian dimension had caused the question to surface in the British Cabinet in May 1946, owing to the Italian government's demand that the DPs be removed from Italy at the earliest date and to the parallel requests from AFHQ to reduce its manpower in the region. There was some concern in London and Rome about the continued existence of these camps since some of the more extreme anti-communist elements among the inmates had shown an inclination to exploit their position to mount cross-border raids into Yugoslavia and generally act, at worst as a source of counter-revolution, and at best as a force for stirring up trouble and instability in the region. On the humanitarian front, there was also a danger that if responsibility for these people were handed over to the Italian government after the signing of the peace treaty, the Italians would be pressured by Belgrade into handing over the Yugoslav DPs en masse. A Foreign Office memorandum to the Cabinet advised that taking these factors into account, every possible effort had to be made 'on the grounds of high policy and in the interests in the long run of Anglo-Russian relations' to settle the question without involving the Italian government.[60] The Cabinet were disinclined to be alarmed by Foreign Office doom-merchants and decreed, on 30 May, that all non-Italian refugees would indeed be handed over to the Italian government on signature of the peace treaty.

A similar discussion had also been occasioned in Washington at this time by the reports being received by the Chargé d'Affaires in Belgrade, John Cabot. The latter was already exercised by the continued absence of an Ambassador, the incumbent Richard Patterson having been largely absent since the autumn of 1945.

Cabot observed, in a telegram dated 5 May, that 'the Yugoslav government is justified in feeling that we have not scrupulously respected our commitments and that it is therefore incumbent upon us to bestir ourselves now'.[61] In conclusion, he remarked upon the devastation he had witnessed in Montenegro and Dalmatia, much of which had been caused by the Italians, and observed that this alone explained Yugoslav bitterness at the apparent failure of the western Allies to honour their pledges. However, the Truman Administration was no more inclined to give priority to this matter than the British Cabinet: the official American view, advanced firmly by the State Department and represented by government spokesmen, was that Italo–Yugoslav relations were destined to be difficult regardless, and there seemed little point in paying this aspect of the problem too much attention.[62]

Nevertheless, it was the imminence of the signing of the Italian peace treaty which raised this question once again onto Bevin's agenda. In the meantime a delegation from the Intergovernmental Committee on Refugees (IGCR) led by Professor George Royse, a former OSS officer and Balkan specialist, had visited Belgrade to discuss the whole DP problem with Yugoslav officials. The result – known as the Royse Report – outlined a plan for screening teams which would determine which of the camps' inmates were culpable beyond reasonable doubt and have them screened before a Judicial Tribunal before repatriation. This mission which, after some debate, was headed by Bevin's choice, Fitzroy Maclean, left for Italy at the end of January 1947. Although it was in the pay of the War Office, the Mission was essentially a political instrument in so far as it was intended by the Foreign Office to mediate an Italo-Yugoslav and Yugoslav–western dispute. Maclean was not at his task long before he requested permission to make an official visit to Belgrade to barter with Tito directly. He was overwhelmed by the enormity of the task and felt that the imminence of the Italian peace treaty made it only sensible that time be bought with the governments concerned through negotiation of an ad hoc agreement.

This idea foundered, not in London, where the realism of this suggestion was immediately recognised, but in Washington. The Americans, who had after some prevarication, agreed in principle to send a team to join the existing mission, had objected all along to Maclean as leader of the Special Refugee Commission owing to his association with the rise of the Tito regime which had provoked considerable protest from pro-Serbian Americans when the appointment became known. How far the Maclean issue was indeed a real difficulty, and how far an excuse for the Americans to dodge commitment is questionable. American suspicions about the motives behind British diplomacy concerning the DPs had been aroused during the early months of 1947 by the British failure to take them into their confidence before sending Maclean to Italy.[63] But American policy on the issue, in so far as there was a policy, derived from the convenient conviction that the problem was primarily a British concern and something with which the United States did not wish to be saddled. As regards repatriation, the Americans had never recognised the necessity for playing a role beyond the rounding up of certain war-time collaborators, in particular Milan Nedic and Dragi Jovanovic, a year previously. Ante Pavelic had slipped the net and escaped with the assistance of Franciscan monks to safety in South America.[64] American disinclination to become any more involved in this mire over a few hundred quislings and war criminals was publicly expressed by Dean Acheson in a press statement at the end of April.[65]

Realising that American participation in an approach to Tito was unlikely to be forthcoming after all, and anxious to be rid of the problem, Bevin now sanctioned Maclean's visit to Belgrade. Meanwhile, negotiation of the Austrian Treaty had begun in earnest at the Council of Foreign Ministers in Moscow in March when the Yugoslavs had added to their claims for cash reparations from Austria, by demanding sovereignty over Styria and Southern Carinthia in the Danube Basin. In making these claims, Belgrade had good grounds for citing the activities of particular Austrian nationals. Shortly before the CFM opened in Moscow, the Austrian-born commander of Army Group E which had occupied the Balkans, General Alexander Lohr, had been tried and executed in Belgrade for war crimes. Lohr had presided over some of the worst excesses in Yugoslavia, including the massacres and deportations from the one-time Partisan stronghold at Kozara in July 1942. During the preliminary conference of deputies, the Yugoslavs had also accused the Austrian delegate, Hans Piesch, Governor of Carinthia, of collaboration with the Nazis. Piesch, who was duly dismissed, was shown to have been an official working in Himmler's Race and Resettlement Office.[66]

Although the Soviet Union had sided initially with Yugoslavia (thereby giving the Yugoslav claims weight they would otherwise have lacked), it now appears that their ulterior objective all along had been to use this as a bargaining chip to give them leverage in the question of German assets. During the Moscow CFM, behind-the scenes negotiations with western diplomats were encouraging enough for the Russians to distance themselves somewhat from Yugoslav claims. Finding themselves isolated, the Yugoslavs sought ways to discredit the Austrian Foreign Minister, Karl Gruber, through the identification of further 'war criminals' among his negotiating team. Indeed, it was at this point that the Yugoslavs appear to have begun to make their case against Kurt Waldheim, then one of Gruber's assistants. It was a determination to bolster Gruber's position against this onslaught that was a factor in British determination to ensure that everything possible was done to round up and repatriate the most guilty parties through extension to Austria of the screening system which had been implemented in Italy. In the meantime, Maclean was briefed to negotiate an agreement to cover DPs in both Italy and Austria.

Maclean travelled to Yugoslavia in June, briefed to secure an agreement with Tito which would put a definite time limit on British obligations to locate and surrender quislings. After an opening round of talks with Yugoslav officials, Maclean flew to Slovenia for an informal visit with Tito himself. The Yugoslav dictator did not limit himself simply to the DP question, but used the occasion to air a wide range of grievances against both Britain and the United States. However, he also observed that any improvement in their relations was dependent upon a fundamental change in the relationship of Soviet Russia and the United States. Maclean responded that the grievances were not on his side alone and that he was personally very unpopular in Britain, which was so for a variety of reasons: among them the downing of unarmed American aircraft, the trial and execution of Mihailovic and the imprisonment of Stepinac and, not least of all, the consistently hostile attitude of the Yugoslav government towards its former allies. These things, he said, made it very difficult for the British government when dealing with DPs, since the electorate and press were prejudiced and could not be prevented from making such opinions felt.[67]

The personal visit had cleared to some extent the obfuscations of Yugoslav bureaucracy and Maclean, on his return to Belgrade, found Simic noticeably more amenable. The draft agreement drawn up at this meeting was, however, substantially revised in London over the summer and Maclean returned to Belgrade in September to begin the process all over again in what he was subsequently to describe as a 'thoroughly Balkan atmosphere of distrust, controversy and blackmail'.[68] This time he went to talk with Tito directly in Zagreb, which resulted in an agreement signed by Tito and the British Ambassador to Yugoslavia, Charles Peake, in Bled on 8 September 1947, which secured the principal British objective of limiting in scope a time-scale to their obligations.

The improved atmosphere which accompanied this signing was reflected during the visit to Belgrade by Philip Noel Baker, now Secretary of State for Air, to open a British book fair held in the Yugoslav capital. In the meantime, a more conciliatory pose had been struck by Tito's government in relation to Anglo-Yugoslav economic relations and in regard to the compensation question in particular. Indeed, while Soviet rejection in July 1947 of the American invitation to participate in the European Recovery Programme confirmed the division of Europe, it also made more urgent the search by states in the Soviet sphere for trade agreements with the West. By August, the Yugoslav Government was once again anxious to maintain and expand such relations; although ambitious trade agreements had been signed or renewed with the Soviet orbit, the brutal fact was that the machinery required for fulfilment of Yugoslavia's five-year plan would not be forthcoming from this source. Accordingly, a second Yugoslav trade delegation was sent to London to negotiate a long-term agreement. From the British point of view, the timing was fortuitous: since the beginning of the year the Treasury had been keen to develop all possible sources of soft-currency supplies owing to the imbalance in dollar payments. Eastern Europe promised to be a good source for such supplies, especially for agricultural produce. In negotiating with the Yugoslavs, Britain sought to secure maize from the 1947 harvest, while also hoping to persuade them to become a long-term source of cereals and other agricultural produce. These needs had been made rather more pressing by the breakdown during the summer of the Anglo–Soviet trade negotiations. Once again, however, it was Yugoslav intransigence on the question of compensation which led to the temporary abandonment of negotiations in December and a return therefore to the stalemate of the previous years.

It was soon to become clear that there had been a sub-text to the Yugoslav dialogue with the British during the summer of 1947. This new confidence in Yugoslavia's relations with Britain was to be short-lived – acrimony over the DPs accompanied the breakdown of the trade talks. In December, Belgrade denounced the

Bled Agreement, which came as little surprise in London and was correctly interpreted there as the produce more of Soviet dictates than the wishes of the Yugoslav government itself. Some years later, Tito was to confide to the British Ambassador during an informal talk that this was the last thing his government had done to please Stalin and if that is true the process of deterioration which now beset Soviet–Yugoslav relations began shortly thereafter.

6

A New Cold War Perspective: Tito's Separate Road

During the early months of 1948, the western world was seized by what the French call a *grande peur*: 1947 had brought the collapse of the projected post-war settlement and the first hesitant steps, on either side of the Iron Curtain, towards construction of a new framework for international politics. It remains difficult to establish where action and reaction took place: consolidation of both western and eastern Europe was conducted almost contemporaneously, and the starting point for what was clearly a chain reaction continues to be a subject for conjecture. The debate turns partly on the view taken of the aims and intentions of the western powers (and particularly the British and Americans), and partly on the view taken of Stalin. In the absence of adequate documentary evidence from Russian sources, interpretations of Stalin's policies are still largely tentative.

The winter of 1946/47 had been particularly harsh in Europe and the bleak wintry conditions had, by mid-February brought Britain to an economic standstill. With financial reserves running out, rationing below war-time levels and industry at a standstill, Britain had to rationalise her overseas commitments. On 21 February, the British had informed the Americans that they would be ceasing provision of aid to Greece and Turkey in six weeks and that they hoped that the Americans would assume their burden. The Americans duly served notice of their commitment to western Europe in a process which began in mid-March with the announcement of American aid to maintain the right-wing regimes in Greece and Turkey, and consolidated when the Secretary of State, George Marshall, professed American willingness to assist with European economic recovery. After this statement, Bevin and Bidault sought a European conference to draw up the recovery programme called for by Marshall: Molotov was invited to this conference, which was held in Paris in July 1947. All along, the Americans intended that this programme should be confined to western Europe and the act of inviting the Russians to participate was a calculated risk: had the Russians agreed to join in, the amount of money required from Congress to get the Marshall Plan off the ground would have been so enormous that the Plan probably would have foundered from lack of Congressional support. If the Soviet leadership wanted to discourage the division of Europe, an indication of interest in taking part would have been a step in this direction in so far as it might have halted, or at least delayed, the establishment of Marshall aid. Either Stalin miscalculated, which is possible, or he had already concluded that co-operation with capitalism, a useful war-time expedient, was a policy which he was ready to abandon. Molotov walked out of the conference and later claimed to Djilas that after initially favouring participation, he had been instructed by the Politburo to oppose the Plan.[1] Perhaps, in order to test the loyalty of the people's democracies of eastern Europe, Moscow did not immediately forbid attendance at the preparatory conference in July. Indeed, the Czechs and the Poles indicated their intention to accept the invitation, but the Czech leaders, in Moscow on other business, were told that participation in the conference would be interpreted in Moscow 'as an act specifically aimed against the USSR': both the Czechs and Poles abruptly announced their decision not to attend after all.[2] Stalin probably hoped for the economic collapse of Europe, which would explain his apparent determination to allow the German question to drift without agreement. This, at least, was the view of Soviet policy being taken by both the British and Americans by the end of the Moscow CFM in March, and this belief provided the immediate impulse which led to Marshall's announcement in June. Some evidence in support of this is contained in the memoirs of Nikita Khrushchev who recalls that in Moscow, the hope existed that revolution would occur in Europe which would bring the end of capitalism there, as predicted by Marxist–Leninist teaching: 'Just as Russia came out of World War I, made the revolution and established Soviet power, so after the catastrophe of World War II, Europe too might become Soviet. Everyone would take the path from capitalism to socialism'.[3] They were disappointed: American economic power had been brought in to prevent such an eventuality and Moscow turned instead to consolidation of its own sphere. The symbolic gesture towards this end was made at a conference held in September 1947 at Szklaska Poreba in Poland, which established the Cominform (Communist Information Bureau).[4] The headquarters of his new organisation, which described itself as a co-ordinating body for national communist parties and included amongst its membership not just the Soviet and east European communist parties, but also those of France and Italy, were to be in Belgrade. It was this factor which seemed from the western perspective to make the Cominform sinister. In practice, the Cominform was totally dominated by the Russians and was used by them as a mechanism to tighten their hold on their own sphere. The Soviet ideologue, Andrei Zhdanov, who chaired the meeting, took the opportunity to proclaim the division of the international system into two camps: that of 'imperialist and anti-democratic forces', and that of 'democratic and anti-imperialist forces'. However, its potential as a mechanism through which the Soviet Union might also disrupt ERP was also self-evident and the Italian and French delegates to the conference left Poland with instructions to direct their efforts towards this end.[5]

There is much evidence to suggest that the Russians had embarked on a programme of consolidation of their sphere from early in 1947, possibly even before Truman's announcement in March. Elections held in Poland on 19 January had ensured the exit of the remaining 'democratic' elements of the Polish Peasant Party, and particularly its leader, the deputy Prime Minister and former member of the government-in-exile, Stanislaw Mikoljczyk. Later, Mikoljczyk was denounced as a foreign spy and collaborator, along with other socialist leaders who were charged in the courts with treason and removed. In the countryside, the remnants of the anti-communist resistance was destroyed and in October, Mikoljczyk, who had been acting as a focus for opposition, fled for his life.[6] The pattern was similar in Hungary where the former secretary-general of the non-communist Smallholders Party, Zoltan Tildy, was arrested early in 1947; in May, the premier, Ferenc Nagy, was implicated in his confession and chose exile. As the communist politicians tightened their hold over the Hungarian government, non-communist parties and politicians were destroyed in the purges that followed. Harsher methods still were employed in Bulgaria and Rumania. The political scene in Czechoslovakia was finally transformed by a coup d'état on 20 February 1948 which brought the downfall of the President and inter-war statesman, Edvard Benes and his replacement by the former Comintern, Klement Gottwald, who had been serving as Prime Minister since 1945. Meanwhile, the Russians had persuaded the Finnish government, with whom they had signed a peace treaty in 1947, to negotiate a Soviet–Finnish Treaty of Mutual Friendship and Assistance which effectively recognised the special relationship between the two countries implying Finnish acceptance of the Soviet position in the cold war.

The British were concerned about the events to the east and relative weakness of the Anglo-American position in Europe; towards the end of the Council of Foreign Ministers meeting in London at the end of 1947, Bevin broached with the Americans his idea of setting up a system for western defence. This was followed by a more detailed proposal which had been prepared by the Foreign Office and was submitted to the State Department for comment in mid-January 1948. The Americans almost immediately concurred, but with the proviso that the initiative come from the Europeans. Thus, the Brussels Pact, which was signed on 17 March by Britain, France and the Benelux, provided for the joint defence system whereby an attack on one signatory would bring the others to its aid. Five days later, British and Canadian delegates met with American officials under conditions of extreme secrecy at the Pentagon in Washington where the discussion centred on the possibility of forming a North Atlantic Alliance. The timing was fortuitous since the coup d'état in Prague had provoked a crisis of confidence in the Truman Administration; the 'Spring crisis', as it was known, was occasioned by fear that renewed war in Europe was possible, a war for which the military were unprepared. Although the immediate anxiety in Washington had waned by April, the closure of ground traffic routes into Berlin from the west by the Russians at the end of May gave substance to fears regarding the precarious balance of power in Europe. At the end of June, the Soviet Union brought into the open its quarrel with the leaders of Yugoslavia, the country which hitherto informed western opinion believed to be designated as the leader of east European communism.[7]

Yugoslavia was banished from the Cominform by a communiqué issued on 28 June 1948, at a Cominform meeting in Prague.[8] The choice of date, the anniversary of the battle of Kosovo, which held great symbolism in Serbian nationalist mythology and was also the anniversary of the assassination of the Archduke Franz Ferdinand in Sarajevo which sparked off the First World War in 1914, could have been simply a crass choice, or designed (as is likely) to be especially provocative. The communiqué called upon the 'loyal' elements in Yugoslav communism to bring the leaders – Tito, Kardelj, Djilas and Rankovic were mentioned by name – to reason or overthrow them. The document had been prepared at a secret meeting of the Cominform in Rumania some ten days earlier and the delay in its publication was apparently due, in part at least, to Moscow's determination to have representatives of all the satellites sign the Warsaw Declaration on Germany which took place on 24 June. Once Simic had done so on behalf of Yugoslavia, the way was clear. In summary, the communiqué indicted the Yugoslav leadership for errors in both foreign and domestic policy; they had taken an independent line in foreign policy and had resisted penetration of the state by Soviet agents; they had attempted to conciliate with the western powers and had treated the Soviet Union on the same footing as other foreign countries, and even shown signs of regarding it as more dangerous to Yugoslavia than the western powers. On the domestic front, they had failed to follow the Marxist ideological teaching with regard to the class struggle in the countryside, and to prepare the way for nationalisation of the land, or to liquidate the small peasant farmer class. In an attempt to cover these areas, they had rushed through a programme of hasty and ill-considered legislation which threatened the whole outcome of the Five Year Plan. Finally, they had failed to maintain the rigid communist control of the popular front. These criticisms were linked together by the common theme that the Yugoslav Politburo was culpable essentially for trying to resist complete domination by Moscow.

The Yugoslav Government responded quickly to indicate that it did not intend to yield: an appeal was published by the KPJ appealing to the loyalty of the party members, and to Yugoslav opinion in general, for support, and indicated their intention to produce a party programme which would proclaim their independence of Soviet hegemony, to continue in their advocacy of a south Slav federation and to seek good relations, not just with the east but with the west also.[9]

The dispute almost certainly had its origins in the war: the partisans had contributed significantly, if not to the extent they later claimed, to the liberation of Yugoslavia and although the Red Army was the real liberator of the region, its efforts took it only across the north-eastern part of the country, and as such Yugoslavia was spared a Soviet occupation. April 1945 had marked the high-water mark of Soviet–Yugoslav relations when their respective governments signed a twenty-year treaty of Friendship and Mutual Assistance, but only the briefest interval elapsed before Yugoslav foreign policy ventures were placing this alliance under considerable strain. The western powers had regarded the Trieste crisis of May 1945 as an unhappy start for post-war relations with Yugoslavia. The Russians had probably taken a similar view: but despite Stalin's evident displeasure, Tito continued to press his claims to the region, as well as persisting with his ambition to annex the southern parts of Carinthia and Styria from Austria, and was publicly incensed when Stalin agreed with the other three major powers that minor war-time allies could not have representation equal to that of the Big Four at the peace conference. Tito had then angered Stalin further by his negotiations with the Bulgarian leader, Georgi Dimitrov, for a South Slav Federation and, by his support from the communist guerrillas of General Markos in Greece, as well as continued interference with Albania with which he again persisted without, so the Russians were to claim, first informing the Kremlin.[10]

Emphasis is generally given by scholars, with some reason, to the foreign policy aspects of the problem.[11] But Tito was showing an independence too in internal affairs which was not insignificant and fitted in with the general tendency towards wilful independence which Stalin, who could be satisfied only with unquestioning obedience, was unlikely to find acceptable. Tito had declared his intention in 1945 that Yugoslavia should not be dependent on anyone ever again,[12] and this ambition encouraged his determination to transform Yugoslavia's predominantly agrarian peasant economy into an industrial one with its emphasis on capital rather than consumer goods. In order to address this task he had produced at the end of 1947 a five-year plan which was designed to lay the foundations for achieving this industrialisation. Stalin did not approve: Yugoslavia's assignment in the Soviet design from the satellite countries meant, effectively, that she would remain primarily an agricultural state and would continue thereby to be poor and backward and, ultimately, in the Marxist scheme of things, weak. This was a problem both for Tito personally, and for other members of his Politburo because it would be necessary in time to explain to the Yugoslav people why the need for smelting mills and dams and electrical development had been overestimated, and, furthermore, why it was now considered better not to build factories. Moreover, the teachings of Marx and Lenin, by which the Yugoslav government justified itself, dictated that the leading political role belonged to the working class who were, with eighty per cent of the population working on the land, very much in the minority. For their part, the peasants were already restless and angry as a result of Tito's vigorous collectivisation programme, but perhaps more important than this was the consideration that the majority of the Partisan army, which had assisted Tito in his rise to power, had been peasants.[13] In the military field, the Soviet Army had sent a number of its officers to Belgrade (at high salaries paid by the Yugoslav Treasury), to advise their Yugoslav counterparts. For their part, the Yugoslav military were anxious to receive new weapons and to be shown how to handle them, but they already had first hand experience of fighting and believed that there was little that the Red Army could teach them when it came to waging war in the Yugoslav terrain. A Soviet promise to supply the Yugoslav army with modern equipment had been one product of Tito's visit to Moscow at the end of May 1946, but behind the scenes Tito was angered by Stalin's wish that Russian intelligence agents should be permitted to operate within the Yugoslav army.[14] Indeed the Russians attempted to recruit agents at all levels in the Yugoslav political machine, and to give orders directly without reference to the Yugoslav leaders; this prompted Tito to say to his Politburo colleagues that he would not tolerate spy networks, and steps were taken to make such actions more difficult. Inevitably, this evidence of Yugoslav discontent reached Moscow. Sometimes Soviet missions found that they could no longer get immediately any and every fact about the Yugoslav internal situation, a means to the end of supervising developments within the country. Moreover, a suspicion probably arose in Moscow that the interest in a Balkan Federation, which Yugoslavia shared with Bulgaria, might be aimed at co-operating satellite actions in the region to offset Soviet pressure.[15] Given this situation, and the paranoia and insecurity of the Stalin regime, it could only be a matter of time before Tito was called to account. However, it was naturally the foreign policy aspects of Tito's policy which had first called the attention of western diplomats to the fact that Yugoslavia was inclined to pursue her interests more strongly than at all times Stalin appeared willing to support. Aside from the frontier disputes, the major questions involved matters of regional security and stability, questions in which the British and Americans had a close interest.

Tito's Balkan Agenda

Since the end of 1944, British officials had been aware that Tito was interested in creating some form of union or federation between Yugoslavia and Bulgaria which might also be widened to include Albania. This project had a long history dating to the nineteenth century, and, as we have seen, was toyed with by representatives of factions within the Balkans states, and also by international bystanders, including Britain, during the inter-war years. While the great powers saw it as a possible solution to the twin problems of instability and regional security, certain Balkan politicians promoted the idea as one which might also have the advantage of increasing their own powerbase in addition to the prospect of a dilution of internecine strife which it also offered. Federation with Bulgaria had been part of Mihailovic's vision for post-war Yugoslavia; it had also been incorporated in Tito's plans.[16] The proposal was formally raised at the Yalta conference in February 1945 when the British delegation stated that such a bilateral agreement between Bulgaria and Yugoslavia was unacceptable, although they indicated that they were not necessarily opposed to a loose federation of the Balkan states.[17] What concerned the British, of course, was how such a development would affect Greece. At the heart of the Balkan problem was the region of Macedonia, which contained elements who considered themselves connected respectively with Yugoslavia (through Serbian links), with Bulgaria or with Greece. Any political grouping which sought to co-opt Greater Macedonia, that is a Macedonia which would incorporate the Macedon lands now belonging to northern Greece, would cut across the Soviet–British division of influence, to the detriment of the British sphere. Since 1940, when Britain had become involved in Balkan affairs as a result of her intervention to save Greece from invasion, British policy had hardened against such developments. The polarisation of Europe, which made victory in the civil war in Greece a cold war objective, rendered any talk of Balkan Federation increasingly an object of suspicion in London, and later too in Washington, and in both the determination that Greece should not be further unsettled by an attempt by her northern neighbours to separate Macedonia was a *sine qua non* of policy.

Between 1945 and 1947, the scheme had been given further consideration in Belgrade and Sofia, where it had developed into something rather more ambitious than that suggested at Yalta, and now involved complete union of Yugoslavia, Bulgaria and Albania. Rumania too was being drawn in. At the same time, Tito was attempting to establish himself as leader of this grouping. In October 1943, Tito had written to Vukmanovic-Tempo who was the Partisans' link with the resistance in Macedonia: 'In our opinion, and also in that of Grandpa [the Comintern], we should be in the centre for the Balkan countries, both in the military and the political sense'.[18] The Partisans had taken steps to establish themselves in the role by maintaining close links with the Albanian communist resistance, a role with which they persisted in the post-war years, establishing joint-companies along Soviet lines as channels for aid and trade. At the end of 1947 they sent two divisions into Albania, significantly without consulting Moscow. These forces were, so Belgrade claimed officially, intended to protect the Albanians from Greece. In reality, the Yugoslavs had recognised that the Russians were already taking steps to reverse Tirana's policies towards Yugoslavia, and were attempting to strengthen their position before this process went too far.[19] Similarly, Yugoslav aid for the Greek guerrilla resistance, though partly derived from revolutionary solidarity with the EAM and KKE, also had, so Djilas recalled, the additional aim of securing Greek Macedonia in return in the event the KKE succeeded in taking power in Athens.[20] This seemed to be one step nearer at the end of 1947 as the Greek rebels announced that a 'Provisional Government' headed by General Markos Vafiades had been formed in the 'free mountains' of Greece.[21]

For the scheme to advance, however, it would require Moscow's approval and it is by no means clear that this was ever going to be forthcoming. Soviet support for the scheme was at best lukewarm: in February, as the Czech crisis was coming to a head, Stalin reproved Dimitrov for his persistent support of Tito's project for federation as well as his advocation of a customs union with Rumania. This disapproval had been given public expression through an article in *Pravda* on 28 January which was a direct reproach to Dimitrov, who at a press conference on 17 January following conclusion of the Bulgarian–Rumanian treaty of alliance, had declared that 'when the question is ripe . . . then our peoples of the People's Democracies of Rumania, Bulgaria, Yugoslavia, Albania, Czechoslovakia, Poland, Hungary and Greece – remember

Greece also – will decide it'.[22] Tito was similarly admonished, but whereas Dimitrov was suitably contrite, Tito made no apology. In the meantime, Djilas had been sent to Moscow in January 1948 to answer Stalin's demand for an explanation of Yugoslavia's policy towards Albania, only to be told by Stalin that they could swallow Albania. However, Stalin added at a subsequent meeting held at the Kremlin on 10 February, this time attended by Kardelj as well as Djilas and the Bulgarians leaders, that this could not happen until a federation with Bulgaria had been achieved.[23] Having admonished the Bulgarians and Yugoslavs for peremptory indications of their federation policy, he now told his Balkan suppliants that they should drive ahead to achieve this quickly. Djilas records, with hindsight, that he sensed disingenuity, and indeed Stalin's behaviour seems to belie at best a lack of certainty, and at worst a hidden agenda. Kardelj was obliged to sign a treaty to the effect that Yugoslavia would consult in future before taking any foreign initiative, but the Yugoslav foreign minister then declined to formally accept Stalin's directives regarding the federation without first consulting Tito.[24] The latter had been summoned to this meeting but suspecting trouble, had sent his deputies. Dimitri Volkogonov has suggested in his biography of Stalin that it was these acts of defiance on the part of Tito, which provided Stalin with the first sense of real opposition to his wishes since the 1930s, which provoked the sharp reaction that now followed.[25] It is also possible that Stalin saw in the mechanism of Balkan federation a means through which he could dissolve the Yugoslav (and other Balkan) leaderships and create a new political entity.

However, the scheme must also have been open to objection in Moscow. The inherent obstacles to achievement of such a federation were still very much in existence: traditional rivalries and the unequal political and economic development of the prospective members were self-evident difficulties and Stalin may also have considered the possibility that such a grouping of states might develop a regional solidarity and collective sense of independence which would cut across Russian designs to dominate the region. This was certainly how British diplomats analysed Soviet policy towards this question during the winter of 1947/48. Their attention had been drawn to the acrimony in the Soviet camp by the removal of posters of Tito in Bucharest at a time when the Rumanian leaders were in Moscow negotiating a treaty of friendship, effectively one of the first visible signs that Moscow was dissatisfied with Tito's leadership.[26] London remained implacably opposed, but recognised that there was nothing that Britain could do to prevent it happening, at least as long as it remained confined to the Soviet sphere. Indeed, long experience of observing the Balkans inclined Foreign Office officials to conclude, wisely, that the likelihood of these states burying their jealousies and rivalries long enough to get such a scheme off the ground, was probably remote.[27]

Aside from Tito's demands for frontier revisions, the initiative which probably disturbed the Russians the most was their policy towards Greece.[28] The predominance of British influence in Greece seems to have been accepted by Stalin, who apparently stood by his word to Churchill in October 1944 not to interfere. This had, of course, been given in return for effective British recognition of Soviet interest in Rumania and Bulgaria. Stalin is believed to have told the Greek communists that they could expect no material help from the Soviet Union and warned the Yugoslavs off their determined support of the Greek guerrillas.[29] Yugoslav intervention in the Greek Civil War in 1944 almost certainly did not receive Soviet backing. Nevertheless, as fighting broke out in Athens, the Partisans had watched expectantly, all the while directing bitter attacks in speeches and radio broadcasts against British intervention. But, Djilas recalled, the Yugoslavs knew they were treading a thin line with their propaganda which might make more difficult their negotiations with the West and Subasic, and which at this time Stalin was seeking to support; in practice, Tito had been running the risk of incurring the disapproval not only of Britain, but also of Moscow.[30] The civil war was quelled by British intervention in December 1944, but Yugoslavia did not cease to offer a place of refuge for the guerrillas, and when the fighting resumed in 1946, Yugoslavia became the principal source of supply for the insurgents. Stalin took advantage of the presence of Kardelj and Tito in Moscow in February 1948 to inform them that the Greek rising had to fold.[31]

The challenge to Moscow's authority had been thrown down. The Soviet Politburo now opened secret consultations with selected members of the central committees of other communist parties in the Cominform to discuss possible action to deal with the 'independent line' being followed by the Yugoslav leadership. In February the successful coup d'état in Czechoslovakia had consolidated the weak point on the Russian's western front. Bringing the Yugoslav leadership to heal was now being given increasing priority. The correspondence between Moscow and Belgrade which presaged the expulsion of Yugoslavia from the Cominform in June began on 18 March when the Soviet military attaché in Belgrade, General Barskov, informed Tito that Moscow was withdrawing forthwith all military advisers and instructors on the grounds that they were 'surrounded by hostility'.[32] On the following day, Tito was visited by the Soviet Chargé d'Affaires in Belgrade, Dmiter Armjaninov, who informed him that Soviet civilian advisers would also be withdrawn. Somewhat disingenuously, Tito responded with a request for information on these matters: the reply from Moscow, this time signed by Stalin himself, consisted of an ideological attack on the structure of the Yugoslav state and the conduct of its leaders. The reference in the concluding line to the political career of Leon Trotsky indicated what the main line of Moscow's attack was to be: Marxist theory required that the Party control all organs of the state. In Yugoslavia, the Russians claimed, the situation was reversed.[33] The correspondence continued over several months becoming steadily more acrimonious in tone. For evidence, the Russians cited the attitude of Tito as indicated by his speeches at the time of the Trieste crisis in 1945 and again during the negotiations for the Austrian Peace Treaty in 1947. By mid-May, Yugoslavia was being contrasted in all aspects with the other east European states, at which point Moscow declared that the matter was properly to be taken before the Cominform.

Despite the efforts of the Tito apologists to mythologise this period as one in which the Belgrade leadership were genuinely trying to meet the wishes of the Cominform, it is equally likely that Tito, having assessed that membership of Stalin's club meant severe curtailment of not only his ambitions for Yugoslavia but also those he entertained for himself, was making preparations lest circumstances forced him to break away. The principal indication of this is the purge within the Yugoslav leadership itself which took place during May, and was directed at the pro-Stalinist faction. The first to be attacked was the Minister of Light Industry, Andrija Hebrang, regarded generally as one of the most influential members of the Politburo who had enjoyed considerable power within the communist party both during and after the war. Djilas records in his memoirs that Tito had himself threatened to resign during the spring of 1948: 'I could tell,' he wrote, 'by his sly smile that he was indeed testing us; all of us exclaimed that it was out of the question – all but Zujovic who remained silent.'

Sretan Zujovic, the Minister of Finance, was dismissed soon after Hebrang.[34]

Within Yugoslavia hasty measures were implemented to consolidate the government's position. Nationalisation of retail shops originally considered too small to bother about during the nationalisation programme of 1947 was put in hand. Drastic restrictions were placed on the right to resign or refuse transfers in government employment. Details of the previous year's budget were not published, as had been the earlier custom.[35] At the same time the state security service, the UDBa and its head, Aleksander Rankovic, was becoming increasingly omnipotent. Indeed, trials of saboteurs and speculators and other miscreants had never been more numerous or harsher than in the spring of 1948, which also marked a renewed campaign against the continuing anti-communist bastion represented by the Orthodox and Catholic Churches. These activities could not be effectively concealed from western diplomats who interpreted them as signs of a general tightening up in Yugoslavia in line with the communist party practice throughout eastern Europe.

These interpretations were prepared in London without the benefit of knowledge of the as yet unpublished Tito–Stalin correspondence and the result was a synthesis both of their impressions of the current direction of Soviet policy and their concept of Soviet-style totalitarianism. In May 1948, the consensus was that these events were following the pattern typical of the simultaneous purges of left and right which had been witnessed first in Moscow during the 1920s and were accepted as characteristic of communist governed states. Charles Peake contributed to this impression when he wrote, on witnessing Hebrang's dismissal, that while this was 'one of the most important events in the history of the communist regime of Yugoslavia', it was the beginning of 'a purge of genuine "deviationists"'.[36] The notion that the underlying cause of the dispute was not within the Yugoslav leadership but between the Yugoslavs and their would-be 'masters', does not seem to have been seriously considered.[37] The Americans were arguably even less prescient: 'for the first time [the] confidence [of the] local regime in its ability to move forward boldly in the new Stalinist world seems to be faltering', observed Cannon, the American Ambassador in Belgrade: 'Today [the] Yugoslav government seems [to be] groping for those new directions that will give it once again [a] sense of having the lead in [the] Balkans, of being in fact [the] spearhead of evangelical and expansionist communism.'[38] Eager to see evidence of strain in the Soviet bloc which they might attribute to American economic policies in Europe, Cannon was among those who claimed that what he called the 'buoyancy of the regime' had been undermined by a combination of the American policy of revitalising the European economy, economic difficulties within Yugoslavia itself and 'recent political defections'.[39]

The visible indications of the deterioration of Soviet–Yugoslav relations in this period were reflected in the Soviet press which markedly decreased the coverage given to Yugoslav affairs. The *Cominform Journal* had, meanwhile, been publishing its own series of editorials on the subject, coming to a crescendo on 11 June in a thinly-veiled attack on the Communist who 'in fog eulogy and exaggerated self-praise' repressed criticism and overlooked its own shortcomings.[40] Indeed, Cannon suspected that Tito had been severely rebuked in a personal letter from Stalin: 'In the final analysis, it seems unlikely theoretical differences basic cause of developing conflict.' Cannon believed that 'Tito's personal ambition to lead own sphere in South East Europe must have cumulatively irritated and perhaps alarmed the Kremlin . . . On basis available evidence I am convinced that definite split exists.'[41] Among the first indications that this was indeed the case appeared in the form of an article by the KPJ ideologue, Mosa Pijade, published in *Borba* on 12 June. Pijade rigorously defended the KPJ's vanguard role in the Yugoslav people's front, reflecting the severity and directness of the criticism to which the leadership had been subjected in recent months. A further indication appeared in Tito's response to Moscow's Note concerning the forthcoming Danube conference. A conference to work out a new convention regarding the regime of navigation on the Danube River had been scheduled to be held in Belgrade on 30 July: on 12 June, the Soviet government suggested that the conference be held in some other Danubian capital; the Yugoslavs confidently asserted that the conference should and would be held in Belgrade as planned.[42]

The British were surprised, if not startled, by this news. Yugoslavia had been evaluated by the Foreign Office's Southern Department in early 1948 as 'undoubtedly the prize pupil of east-European states within the Soviet orbit'. London believed that the proposal to establish the Cominform headquarters in Belgrade had confirmed Yugoslavia's pre-eminent status, and that Tito had 'largely been entrusted with the responsibility of consolidating eastern Europe'.[43]

The causes of the quarrel seemed in London rather more obvious: Stalin, in his attempt to consolidate Soviet hegemony throughout east and south-east Europe had stumbled on the strong nationalist and individualistic characteristics of Tito and his colleagues. Although in recent months Tito had apparently made some efforts to meet Moscow's demands, he could not or would not take these measures far enough. On the Soviet side, so the British believed, Tito's self-assured and independent posture posed a threat to the consolidation of the bloc. What made them distrustful, however, that the episode was what it seemed, was the fact that the Russians had failed to so arrange matters that a coup d'état could follow immediately upon the issue of the communiqué: 'It seems inconceivable,' wrote Wallinger, 'that the Kremlin should have taken a chance in this matter, having regard to the strategic importance to the orbit of Yugoslavia.' Indeed, Anna Pauker, foreign minister in Rumania, took occasion of the Danube conference to remark to Peake, with whom she was on particularly good terms, that if Stalin had realised what Tito's reaction would be he would have approached the problem differently.[44] This being so, they reasoned, the Russians must expect Tito, once faced with the condemnation of all his communist colleagues, to recant or resign.[45]

The Foreign Office analysis of the dispute is important because it contained a thesis regarding Tito as leader, and his role in Yugoslavia, which can be traced to the war. The causes for the dispute were identified as two-fold: the first of these centred on the personality of Tito whose arrogance and independence had unquestionably irritated Stalin to such a degree that a showdown had become inevitable. Indeed, some have argued that it was it was precisely this, and in particular his evidently growing popularity within Yugoslavia, which provoked Stalin to turn on him.[46] The second concerned the obstacles Tito placed in the way the Kremlin's foreign policy. Since the announcement of the European Recovery Programme and the creation of the Western Union, the Russians had been seeking the closest possible unity in the foreign policy aspect of their sphere. Like their American counterparts, the British conjectured that Yugoslav obduracy regarding the Austrian Treaty and Trieste, assuming that Moscow had seriously desired to seek a compromise with the west as a factor in their recent 'peace offensive', as well as their interest in Greece, had placed a significant part in shaping current Soviet thinking. Tito was evidently being held personally responsible. In a paper submitted to Bevin as a briefing on the present Yugoslav crisis, the Foreign Office concluded that it seemed that 'even if the present differences are composed by some compromise which western thinking would consider inconceivable, the fear would remain and Tito and his fellow-leaders of Yugoslav communism could never be really accepted back into Moscow's fold. Confidence between them has been destroyed forever.'[47]

Bevin was initially unimpressed by the dispute and inclined to regard it as of little significance in policy terms. The Yugoslavs had been the most aggressive of the east European governments in attacking British post-war policy, and he felt that it required more than the publication of an acrimonious exchange of correspondence to constitute convincing evidence of a genuine separating of the ways. A survey of the situation in central and eastern Europe, which Bevin asked the Foreign Office to draft for submission to Attlee at the end of July, and which carried evidence of Bevin's input, concluded in respect to Yugoslavia that 'it would be a mistake to read too much' into the Soviet–Yugoslav dispute which was probably little more than a family quarrel.[48]

Strategists were also at work assessing the potential value or impact for British interests of a genuine breach in the Cominform monolith. In the summer of 1948, they concluded that its potential was uncertain until more was known about the nature of the dispute and the likelihood of a rapprochement.

If Yugoslavia's independence was sustained, then the Chiefs of Staff argued that it would be reasonable to assume that pressure might ease on both Greece and Trieste, and that the proposed South Slav Federation, with its inherent threat to the *status quo* in Greece, would not materialise. The implications for British military planning were subsequently put before the Chiefs of Staff in a JIC paper submitted on 24 September, still withheld from the public domain.[49] The immediate priority seemed in London to be to co-ordinate any response with the Americans. Indeed, if the dispute were genuine then it could only be a matter of time before the Yugoslavs turned to the west for support and new sources of supply to replace those formerly provided by the Soviet sphere. In this event, it would be the United States and not Britain which would have the wherewithal to assist Tito in maintaining the Yugoslav state as an independent entity.

If British policy towards the dispute might be characterised as a case of masterly inactivity, that of the United States was much more a progression in a series of abrupt advances. The advice from the Embassy in Belgrade, as is so often the case, was somewhat in advance of the cautious wait and see approach being adopted in Moscow. The habitually perspicacious Cavendish Cannon, among the first western diplomats to perceive the existence of fundamental differences between Belgrade and Washington, was inclined to argue that western support for Yugoslavia would have a major influence on the course of Soviet policy since no event 'could be more momentous for the attainment of our foreign policy objectives than the permanent alienation from the Soviet Union of this key regime'.[50] The American military attaché was similarly impressed, and recommended to Washington the 'boldest possible exploitation of this defection in keystone of Soviet satellite structure'.[51] Tito, he argued, could not hold out long against Soviet pressure unless some form of outside assistance were provided, and that if such aid were forthcoming, 'he would have good prospect of a success which would lead to solution of our major problems in Europe'. The naiveté of this statement, to say nothing of the optimism it betrays, is breathtaking. Nonetheless, the Tito–Cominform split was indisputably the most significant event to occur behind the Iron Curtain with the exception of the Berlin crisis, and it was right for officials to recognise it as having much potential.[52]

The American posture was defined in a paper of 30 June, prepared by the Policy Planning Staff (PPS) of the State Department which had been created recently by George Marshall for the purpose of future planning, but also to reappraise existing policies. The first head was the former Chargé d'Affaires in the American embassy in Moscow, George Kennan, who was considered by senior officials in the Foreign Office as 'possibly the ablest man in the State Department as far as Russia is concerned'.[53] Kennan welcomed the Tito–Cominform split as confirming his analysis that the Soviet Union's imperial policies would lead it inevitably to clash with the nation and personal interests of its subject peoples.[54] The paper prepared by his staff on the current Yugoslav crisis opened with the assessment that 'for the first time in history we may now have within the international community a communist state resting on the basis of Soviet organisation and principles and for the most part on Soviet ideology, and yet independent of Moscow', but argued that the need for extreme circumspection remained paramount until a more definite pattern emerged: 'it would . . . be a frivolous and undignified error on our part to assume that because Tito had fallen out with Stalin he could not be considered our "friend"'.[55]

There were several points involved here. The first concerned the question of precedent: Kennan argued that Titoism should not be regarded as an isolated phenomenon but a precedent to be encouraged elsewhere: Yugoslavia was just the first to break away from the Soviet orbit. Moreover, as officials on both sides of the Atlantic were quick to advise their government masters, the attitude adopted by their governments would have a considerable influence on whether the rift between Tito and Moscow would indeed spread to other members of the Cominform. An ill-judged move or public statement could merely serve to weld the other members more tightly to the Kremlin. The American Embassy in Belgrade suggested at one point the idea of issuing a public statement indirectly supporting 'small nations', but on learning of this Bevin requested through the American Ambassador in London that such statements be withheld for the time being, fearing that actions of this sort would merely lead to complete oblivion of all local autonomy and ultimate absorption of the region by Soviet Russia.[56] The Tito–Cominform dispute led the British and Americans to devote great resources to ways of encouraging further dissidence in the satellites on the basis that 'Titoism', as it became known, was a phenomenon that could be encouraged to take root elsewhere, a conviction which led to the evolution of policies known respectively as 'liberation' and 'roll-back'.[57] At the Russia Committee meeting of 25 November, Ivone Kirkpatrick, then responsible for development of the propaganda offensive, asked whether it might not be possible to start a civil war behind the iron curtain and by careful assistance to produce a state of affairs in Albania, similar to that in Greece.[58] A sub-committee was duly set up, tasked to examine ways of undermining eastern Europe, particularly south-east Europe, mention being made specifically of Yugoslavia and Albania. This sub-committee's report concluded that priority for such activities be given to Yugoslavia, the Soviet zone of Germany and Albania, as well as to implementation of economic measures: 'Of the countries lying on the periphery of the Soviet orbit, Yugoslavia is by far the most important for our purpose . . . If this opening is thus exploited, a sort of chain reaction among the satellites might be started.'[59] A draft paper for submission to the Defence Committee was prepared and sent up to Bevin for approval in early February 1949. Bevin had reported to the Russia Committee through Frank Roberts (since 1947 his Private Secretary), that he wanted British policy to concentrate on three primary and closely related objectives in south-east Europe: to take even more energetic steps to save Greece, to give discreet encouragement to Tito and so to maintain the Yugoslav–Soviet clash, and to detach Albania from the Soviet orbit.[60] He rejected at this stage the proposal to institute active subversion, particularly in the light of the present North Atlantic Treaty negotiations. However, intelligence information revealed that the Americans were already actively attempting to infiltrate former Cetniks into Yugoslavia. These activities were apparently being conducted at the instigation of the Army Department which was somewhat more hawkish than the State Department evidently wished. The British were appalled, regarding such missions as 'inconceivably stupid' and 'idiotic', which would serve only to rouse all of Tito's worst suspicions about America's real aims in the region. Furthermore, the Yugoslav security services were aware of these infiltrations and had already rounded up large numbers of would-be counter-revolutionaries. Bateman recommended that the Foreign Office indirectly reveal their knowledge of these activities in the hope that this would be sufficient to warn the Americans off.[61]

Albania evidently was a different question however. On 14 March, Bebler had indicated obliquely to Hector McNeil that while Yugoslavia would not seek to interfere in either Macedonia or Albania, in the latter the situation was potentially 'of interest' to the West, and that they might further their interests by rescuing the Albanian Communist Party General Secretary from the jail in which he had been languishing since the previous autumn, and set him up as a rival to Hoxha.[62] Clearly the Belgrade government had its own interests in at least neutralising the Albanians as allies, and probably agents, of Stalinism. However, this was the first excursion by the Tito government into political issues since the split and this approach left the British puzzled about its meaning? Was this intended to create an opportunity for Tito to go into Albania, and could Bebler be trusted as the mouthpiece for Tito's intentions? The central dilemma remained that while all were agreed in London on the opportunity provided by the Tito–Cominform split, the question they were unable even now to answer was how best to exploit it: 'If we are too forward,' Wallinger wrote in comment on American overt and covert activities, 'we risk destroying what we want to support.' Cavendish Cannon, despite his disapproval of the number of military attachés now being assigned to his Embassy in Belgrade, was known to believe that delay in acting on this 'opportunity' was risky, but the British were inclined to the view that haste was even more risky: 'backing of anti-Soviet elements would be playing straight into the Soviet hand'.[63] Peake was particularly forceful in arguing that no action be taken which might give credit to the belief in 'imperialist warmongery' in Yugoslav minds, and that this included drastic interference in Albania, particularly if it involved the return of King Zog.

None of this prevented the British and American intelligence agencies mounting one of the tragic and misguided missions to which these strange and tense times gave rise. Julian Amery, and several of his former colleagues in SOE, had come up with an idea for an operation to instigate a rebellion in Albania.The Hoxha regime was believed to be weak, unpopular and isolated and, so Amery argued, could be overthrown by well-trained Albanian exiles. In part this was an outgrowth of the 'liberation policies' being evolved on both sides of the Atlantic; how far this particular operation was connected with Bebler's approach is unclear. Amery knew that what he had in mind would provoke the strongest opposition from Tito; in proceeding he was also flying in the face of such wily Balkanists as Fitzroy Maclean and Franklin Lindsay. When Bevin was told of this plan, he agreed so long as the Americans would join in and meet the costs.[64] The operation finally took place in late November 1949, when 60 Albanians were infiltrated to organise and lead a rebellion against Tirana using the million or so Albanians living in Kosovo. In fact, there was no popular will for such a rising and this was the primary cause of the mission's failure, although it had also been sabotaged from the outset by its joint commander, Kim Philby, who had ensured that Moscow had advance warning.[65]

In practical terms, the western powers were in many respects impotent to influence events in the Balkans. The situation depended wholly on Tito, much as it had during the war: perhaps the greatest difficulty both the British and Americans had in policy-making towards Yugoslavia in their anxiety to exploit the perceived opportunities for the west to build political victories against the Soviet Union in the Cold War which seemed to be offered by the Cominform split, was in coming to terms with that fact. In a sense they remained, as in the first three years following the war, relatively limited in the degree to which they could develop an active policy in the region. Until the spring of 1949, economic aid, in discreet and carefully restricted quantities was the only effective mechanism for demonstrating support for Yugoslav neutrality. It was a policy which required subtlety and a great deal of patience, but its importance for incremental detachment of Yugoslavia from the Soviet block and maintaining her as a stable bastion of neutrality in the Balkans was enormous.

7

Limited Commitments: Keeping Tito Afloat, 1948–1949

In order to explain the evolution of economic aid to Yugoslavia it is necessary to go back to the summer of 1948. Following the rupture in the Cominform a somewhat contradictory situation existed with respect to Yugoslavia's position in the international community and the policies of Britain and the United States towards her. Despite Yugoslavia's expulsion from the Cominform and the Soviet hostility towards the Yugoslav leaders, Tito's foreign policy remained generally consistent with that of the Soviet bloc. The emphasis of the Yugoslav government statement immediately after the expulsion was announced was on their determination to maintain present external and internal policies: both Djilas and Vlahovic went into print in *Borba* in early July, predicting a continuation of Yugoslavia's tough line towards the West and even gilded this particular lilly to the extent of predicting some form of conciliatory move with the Kremlin.[1] Whatever the differences, theoretical or otherwise, that Tito might have with the Russian leaders, his regime was legitimised by Marxist–Leninist doctrine and Tito, despite Soviet criticism, wasted no opportunity to remind the world of his continued commitment to communism. Nevertheless, it was becoming increasingly clear that Stalin was determined to engineer the removal of Tito and his entourage, and would be likely to use all means short of war to achieve this purpose. Assassination became an ever-present danger for Tito and contemporary accounts confirm that Stalin expected that it would be easy to depose him: 'I will shake my little finger,' Stalin is reported to have said, 'and there will be no more Tito.'[2] However, if this is what Stalin believed, then he had failed to understand the dynamics of Yugoslav nationalism – or supranationalism – and the significance of this for Tito's position.[3]

Hostility from powerful neighbours served only as a unifier and a means by which Tito could heighten his power.

The break with the Cominform left Yugoslavia isolated militarily and economically. Numerous border incidents occurred but the country itself, with the exception of minor civil unrest in Bosnia, was quiet.[4] Soviet pressure began to drive Yugoslavia towards the West. The immediate crisis concerned the Yugoslav economy, which was highly dependent upon imports from the Russian sphere; having little connection with the outside world was therefore especially vulnerable; once the Russians cut off the source of supply, Yugoslavia would in time be forced into submission unless, of course, Tito was prepared to compromise and seek large-scale trade with the western Powers and that they, in turn, would be prepared to participate. Stalin might well have reasoned that such a move on Tito's part would undermine his credibility in Yugoslavia, and that disruptive forces within Yugoslavia itself would operate to undermine his position. The interests of the West, as British officials perceived in July 1948, could be served best by the separation of a Tito-governed, unified Yugoslavia from the Soviet sphere, as encouragement to the others to assert their independence once they felt themselves sufficiently strong. In this sense the ideological orientation of the Yugoslav government was of little concern and it was Yugoslav independence per se which became, by the autumn of 1948, the objective of policy.

One thing seemed fairly clear: Yugoslav independence was not something over which the West would go to war. There was an assumption in London and Washington at this time that the process of detaching Yugoslavia from the Soviet Union was not worth a fight. Policy towards Yugoslavia, which in time came to include military aid, was pursued with all means short of war. In the summer of 1948, the first priority was to ensure that Tito remained in power and shoring up his regime economically was the immediate means to this end. Yugoslavia, an industrially backward country, decimated by war and denuded by Soviet activities in its aftermath, would be in need of economic assistance from the West in order to survive: this was the principal problem on which the British concentrated until the conclusion of the long-term trade agreement and the beginning of American aid at the end of 1949. That they did so was critical to Yugoslavia's short-term survival and probably to her long-term cohesion.

The immediate question was to the extent `of the assistance and timing of the offer. It was by no means certain in the summer of 1948 that the Tito–Stalin quarrel was irreparable, or that the Tito government would succeed in remaining in power even with the benefit of financial and economic assistance from the West. Lurking in the shadows was the danger that once aid was given, Tito would recant or be overthrown, and the Soviet sphere would accrue whatever benefits had been handed to the Yugoslavs. Another possibility which was also raised in the minutes of officials required to analyse developments in the Soviet sphere was whether the whole episode had been staged by the communist bloc, precisely so as to acquire western assistance and technology.[5] Although this argument was not given much credence in Britain, it was nonetheless a contingency which had to be weighed in the balance. There was also the question of timing: when and how should assistance be offered. Any overt show of support for Tito could be damaging to his position as a communist ideologue, betokening ideological compromise with capitalism, which while unlikely to lend much additional ammunition to outside forces – Tito had already been accused by Stalin of being the agent of the West – might damage his status within his own fortress.

The Yugoslav government had its own timetable for the revision of its relations with the West. They claimed that they had been puzzled by the failure of the western powers to soften their policies towards Yugoslavia during the first six months of 1948 since they were sure that they had been aware the tension was increasing between Belgrade and Moscow. Particular concern was expressed lest the British and American press and radio stations started holding out glowing promises of future aid or violently attacking either Tito or the regime, either of which would have had a detrimental effect.[6] From the beginning of July onwards, clandestine contacts were established apparently at Yugoslav instigation, as channels through which Tito could communicate his true intentions while simultaneously maintaining a public façade of injured estrangement. The speed with which these were activated seems a further indication that Tito had a well thought out plan for establishing Yugoslavia's independence should the need arise. During the course of these conversations, it was made clear to British and American diplomats that for the time being, the Yugoslav government would maintain its present course. At the first party congress held since the war, Tito spoke for nine hours before the 2,300 delegates and although he defended his position, he did not openly criticise the Soviet Union.[7] In private, however, Tito let it be known that Yugoslavia might now be interested in participating in the European Recovery Programme and that he wished to halt the drain on resources constituted by support for the Greek guerrillas at the earliest opportunity.[8]

In the Foreign Office, Geoffrey Wallinger, who was the principal commentator on Yugoslav affairs in this period, was in agreement with Charles Bateman, his head of department, that Yugoslav protestations could not be accepted at face value at this stage.[9] In a letter to George Sappington at the American Embassy in London dated 10 July, he explained that it was the British view that the Yugoslavs should be required to make some demonstration of the sincerity of their intentions by their actions. The sudden interest of Belgrade in the European Recovery Programme, while probably motivated by genuine economic difficulties, might just possibly be part of the Soviet Union's policy of undermining ERP. This notwithstanding, the British had identified certain steps which they believed could be taken immediately to help maintain the break, for example, the Yugoslav government had attempted to purchase 20–30,000 tons of crude oil form the AIOC and while provision of this would confer no lasting benefit, it would help to keep Yugoslavia functioning for the time being.[10] The State Department was in substantial agreement with this, but was keen to encourage its Embassy's informal contacts with Yugoslav government officials and instructed Reams to convey American willingness to consider the possibilities of improving Yugoslav–American trade and economic relations when the moment was more opportune.[11] Marshall directed that the Embassy take no initiative in this regard until the situation had solidified.

The Danube Conference, due to be hosted by the Yugoslavs in Belgrade at the end of July, seemed to offer the three major western powers, who were entitled to send delegates as riparian powers, the first opportunity to observe the Russians and Yugoslavs together since the split. The Foreign Office were hopeful that the behaviour of the other Cominform members towards each other, and perhaps even the posture of the Yugoslav government on the question of the Danube, might give some solid indication as to the direction of Yugoslavia's relations with both the Soviet sphere and the West. The conference was the direct result of a resolution of the CFM passed at its meeting in New York in December 1946, that the four controlling powers could call a conference to work out a new convention regarding navigation of the Danube river within six months of the coming into force of the peace treaties with Rumania, Bulgaria and Hungary.[12] This had happened in September 1947 and it was only after some delay, at the request of the western powers, that the conference was finally convened. When the Russians attempted to have the venue changed in June, and the Yugoslavs were unable to make the necessary preparation in the time available, one Foreign Office official suggested that the West might exacerbate the quarrel by taking the Russians up on their proposal. Wiser counsel prevailed, however, for it was hardly in the West's interests to undermine Tito in this way.[13]

The outcome of the conference was never in any doubt. The interests of the western powers were somewhat tenuous, stemming as they did from a desire on the part of the British and French to revive their pre-war trading position, and on the part of all three to fly the flags freely on the river as a means of pushing at the Iron Curtain and maintaining the principle of freedom of navigation on European inland waterways.[14] Since the cessation of hostilities, however, a Central Rhine Commission had been set up successfully without any representation from the Russians; it was to be expected that Moscow would similarly ensure that no western representative should sit on the body that would control a vital waterway running through much of their sphere of influence. On this basis, and given the fact that the Russians would give their support to the east and south-east European states, the western powers could predict with confidence that they would be heavily outvoted by seven to three. In order to minimise the possible loss of prestige inherent in this, they sought to play down the significance of the conference through the diplomatic gesture of sending their ambassadors in Yugoslavia to the conference table rather than matching the rather grander ministerial delegation which had set out from Moscow.[15]

In the context of political developments within the Soviet sphere it was the atmosphere of the conference which was its most interesting aspect. Although the Yugoslav delegation followed their Russian counterparts closely in speeches and voting, their isolation outside the conference room, both from the Soviet representative and those from the satellites, was all too apparent. However, during the course of a conversation with a clandestine contact, Anton Bebler remarked that while it suited the Yugoslav government to follow Vyshinsky's line on the Danube, Yugoslavia was otherwise maintaining her independent line in foreign policy. Indeed, Tito himself was conspicuously absent from Belgrade, having retired to his hunting lodge at Bled. The rest of the Yugoslav Politburo had similarly dropped out of sight for the duration of the conference.

Shortly after the conference concluded, the Yugoslavs published the texts of their correspondence with Moscow which had preceded the Cominform resolution in June. The Soviet version appeared in print not long afterwards, marking a further sharp deterioration in Soviet–Yugoslav relations.[16] In September, the dispute had taken a further turn when there appeared in *Borba* three articles, which, though unsigned, appeared to have been written by Tito himself.[17] The significance of these lay in the fact that the constant theme of the orthodoxy of the Yugoslav attitude was now accompanied by a condescending manner towards Stalin himself who was referred to simply as *one* of the great leaders of Marxism–Leninism. The slanging match rumbled on through the autumn, but there was increasingly tangible evidence that the dispute was genuine. Within Yugoslavia there prevailed an atmosphere of stability and calm, although not all in Yugoslav government circles had toed Tito's line: two ambassadors, three generals and five officials in republican cabinets, as well as a small number of lesser personalities, were known in the West to have defected to the Soviet camp.[18] The slow progress of the Soviet–Yugoslav trade talks, and the imposition of economic sanctions against Yugoslavia by the Soviet Union in December, seemed to bring confirmation that the rift would endure.

Negotiations for an Anglo-Yugoslav short-term trade agreement had been deadlocked since the Spring 1946, owing to the inability of either side to compromise on the question of compensation for British-owned property sequestered by the Yugoslav Government during its nationalisation programme. This had become a matter of principle for the British, and they had made it clear that the trade agreement would not be signed unless the compensation issue was settled at the same time.[19] A fresh attempt to settle the question was made in August 1947 which originated with an offer on the part of the Yugoslavs to settle the compensation question. Once again, the negotiations quickly reached a stalemate. The original British draft had centred on a sizeable import of maize from Yugoslavia, maize being a crop of which supplies were urgently needed in Britain at this juncture, particularly since the outcome of negotiations with other major maize exporters, especially the Soviet Union and the Argentine, was uncertain. In return for cereals, the British had offered to supply significant quantities of capital goods. The Yugoslav government, however, was unimpressed: their delegation swiftly rejected the British draft and, during the early part of December, tabled one of its own, by which time Britain had not only concluded agreements with the Argentine and the Soviet Union, but was also reconsidering the wisdom of supplying capital goods to Yugoslavia. The original British draft had therefore been largely superseded, and since the Yugoslav proposals were considered in London to be totally unacceptable, the negotiations collapsed.[20]

The Foreign Office, frustrated by the lack of progress, instructed Peake in April 1948 to complain to the Yugoslav Ministry of Foreign Affairs, citing the methods and personality of the Yugoslav's chief negotiator, Sretan Kopcok, as the principal reason for the lack of any advance.[21] Apparently his remonstrance did not fall on deaf ears; when the Yugoslav team returned to London to resume negotiations at the beginning of May, Kopcok was noticeably more willing to co-operate.[22] Nevertheless, the main stumbling block to an agreement remained unresolved, since the Yugoslavs persisted with their refusal to agree to the inclusion in the draft of any figure of compensation for British properties. Nor would they agree to a clause providing for a token payment. At an inter-departmental meeting held at the Board of Trade on 6 May, it was agreed at ministerial level that the question of compensation was so fundamental to the British position that there was effectively no way forward so long as the Yugoslavs continued with their obduracy.[23]

This experience was shared by the Americans and it is necessary to say something here about their position in this, partly because of the light it sheds on Yugoslav policy, but also because British and United States policies towards Yugoslavia were now formed increasingly in co-operation, and in nothing was this more so than in preparing the ground for the extension of economic aid. The latter, who had not embarked upon trade negotiations with the Yugoslav Government after the war, had encountered similar difficulties as the British when attempting to secure compensation for their property. Despite the bargaining counter the Americans held in the $48 million of Yugoslav assets frozen in the United States since April 1941, the Yugoslavs had not apparently felt sufficiently anxious to retrieve these assets to overcome their reluctance to settle American compensation claims which were held out as the *sine qua non* for an agreement.[24] Negotiations had been opened (again at the instigation of the Yugoslavs) in Washington in May 1947, but a year later the best Yugoslav offer amounted to just $5,181,000 in compensation for nationalised property and the equivalent of $300,000 in Yugoslav currency in settlement of Lend Lease and other forms of relief for which the Americans were also demanding recompense. The inadequacy of this offer is self-evident in the fact that the private claims regarding nationalised properties alone amounted to some $50.3 million.[25] However, a moderation of the Yugoslav attitude had been detected by American officials in Belgrade early in 1948, coincidentally, as later became known at the same moment that Soviet–Yugoslav acrimony became sharper. In January, Tito had intimated to Cavendish Cannon that, above all, the Yugoslav government wanted to secure the release of Yugoslav assets in the United States.[26] Although this attitude was not immediately reflected in the approach of the Yugoslav delegation in Washington, their approach had now become less belligerent. Suddenly, without any apparent reason, towards the end of May, rapid progress occurred and by the second week of June an agreement had been drafted which provided not only for the settlement of outstanding claims for pre-UNRRA aid and Lend Lease supplies, but also satisfied American demands for compensation with respect to private property. The Yugoslav government, which by this stage was being purged of pro-Stalinists, was seeking not perhaps so much an improvement in relations with the West, as the retrieval of urgently needed finances which might assist the government in establishing Yugoslav independence of the Soviet Union. It is also further evidence to suggest that Yugoslav departure from the Soviet camp may not have been as unanticipated in Belgrade as the Yugoslavs wished the world to believe. Concern that Yugoslavia should not be seen to be consorting with the West immediately on the announcement of a difference of opinion with Stalin probably dictated the timing of these advances. The agreement, which amounted to some $17 million (as against the $20 million for which the Americans had originally bargained) was signed in Washington on 19 July and all Yugoslav assets in the United States were duly unfrozen.[27] The timing of this announcement, which came so shortly after publication of the Cominform Communiqué on 28 June, seems more than coincidental.

Other events also indicated that the Yugoslavs were anxious to put their relations with the United States onto a more satisfactory footing. At the beginning of July, Tito had contacted the Americans clandestinely in Belgrade, in order to express an interest not only in reviving trade links with the United States but also the possibility of Yugoslav participation in the European Recovery Programme at some future date.[28] The idea of making some positive indication of support for Tito was attracting acceptance in a number of quarters: the Under Secretary of State for the Department of the Army, Richard Patterson, argued somewhat rashly that the strategic value to the United States of an independent Yugoslavia was sufficient to merit the extension of economic aid forthwith.[29] Somewhat less incautious, but nonetheless enthusiastic, was the American Chargé d'Affaires in Belgrade, Reams, who had been on the receiving end of recent Yugoslav contacts, and was keen to make further contact with Tito's envoy.[30] Reams' excitement at what he described in his correspondence with George Marshall as 'this brilliantly fluid situation',[31] was supported by military and naval attachés, and also by the American Special Representative in Europe, Averell Harriman, one of the most experienced American officials in the field of Soviet affairs. After reading the telegrams from Belgrade, he wrote to George Marshall to recommend that Reams be encouraged to seek immediately another meeting with the Yugoslavs in order to indicate American willingness to discuss the possibility of improving economic relations which, he suggested, might 'stiffen Tito's resistance to Kremlin pressure'.[32] The Secretary of State was first amongst those who argued against such an approach: Marshall recognised in the situation a fluidity which cautioned him against such a dramatic shift in American foreign economic policy. Despite the recommendations of Harriman and others, he remained firm in his view that any initiative concerning economic assistance that might be forthcoming from Belgrade should be handled with the utmost circumspection.[33] This cautious wait and see approach was the determining factor in American policy towards Yugoslavia for the remainder of 1948.

The Yugoslavs were undeterred by the lack of an immediate response. Before the end of July, Tito had taken advantage of an informal meeting with George Olson, the former Governor of California, who was then visiting Yugoslavia, to reiterate Yugoslav interest in a trade agreement. He pointed out that overtures to this effect had so far been received unfavourably in Washington and warned that Yugoslavia would not accept any proposals which included political conditions. Having refused to be dominated by Moscow, Tito was not now going to permit the US – or the British – to assert a dictatorship of their own. Tito also emphasised his conviction that, in time, Yugoslavia would be vindicated in the quarrel with the Cominform and that there was no intention on his Government's part to change the line of attack. Once again, an interest was expressed in the European Recovery Programme and, in particular, in Olson's statement that the Marshall Plan was designed solely to stabilise the world economic condition and, contrary to Soviet propaganda, had no political motivation.[34] Olson's subsequent report of this conversation did little to ally Washington's suspicions, however, and while the Americans sanctioned supplies of short-term economic aid in the form of consumable goods so that the Yugoslav economy might be saved from imminent collapse, it was without the provision of long-term benefits. They were officially going to 'wait and see' before offering anything more substantial and sought to defuse any 'inappropriate speculation' in the press by announcing only that it was taking note of Tito's request.[35]

In London, Foreign Office officials had awaited the American reaction to developments in Belgrade with interest and not a little apprehension. It was important for British purposes that the United States should not take any action which might prejudice either the position of the Western Powers, or that of Tito himself. The British had concluded that it would be imprudent to make any significant alterations to their present policy until the situation had solidified, and reasoned that supplies of consumable goods only might usefully be supplied in the short term in order to keep Tito going long enough for the West to assess the nature of the dispute.[36] The Yugoslavs had tested the British attitude towards the question of economic aid early in July by placing a request through the Anglo-Iranian Oil Company for some twenty thousand tons of crude oil for which they had offered to pay in dollars.[37] Oil was a commodity of which Britain had more than sufficient stock and the sale of it in this instance would enable Britain to earn dollars without conferring any lasting benefits on Yugoslavia. Nevertheless, Geoffrey Wallinger of the Southern Department recommended initially that it would be worthwhile to at least attempt to extract some political concession from the Yugoslavs in return. The AIOC should be advised to say that they had encountered opposition to the sale from Government departments who were unhappy about Yugoslav intransigence over the trade and compensation issues. Bevin, however, indicated his doubts about the wisdom of such a manoeuvre, and instructed his officials to let the sale proceed without hindrance; if the Yugoslavs really wanted to conclude a trade agreement with Britain, so Bevin reasoned, this would come about in due course without such exertions.[38]

Bevin's view of Yugoslavia's predicament as a cold war issue was straightforward: the changed circumstances of Yugoslav–Soviet relations made it more desirable than ever for British traders to establish links with Yugoslavia which would open the possibilities of long-term connections between that country and Britain. Once such links were established Tito's actions might be tempered a little out of consideration for what could possibly become a vital supply line.[39] Some transactions of this nature were in fact already taking place between the Yugoslavs and individual British traders. The Board of Trade had no objections to these activities: in no cases were raw material or capital goods involved, and the process was having the effect of generating sterling balances in Britain out of which the Yugoslavs might be persuaded, eventually, to settle the compensation claims.[40] Mindful of the recent American experience, Orme Sargent was less sanguine. Provided Tito continued to stand firm on the major dispute, he considered that it would be better to discourage the establishment of too many private commercial contacts, at least for the time being when Yugoslav independence remained a politically sensitive issue for Britain.[41]

The Danube Conference in August had created an interlude in the general discussion of the future of Anglo-Yugoslav trade,[42] but shortly after the conference had broken up, the Yugoslav Government initiated fresh talks with considerable vigour. The British Embassy in Belgrade was informed unofficially that the Yugoslav Trade Delegation in London had been instructed to reach an early agreement concerning short-term trade, and that there would no longer be any difficulty over the £4.5 million which was considered in London the lowest acceptable figure for compensation.[43] This communication had evidently been made on excellent authority: within a month the short-term agreement which had been stalled for two and a half years, had been settled and a figure for compensation agreed.[44] These documents were eventually signed in London on 23 December 1948. The first, the Trade Agreement, provided for an exchange of goods between the two countries during the year ending 30 September 1949; Britain would receive imports from Yugoslavia amounting to $14.7 million, including timber and foodstuffs, and would export to the value of £11.3 million in the form of raw wool, cotton yarn, oil, rubber, chemicals, steel and miscellaneous machinery. The second agreement concerned compensation for expropriated British property for which a sum of £4.5 million would be paid. This was considerably higher than the figure the Foreign Office had considered likely to be offered, a measure perhaps of the importance of the agreement to Belgrade – and probably to Tito personally. A token payment of £400,000 would be made immediately with the balance to be negotiated at the same time as the long-term agreement. A clause was to be included in the latter which would put a time limit on the final settlement. A third agreement related to money and property in Britain and Yugoslavia which had been subjected to 'special measures in consequence of enemy occupation of Yugoslavia', and included Yugoslav national assets in Britain which had been frozen during the war.[45] The agreement was to be renewed in July 1949, while negotiations for a long-term agreement were expected to begin 'at an early date'. The documents also envisaged the fostering of the shipping trade and establishment of shipping agencies.[46] The publicity surrounding these agreements was tailored at Yugoslav request to present them in purely economic terms. It also suited British purposes: the Southern Department believed that the British position in terms of cold war politics might benefit generally if it could be demonstrated that Yugoslavia had been granted favourable economic terms without any political ramifications.[47]

Since the publication of the Cominform Communiqué in June, Bevin had pursued a policy of keeping Tito 'just afloat'. The events of the following four months had not substantially altered this view. When policy was reviewed again at a meeting held between Bevin and the then President of the Board of Trade, Harold Wilson, during the third week of October 1948, Bevin encountered little difficulty in persuading his Cabinet colleague that Yugoslavia should be given only enough economic assistance to prevent collapse of the economy, and that this should remain the guiding principle of British policy until the situation had become clearer. In practice the notion of keeping the Yugoslav economy just afloat was to remain the determining factor in British policy towards Yugoslavia until the end of 1949.[48]

While the Anglo-Yugoslav Short Term Trade Agreement had been under discussion in London, the Yugoslavs had also been making further overtures to private enterprises in the United States with a view to securing a number of much needed industrial materials. During September, for example, three oil well equipment suppliers had been approached by the Yugoslav Embassy in Washington regarding purchases of drilling and auxiliary equipment, for which the Yugoslavs offered to exchange certain minerals and ores. Although the State Department was inclined by the autumn of 1948 to disregard elaborate conspiracy explanations of Yugoslav behaviour, officials in the Department of European Affairs were wary of these Yugoslav probes: their principal concern was with the much more rational concern that Tito might yet be toppled from the seat of power, either by malcontents within Yugoslavia or by external influences and that, should this happen, a Soviet puppet government would probably take its place. The Russians also were in urgent need of the materials being sought by Yugoslavia, and would greatly benefit if American exports of this nature should fall into their hands.[49] Furthermore, the Yugoslav Government was persisting with its anti-Western foreign policy statements in the Security Council, which were being reinforced by the public pronouncements of senior politicians, in particular the Foreign Minister, Edward Kardelj, who had declared at the Yugoslav Communist Party Congress in July that Tito would continue in his support for Soviet 'anti-Imperialist' policies.[50] Yugoslav requests for industrial equipment were not considered attractive propositions by State Department officials, unless the Yugoslav Government felt them to be sufficiently important to justify further concessions of a more political kind.[51] The firms concerned were asked, therefore, to convey the sense of this when they turned down the Yugoslav requests, and to emphasise American interest in promoting trade.[52]

This decision provoked an immediate, and strongly worded telegram from Cannon who was greatly disturbed by this decision.[53] By September 1948 American diplomats in Belgrade were sufficiently convinced of the stability of Tito's Government to argue that Washington should be considering the possibilities of pursuing a more active policy towards Yugoslavia than had been thought appropriate hitherto. The principal difficulties facing the Yugoslav Government were food shortage, high inflation and the deterioration of plant and equipment: of these, the American Embassy believed that the latter would prove to be the most significant and emphasised the urgent need for tractors, trucks and machinery parts so that civilian transport, agriculture, mining and timber output might be maintained. These were weaknesses which made Yugoslavia particularly vulnerable to Soviet sanctions, the success of which would depend, so the Embassy argued, upon the extent to which the United States and Western Europe were prepared to block the opening up of new sources of supply. For the time being, however, it was felt that an overt approach by the western governments would compromise Tito's position. If the State Department wished to widen the breach through economic assistance to the Yugoslav Government, the most suitable means to this end would be the quiet relaxation of American export controls, combined with a favourable inter-Departmental consideration of export license applications for goods of a non-military nature. Furthermore, the Embassy recommended that the State Department might encourage some of the west European governments to redirect their policies towards Yugoslavia within the 'spirit of the broader trade objectives of the European Recovery Programme'.[54]

Although this telegram reflected a pattern of thinking which was somewhat in advance of the position being maintained at that time by officials in both London and Washington, it was to such methods that British and American policies turned as these policies evolved during the winter of 1948–9. One obstacle in particular stood in the way of a more flexible economic policy towards Yugoslavia on both sides of the Atlantic, in the form of broader constraints on east–west trade imposed by the European Recovery Programme and the American legislation regarding export licensing (as embodied in the Foreign Assistance Act of 1948) by which it was complemented. This legislation, which was to be implemented by the European Co-operation Administration (ECA), owed its immediate origins to a paper submitted to the United States National Security Council (NSC) by Averell Harriman, then Secretary of Commerce, in November 1947.[55] Its central recommendation was that all shipments from the United States which would contribute to Soviet military potential should be terminated immediately, and that as a general rule exports to Europe should be controlled and shipments permitted only when there was 'adequate justification' for the commodities, and no danger of American interest or the objective of European recovery being adversely affected. Shortly after this paper had been presented, a working party within the State Department produced a complementary paper entitled 'The immediate United States economic policy towards eastern Europe' which argued that Soviet policy was directed 'primarily at the increase of military potential', and that all indications suggested that the Russians intended to do all in their power to sabotage ERP. After due consideration of these papers, the Administration announced through the Department of Commerce that as from 1 March 1948, all commercial shipments of commodities to Europe would require individual licenses.[56] In practice this would mean that licenses would be issued routinely wherever the destination was a member of the Organisation for European Economic Co-operation (OEEC) whereas they would be turned down in the case of countries of the Soviet sphere. However, this attempt to prevent material of war reaching the Soviet sphere could only be effective if imports from western Europe as well as those from the United States were subject to restrictions. This would not be easy to negotiate.

The American Department of Commerce had set up an Ad Hoc Committee in May 1948 to evaluate the control of trade and its implications for American foreign policy, and to assess the various economic instruments that might be applied. This sub-committee identified three major objectives of American trade policy towards eastern Europe: to assist the west European economy in obtaining the necessary imports from eastern Europe; to prevent (or delay) further increase in the war potential of the east European economies; and to ensure an adequate flow of manganese, chrome and (to a lesser extent) the plutonium group of metals and other essential commodities from eastern Europe to the United States.[57] The principal recommendation to emerge from its deliberations was that four priority classes should be defined into which commodities could be (tentatively) divided. The most sensitive items would be placed in category 1 (subdivided into 1A and 1B) to include all military and semi-military commodities. Such a system was, however, going to be difficult to operate under normal circumstances and where a particular flexibility was called for, it would be a positive hindrance.

British policy towards economic relations with the Soviet sphere was based on the premise that promotion of trade to the 1939 level was an objective of the ERP, as well as being fundamental both to the success of ERP in general and to British economic recovery in particular. By the summer of 1948, the British government was, of its own volition, prohibiting the export to eastern Europe of material of military potential. During August, the Foreign Office made a formal request for 'guidance' on the formulation of a common east–west trade policy during August 1948,[58] resulting in formal negotiations which began in London in early September. Similar discussions were later held with other ERP participants. Article 117(D) of the American ECA Charter, set up under the Foreign Assistance Act to administer the ERP, directed the ECA Administrator to refuse delivery, in so far as practicable, to participating countries of commodities which go into production of any commodity for delivery to any non-participating European country which commodity could be refused an export license to those countries by the United States in the interest of national interest.[59] Ministers concerned agreed at a meeting held in the third week of October that American requests should be met by including undesirable export items on a mutually agreed list of commodities for which export licensees would be required for all destinations.[60] An equivalent list to the American List 1A was prepared and handed to the Americans at the beginning of January 1949.[61] It was significantly shorter than the American list which the British considered too 'woolly' to be workable. More importantly, Britain wanted to maintain trade with eastern Europe as far as normal commercial goods were concerned, and did not want commodities to be excluded unnecessarily. Formal adoption of export licensing controls was accepted by the Economic Policy Committee of the Cabinet on 11 March 1949, with effect from 8 April.[62] The American influence, which had weighed significantly in the evolution of these controls, was kept highly secret, as indeed had been the original development of the policy in the United States where Congressional discussion of the issue had taken place in secret session.[63]

In the meantime, the Yugoslavs had greatly increased their demands for a whole range of commodities from the West. So long as the question of export licensing remained under consideration, the Foreign Office and the Board of Trade had agreed that Yugoslavia could have whatever was available on supply grounds of materials for which they asked provided that they did not appear on List 1A.[64] This was fairly consistent with the general policy already being applied with respect to the whole of eastern Europe.[65] During this period the Yugoslav economy was steadily deteriorating as the breakdown of relations with the Cominform states began to take effect. At the end of 1948, Tito gave a clear indication of the direction in which events were driving him; in a speech to the Skupstina on 27 December, he stated that if the Cominform countries did not want to help Yugoslavia industrialise, then she must sell her produce elsewhere in order to buy the machines necessary for completion of the Five Year Plan.[66] Four days later, details of the Soviet–Yugoslav Trade Agreement were announced, revealing that the value of trade between the two signatories would be limited in 1949 to one-eighth of its 1948 value.[67] This news was received in London at the same time as a series of telegrams from the embassy in Belgrade which described the situation in the bleakest terms. Bevin began 1949 by raising the whole question of policy towards Yugoslavia with the Prime Minister in order to initiate a reassessment of the British position with the objective of providing greater assistance to the Yugoslav Government in its efforts to resist Soviet pressure.[68]

Senior Foreign Office officials were particularly concerned that British and American policies on this question should be 'completely in step'.[69] Accordingly, the Americans were duly informed of the Foreign Office intention to review economic policy towards Yugoslavia and that, in the British view, these efforts would be best served if London and Washington could co-ordinate their actions. This proved an opportune moment to raise the issue since the State Department was also rethinking its position. The Yugoslavs had recently offered to sell copper and lead to the value of £15 million to an American firm, which had been strongly commended to the State Department by the embassy in Belgrade as 'an excellent opportunity to develop sound trade with Yugoslavia'.[70] There was a problem, however, since the Yugoslavs were demanding, in return, that the Americans grant export licenses for certain capital equipment. Owing to the restrictions a favourable response would require a major decision on policy. At the same time, Cannon had taken the opportunity to reiterate the case for a general lifting of export restrictions in regard to Yugoslavia. This sentiment was echoed a few days later by the American Chargé d'Affaires in Moscow who strongly recommended that the United States and western Europe should extend trade relations with Yugoslavia without trying to extract political concessions.[71] Such means, he believed, were now most likely to prolong and aggravate the Cominform split and encourage non-communist elements in the Soviet satellite states, while also securing a useful contribution to the Yugoslav economy.

These recommendations were presented to the Policy Planning Staff on 10 February in a State Department paper entitled 'The Economic relations between the United States and Yugoslavia' which argued that the gulf between the Tito regime and the Kremlin was now 'practically unbridgeable' and that if Tito continued in power he would be an 'erosive and disintegrating force . . . within the Kremlin's power sphere . . . a vital weakness in Russia's expansionist plans . . . If Yugoslavia was not given economic aid from some source, there is grave danger that Tito will be overthrown'.

This effective reversal of American policy was approved, after discussion at the NSC, by Truman on 18 February.[72]

The Americans, convinced that Yugoslavia was now in urgent need of economic assistance, were inclined to press for political concessions. The issue they had in mind was Greece: indeed the contradictions inherent in a situation in which the United States was simultaneously sending supplies to Tito and also aiding the Greek Government to suppress the very rebels to whom Tito was giving support, were self-evident. When informing their British counterparts of this change in policy, the State Department emphasised that they would seek to persuade the Yugoslav Government at the earliest opportunity, to cease its support for the Greek communist guerrillas. Meanwhile, as an immediate safeguard, the way had been left open for hasty tightening of controls should Tito fail to 'behave well'.[73] In order to protect the American position further, no direct indication was given to the Yugoslav Government that a change of policy had occurred;[74] instead, the Belgrade authorities would be left to find out for themselves how far restrictions had been lifted.

British officials were unhappy about this American about face. It was generally accepted within the Foreign Office that a sudden relaxation of export controls, such as the Americans had decided to make, was at best an over-reaction and at worst might undermine the very objectives it sought to achieve. Tito, it was argued, was best placed to know when his Government could most safely approach the West without undue prejudice to his own position; only when he had made such a move would it be wise to undertake any dramatic gestures with regard to economic relations.[75] These initial concerns were allayed a little, however, by the American assurances to observe strict secrecy, but the new American policy continued to be viewed with misgivings in London nevertheless. Of course there was little, if anything, that the Foreign Office could do to discourage the Americans since they had only been informed after the decision had been taken. It remained, therefore, for the British to reconsider their own position, bearing in mind the need to keep in step with the United States. Political considerations were the driving force and revisions of the current British policy followed quite quickly. Within a few weeks, the Government departments concerned agreed that Britain should be prepared forthwith to accept orders from the Yugoslavs for all commodities, with the exception of oil well and refinery equipment, ships and harbour equipment in excess of £2 million, and the latest type of penicillin plant which could be used for biological warfare.[76]

While these broad policy issues were being settled, negotiations began in Belgrade on 1 March for an Anglo-Yugoslav long-term trade agreement. The British delegation was led on this occasion by the Ambassador, Charles Peake, with the assistance of advisers from the Board of Trade, the Treasury and Ministries of Food and Supply. Peake's brief was to seek a five-year agreement and to negotiate on strictly economic lines.[77] Any points involving security were to be considered as they arose. The Yugoslavs would be invited to purchase machinery in Britain, or certain raw materials in the Sterling Area, subject to limitations on the General Export Licensing Policy, an arrangement which in practice meant the British could withhold whatever they liked without giving any indication as to how far this might be extended. A monetary agreement and the extension of credit were ruled out by the Treasury, but the Foreign Office correctly interpreted this as a reversible veto and briefed its negotiating team to submit a request for credit in the event that this seemed necessary.

Within a few days of the negotiations opening, serious difficulties had arisen. The Yugoslavs were undaunted by their present economic difficulties and made immediate difficulties over the payments agreement on which they insisted having, unconditionally of payment of Yugoslavia's long-term sterling debt, before the discussions on trade began. The Cabinet Economic Policy Committee had already decided that Britain should not negotiate a payment agreement without settlement of this debt and that there was, in any case, no urgency for conclusion of a payments agreement since trade could proceed perfectly well without it. Knowing this, but believing that the talks would be broken off if a concession were not forthcoming, Peake took it upon himself, with characteristic independence, to begin negotiations for just such an agreement. There was, he argued much of British interest at stake and the Yugoslavs had presented a sensibly based and well-reasoned case.[78] After consultation with his Cabinet colleagues, Bevin managed to secure a modification of the official policy: a firm directive was transmitted to Belgrade instructing Peake to say that the British Government would be prepared to conclude both a long-term agreement and a payments agreement subject to their satisfactory settlement of the sterling bonded debt. Without such a settlement, Britain would not be agreeable to further negotiations of a Payments

Agreement. Foreign Office officials, among them the head of the Southern Department, Geoffrey Wallinger, strongly maintained that the Yugoslavs should be shown that Britain was not prepared to be blackmailed out of a carefully considered position of principle. It was also doubted that the Yugoslavs would, if put to the test, permit the question of a payments agreement, which had relatively little value to them, to be a breaking point. This judgement was shortly shown to have been well founded when the Yugoslavs agreed after all to discuss trade schedules without prejudice to the financial issue.

The more thorny – and politically sensitive – issue of credit was raised by the Yugoslavs at an early stage in the negotiations. The British delegation were authorised to discuss commercial grounds for credit with the objective of obtaining a high level of trade and early liquidation of all compensation payment, and despite initial sympathy within the Foreign Office for the Treasury's argument that Yugoslavia did not have any economic grounds for requesting credit, when the issue came to the fore again at the beginning of May. The Foreign Office was prepared to view the request more favourably.[79]

The Greek Civil War and Western Credit

This change of heart seems to have been closely related to a private meeting between Tito and Fitzroy Maclean during the second week of May. Tito had judged, correctly, that the British would need a concession from the Yugoslav Government if such a substantial grant of credit were to be seriously considered in London. Shrewdly, he chose the issue of Yugoslav aid to the Greek guerrillas as his bargaining counter. The Tito–Cominform dispute had occurred at a particularly low point for the West in the Greek question. Yugoslav involvement in Greece had, since 1945, persistently soured Yugoslavia relations with Britain and the United States. The importance of Greece in strategic terms had been heightened in British eyes by the onset of the Cold War in so far as it was regarded by the Chiefs of Staff as critical for the Royal Navy's command of the eastern Mediterranean, a position based on war-time experience when the loss of Greece and Crete had been severe handicaps.[80] Despite American intervention in 1947, the situation continued to deteriorate. In February 1948, the Minister of Defence, A. V. Alexander, forwarded to Bevin a disquieting appreciation of Communist objectives in Greece as perceived by the British Chiefs of Staff.[81] This paper reiterated the well-worn thesis that the ultimate communist objective was the incorporation of a communist Greece within the Balkan bloc, and their immediate goal as control over the Aegean ports and airfields, especially those of Salonika, which would threaten Anglo-American communications through the Mediterranean. Macedonia and Thrace would be absorbed by Yugoslavia and Bulgaria which would help create maximum chaos in Greece through their support of Markos and the KKE in the continuing civil war. Following the Tito–Cominform split, a Foreign Office discussion paper observed that a communist victory in Greece would seriously jeopardise western defence of vital areas, 'turn Turkey's flank, weaken Italy's strategic position and threaten communications through the Mediterranean'.[82] Soviet policy, it concluded, aimed to control Greece, or failing this to disrupt the political and economic state of the country so as to render it a continuing liability to the West. The task of upholding the regime in Greece was accepted in London as an urgent short-term liability and a long-term commitment.

As we have seen, the Truman Administration mooted the possibility of using the granting of credit to extract from Tito a promise to close the Greek frontier. Yugoslav obduracy during April and May in trade negotiations had caused Bevin to wonder, given the reports on the state of the Yugoslav economy, what Tito might really want from the West. Experience had shown that personal negotiations with the Yugoslav dictator directly were far more effective than weeks of formal talks with appointed representatives who were paralysed by fear of their superiors and lacked the power of decision. To cut through this bureaucratic screen, Bevin asked Fitzroy Malcean to make an unofficial, private visit to Tito with the objective of discussing his requirements. Maclean travelled to Belgrade secretly: at a meeting on 9 May, Tito took full advantage of the opportunity to state Yugoslavia's urgent need of credits from Britain to the value of £11.6 million in the form of 'medium term credit on the British market', which he envisaged would be made of £7.3 million in the first year, £2.3 million in the second year and £2 million in the third.[83]

Although Peake had been keeping the American Embassy in Belgrade apprised of the progress of these negotiations, not all the circumstances influencing British thinking during the early summer of 1949 had been made available to the Americans. That this was so was entirely due to the secrecy which surrounded Maclean's visit in order to protect this channel of communication.[84] Unaware, therefore, of Tito's promise to close the Yugoslav frontier with Greece, the State Department reacted with surprise and not a little disapproval, on learning of the British decision to offer a sizeable credit facility. However they were duly pacified having learnt of Tito's bargain.

Tito was as good as his word. In July, the closure of the Yugoslav frontier to the Greek rebels was announced in Belgrade, a move which effectively quarantined some four thousand guerrillas in Yugoslavia, and drove a wedge between the main concentration of rebel forces in northern Greece. The situation for the Greek government now improved considerably. Yugoslavia had been the most important source of external support to the guerrillas since 1944.[85] Closure of the frontier was a significant concession: subsequent studies of the Greek civil war have placed Tito's defection from the rebel's cause as the main reason that the civil war did not continue into the 1950s.

Aside from the Greek issue, it could be argued, on the basis of Tito's meeting with Maclean, that it was quite possibly necessary for the Yugoslav leaders to be able to demonstrate to their people that they could make a success of their industrialisation plans without the assistance from their erstwhile benefactors in Moscow. A credit facility with a western power without any apparent political strings attached would go a long way towards achieving this. There was, nevertheless, considerable opposition from other government departments which remained unimpressed by the political argument. The Central Economic Planning Staff, for example, had studied the Yugoslav economic plans in some detail and concluded that, on economic grounds alone, they were completely unsound.[86] This was speedily refuted by the Foreign Office which argued that, as Yugoslavia came to rely increasingly on supplies from Britain, there would be more incentive for them to earn sterling and thus produce the capital goods Britain needed. Toward the end of May, the issue was referred to an inter-departmental working party on Yugoslavia which started its consideration of the problem with the premise that credit was not justifiable economically on the basis of the offers made at present. It is a measure of the weight now being given to political considerations, therefore, that the Economic Policy Committee was persuaded to accept, on political grounds alone, the extension of a special credit to Yugoslavia which would reach about £7 million at the end of the third year of the agreement. This was in keeping with the figure for which the Foreign Office had asked in support of the Board of Trade and the Ministry of Food. The sum was hotly contested by the Treasury, which had only approved a limit of £5 million. Initially, Bevin was unsuccessful in obtaining a revision and the £5 million was duly offered, and quickly rejected. Although Peake considered that the Yugoslavs would, if pushed, conclude an agreement without a higher offer, the indications were that the Yugoslav economic situation was rather worse than had been thought, and he recommended that Britain now 'take bold steps to frustrate Russian policy' by offering a more generous level of credit, somewhere between £8 million and £10 million, without asking or being fully informed of why and for what purpose each penny was required.[87] Cautiously, the Southern Department put forward, on political grounds, a request for £7 million, which Bevin succeeded in obtaining from the Economic Policy Committee, but this too was turned down.

Until this point, there had been a general consensus within the Foreign Office which argued that political considerations outweighed economic objections to the accommodation of Yugoslav demands. But despite the strength of Peake's case, there was now some debate as to whether Yugoslavia was worth, in terms of British interests, the level of credit for which he asked. Britain had possibly extended herself far enough, and the price of Tito's goodwill was apparently going to involve a higher level of credit than Britain could reasonably afford. Bateman introduced a note of caution into this debate: 'I think we might, as suggested, go to £8 million, but this is not necessarily the end of Tito's demands. We must stop somewhere and I do not think we would be justified in going beyond eight million.'[88] This view was shared by Bevin, who had registered a degree of discomfiture at having to approach the Chancellor of the Exchequer once more for yet another extension of the credit limit, especially since he had promised that the previous request would be the last. However, he had a strong ally in Wilson, and the advance to £8 million was secured.

In the event, the Yugoslav Government accepted the offer, and agreement on all but a few relatively minor points was quickly reached. The two resulting agreements were finally signed in Belgrade on 23 December. The Trade Agreement was scheduled to operate over a period of five years, during which time goods to the value of £100 million would pass each way. The principal British imports would be timber, non-ferrous metals and maize; exports would include wool, woollen and cotton yarn, chemicals, rubber products machinery and capital equipment. Supplies of raw materials from other parts of the Sterling Area were also covered. In addition, Britain would provide guaranteed credit to the value of £8 million to be repaid over six years, as well as short term (ninety day) credits to the value of £5 million. This was notable for being the largest Government credit granted to Yugoslavia by any western country at this time. The second agreement related to the compensation payment and supplemented the one signed in London the previous year; it stipulated that Yugoslavia would provide the balance of compensation at the rate of £506,000 per year for a period of eight years. The progress of the Anglo-Yugoslav trade negotiations had been followed closely by the United States. Although the American Government had not actively sought closer commercial links with Yugoslavia, trade between that country and private American businesses had increased considerably during 1949. From the latter part of February, when the new economic policy towards Yugoslavia was put into effect, until 27 May, United States Export License applications from Yugoslavia were approved to the total of $17,181,000 which was some 42 per cent higher than that for whole of the previous year. Of the Anglo-Yugoslav trade negotiations, Cannon had expressed the anxiety widely held in Washington when he observed that failure to conclude an early agreement would affect adversely not only Yugoslavia and Britain, but also the United States and other western countries interested in keeping the Tito regime 'strong enough'.[89]

The major revision of American policy did not come until the end of 1949 when the National Security Council adopted a report, subsequently circulated as NSC 18/4 of 17 November 1949. Entitled 'United States Policy toward the conflict between the USSR and Yugoslavia', it reviewed the courses of action open to the United States but envisaged a policy of economic assistance to Yugoslavia on an as and when basis. The important development lay, however, in the military implications. NSC 18/4 recommended that all possible measures to strengthen Yugoslav resistance to military attack should now be examined. By mid-1949, as Yugoslavia seemed to have been saved from economic collapse, so the Soviet Union attempted to step up the pressure by increasing troops concentrations on the borders. Incidents mounted to nearly 4,000 over the 1949–51 period, with 40 Yugoslavs killed.[90] It was the Korean War, which broke out in June 1950, which finally brought respectability to the notion of extending military aid to Yugoslavia; by the end of 1951, some $60 million of military supplies had been transferred.

This policy of keeping Tito afloat, which was initiated by Britain after October 1948, was of major significance both in terms of Yugoslavia's future and also in cold war terms. Yugoslavia was able to establish herself as a neutral, non-aligned state, and sometime go-between in the cold war polices of Europe. The by-product was the cessation of the civil war in Greece. Western aid, which included funding from the International Monetary Fund, facilitated the policy of self-management socialism, instituted in the 1950s and although ultimately its effect was negative in so far as the imbalances and inefficiencies of the Yugoslav economy were never properly addressed, as an episode in the Cold War it was vital in preserving Yugoslavia as a stable entity and provided de facto a relatively inexpensive means of securing the Adriatic for NATO.

8

Trieste: Frontier Making in Cold War Europe

Although a settlement of the sovereignty of Trieste had been included in the Italian Peace Treaty, the situation in the spring of 1947 was far from settled. An Italo-Yugoslav Commission had been despatched to demarcate the new frontier between the two countries; another commission, this one involving the four major powers, was considering how best to finance the proposed Free Territory. The present arrangement, by which Britain and the United States shared the costs, was due to expire at the end of 1947 and financing by the United Nations would begin as soon as the Treaty had been ratified. Local government election had yet to be organised, while the final details for the withdrawal SACMED's forces from the areas granted to Yugoslavia had still to be worked out. The major outstanding problem was a nominee for the post of Governor which required the agreement of the four major powers. Until this had been accomplished, Allied troops would remain in Trieste and the settlement envisaged by the Peace treaty could not be translated into reality.

The Italo-Yugoslav Boundary Commission began the task of preparing detailed demarcation for the future frontier on 17 March. Work progressed smoothly at first, but became bogged down when the representatives began to consider the area around Gorizia. The Russians had already rejected the British suggestion that a Four Power Supervisory Commission should have the authority to determine the frontier in the case of an unresolved dispute, however the Foreign Office, fearing that the frontier would not be settled by the time the peace treaty came into force, asked the Allied Military Government of Trieste to make an immediate report on the nature of the present dispute. At the same time, the

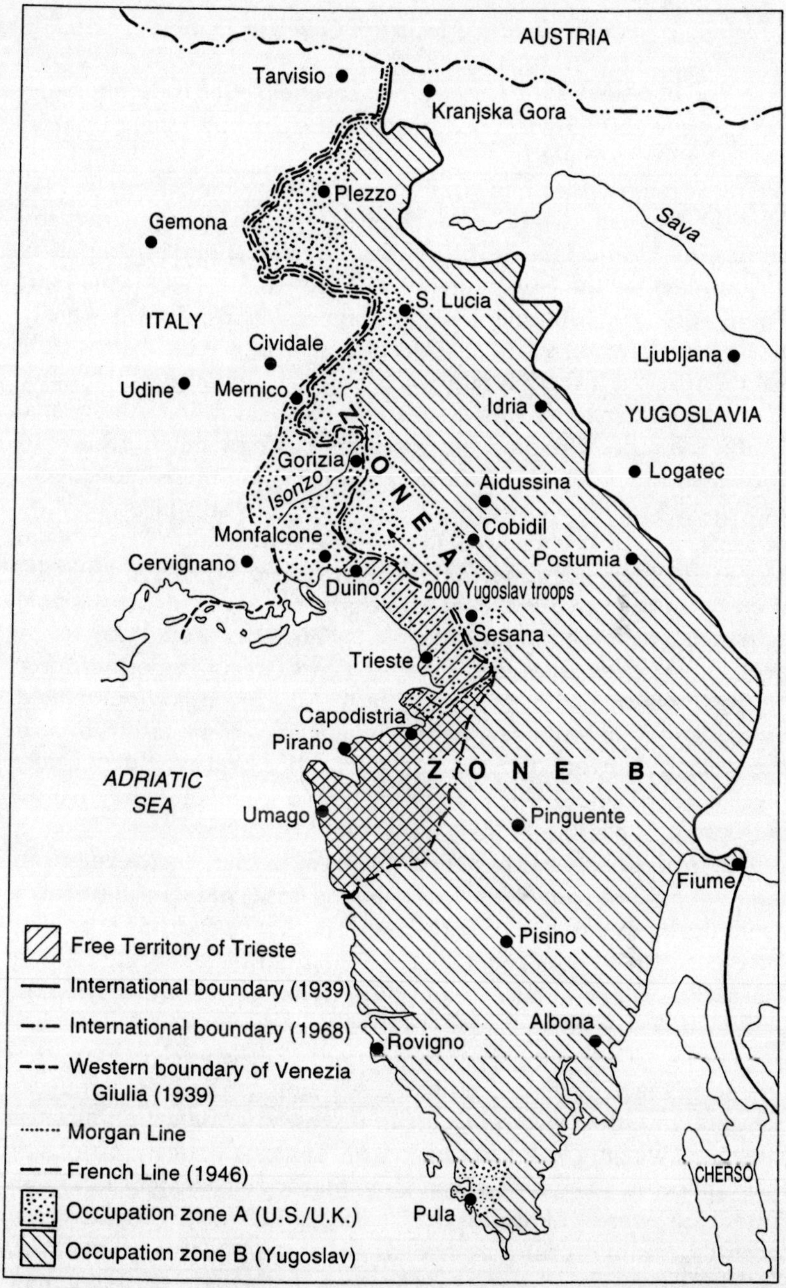

Map 3 The Free Territory of Trieste established in 1947 (Source: Foreign Relations of the United States, USGPO, 1947, volume II, p. 94)

question of whether the western powers could effectively intervene irrespective of the Soviet position, was taken up in Washington with the State Department.[1]

The Foreign Office had firmly concluded by the Spring of 1947 that the Russians would do whatever they could to obstruct the setting up of the Free Territory: they were dilatory in proposing a candidate for the Governorship and unwilling to adopt the Four Power financial Commission's recommendations. It was hardly likely, in view of this, that any attempt to obtain a workable solution through the Boundary Commission would be successful. The present arrangements also suited the British and Americans. Under the present regime, any attempts made by the Yugoslavs to spread communism into Zone A were being countered effectively by Allied Military Government and were also still in occupation of territory which officially had now been awarded to Yugoslavia. Moreover, their continued presence was a lever which could be used to bring pressure to bear on Belgrade to agree to a reasonable settlement of the boundary question. This lever would, however, become worthless should the Italian Peace Treaty come into force before the issue had been settled, since Allied troops were obliged by the Treaty to withdraw within ninety days of its ratification. If the western powers decided that the withdrawal would not take place without prior settlement of the boundary dispute they would be running the risk that their bluff might be called.[2]

American policy was based on the premise that Anglo-American troops should remain on the Morgan Line until complete agreement about the boundary had been reached. The State Department briefed the delegation to the Conference of Foreign Ministers being held in Moscow in March to take the opportunity to re-open the discussion of the whole Trieste question. This had not been anticipated in London, and so when the subject came up, the British delegation were unable to participate in a serious discussion of the issue.[3] Indeed, the Foreign Office was reluctant to discuss the matter publicly at this stage, wishing instead to keep it an Anglo-American affair until the implications had been given more thorough consideration.[4] The Americans were not unresponsive to British misgivings: by the second week of April, they had dropped their plan to remain on the Morgan Line and suggested instead that where no agreement could be reached, the Yugoslavs should be permitted to advance to the French line as agreed by the majority recommendation at the Paris Peace Conference the previous July.[5] Britain, as one of the parties to the original recommendation, could hardly argue with this. The State Department had also acquiesced in British wishes to withhold discussion of the Trieste settlement at the Moscow conference and endorsed the British proposal that the Yugoslav and Italian Governments be asked to approve representatives for delimiting the frontier without waiting for Russian concurrence. In the event, the western powers were reluctant at this stage to adopt quite such a degree of high-handedness and the Russians were pressed for an opinion before further action was taken. However, the determination of the British and Americans to enforce the French line if final arbitration of the boundary dispute proved necessary was not communicated immediately to either the Russians or the Yugoslavs since there seemed to be a reasonable chance that a settlement would be reached without the intervention of the Great Powers.[6]

Much to the surprise of the Foreign Office, it was the Italians and not the Yugoslavs who made difficulties over the delimitation of the frontier. The Italians were also unwilling to accept the French Line and since the Americans were not prepared to force them to concede this point, the option of reverting to the majority decision of July 1946 was no longer open. This notwithstanding, Bevin drafted a strongly worded telegram to be passed to Sforza, urging him to accept the provisional line as agreed in Paris, but before this could be delivered, a telegram arrived for Bevin from Rome which indicated that the Italians hoped to persuade the Foreign Secretary to say publicly that he did not approve the recommendation of the Four Power Commission.[7] The situation was little altered on the eve of the treaty's ratification on 15 September, by when the Italians had taken recourse in the claim that their acceptance of the French Line would result in the fall of the Government. It was felt in both London and Washington that there was a good argument for instructing SACMED to hand over a line more favourable to Italy; in practical terms, however the disparity between the Provisional Line and the French Line was extremely small.[8]

It soon became apparent that the Yugoslavs also were not going to accept the implementation of the Italian Peace Treaty without some show of their dissatisfaction at the provisions for Trieste. On the evening of 15 September, Terence Airey, Allied Commander and Military Governor of the Anglo-American Zone of Venezia Giulia, received a written communication from the General Officer Commanding the Yugoslav 4th Division at Duino, announcing that as the Treaty was in force, the Yugoslav government had instructed him to advance to the French Line at midnight.[9] The Yugoslavs probably intended to bring their detachment into the city so as to activate the latent support of the pro-Slav communist fifth column. This was certainly the view of the British Political Adviser in Trieste, William Sullivan. Airey's reply, however, left them in no doubt that if they entered the city they would be resisted by force.[10] In the event, such incidents as there were on the night of 15/16 September were caused by the pro-Italian elements, perhaps not surprisingly since violent protest by the Italian sympathisers had been on the increase for some time. These activities were potentially self-defeating, however, because they provided the pro-Slavs and communists with a good enough pretext for forcing the issue of control of the city, at least to the extent of insisting upon their participation in local government. In view of the close proximity of Yugoslav military forces, which virtually surrounded the city of Trieste, they might, if provoked, feel justified in resorting to outright aggression.[11]

At the end of September, Airey set down his assessment of the political future of the Free Territory.[12] It was his belief that wherever Yugoslav troops went in Trieste, they would succeed in establishing the communist machine and preparing the area for inclusion in Yugoslavia, a process he referred to repeatedly as the 'Balkanisation of Trieste'. Airey made several recommendations to prevent this: firstly, that Zone A should be kept entirely free of Yugoslav troops and that the best means to this end was for the Western Powers to cease in their co-operation with them. Secondly, he argued that before a civilian governor for the Free Territory was appointed, a strong police force should be built up which the civilian authorities could use to maintain order after the withdrawal of Allied Military Government. These recommendations were generally accepted in London where, from a purely political point of view, it was accepted that all measures should be taken which might prevent Trieste's subversion by the communists. In fact, AMG had been engaged for some months in recruiting a strong police force from the local population, and it was expected that a reliable force of at least some six thousand would be available by the time a Governor had been appointed.[13] The civil administration was similarly being drawn from the Trieste community and operated within the framework of the Italian prefectorial system of government, in contrast to the system in operation in Zone B where the local government administration, the legal system and the police force were, by 1947, all essentially an extension of the institutions which the Tito Government had established in Yugoslavia since the war.[14]

The viability of the Free Territory was, therefore, already open to question owing to political and social factors. To this was added the problem of the economy. Since December 1946, when the CFM had reached agreement on the future disposition of Trieste, both the political and economic situation of the world had rapidly deteriorated. As far as the Free Territory was concerned, it was beyond dispute by the autumn of 1947 that Yugoslavia was opposed to its survival. In a report written at the beginning of October, Sullivan stated ominously that, 'no one here in Trieste entertains any illusions as to the determination of Yugoslavia to secure incorporation into self of the Free Territory sooner or later by fair means or foul . . . '.[15] While officials in London, and Bevin too, were in agreement, they considered that not only the political, but also the economic disintegration in the area had gone so far as to make it extremely doubtful whether the Free Territory could realistically be placed under the administration of a civilian governor who would not have the advantages of the presence of an Anglo-American garrison and a constant supply of American money and goods. There had already been considerable reflection within the Foreign Office as to the viability of Trieste as an economic unit. Before the war, the region had been subsidised by Italy; its proposed separation from the Italian economy, which had largely absorbed its products, was considered likely to cause fiscal and financial difficulties, the solution of which would be hindered by Italo-Yugoslav political differences. The city's economy had previously been based on its status as a port which acted as an outlet not just for Italy but more importantly for the produce of the central European states, and as yet this trade was showing no signs of revival. This was being reflected in the high level of unemployment in Trieste where a hard core of 26,000 out of the 105,000 registered workers in Zone A were out of work. At the same time, the continued uncertainty surrounding Trieste's future, which was partly political and partly due to the adverse economic outlook, was also leading to withdrawal of Italian capital, while communist influence in the trade unions was further exacerbating the problem by getting in the way of efficient use of the Territory's labour force.[16]

In a paper prepared in October 1947, Geoffrey Wallinger concluded that unless Britain and the United States were prepared to maintain the Free Territory at a cost of keeping Anglo-American troops there, and of furnishing economic assistance indefinitely, the British Government must either resign itself to seeing the whole Territory absorbed into Yugoslavia, or try to find some solution by which the Anglo-American Zone would revert to Italy.[17] He did not believe that the barrier between the two zones could be removed if the absorption of Trieste were to be avoided. While the original legal and economic structure had been maintained in the Anglo-American Zone, the other four-fifths of the Territory was to all intents and purposes a communist state. If the two zones were merged, the Anglo-American Zone would, he argued, be submerged by a communist administration. From there it would only be a short step before the population was pronounced as ready to petition the Security Council with the appearance of unanimity for incorporation of the entire Free Territory into Yugoslavia.

The prospects looked gloomy. Under the Italian Peace Treaty, the appointment of a Governor would weaken the western position in the Territory owing to the Governor's dependence on the Yugoslav communist-dominated administrative machine on the one hand, and on the corrupt and inefficient Italian administration on the other. Moreover, he would be obliged to admit the communist police force, riddled as it was with Yugoslav agents, which had been built up in the Yugoslav Zone, into the force of the whole Territory. Airey, together with a senior officer of the economic section of AMG, had both said that there was no hope of overcoming the huge balance of payment deficit and the burden of unemployment except by artificial methods of continual credits. There was little prospect that the United Nations would vote such credits, and the entire cost would therefore have to be borne by Britain and the United States. Britain had already declared her inability to make even a 25 per cent contribution to the budget, which for the time being was to be covered by the United States.[18] In view of this the question to which the Foreign Office addressed itself in October 1947 was how far the Western powers could exert themselves to prevent Trieste slipping, with a semblance of constitutional procedure, into Yugoslav hands: 'If international communism succeeds in absorbing the Free Territory into the Soviet orbit,' Wallinger wrote, 'the moral effects will be out of all proportion to the physical value of the prize.'[19]

For most of the year, the Foreign Office had based its policy on the assumption that both Russian and Yugoslav interests lay primarily, if not exclusively, in the election of a civilian governor as soon as possible, which would bring about the withdrawal of the Anglo-American garrison. In practice, however, neither Moscow nor Belgrade had shown the slightest interest in having a Governor elected, and had even rejected proposed candidates who would hardly have had the strength indefinitely to thwart their purpose once the troops had left. In the middle of September, the State Department suggested to the British that rather than press for an early appointment, the western powers might be best served by the adoption of a wait and see approach in the expectation that the Russians would themselves propose a candidate.[20]

Bevin presented his own views on the matter at a meeting held in the Foreign Office on 24 October.[21] It was his feeling that the Soviet Union and Yugoslavia might really prefer partition of the Free Territory rather than the internationalisation settlement envisaged by the Peace Treaty. There was not much evidence for this as yet, but Bevin said he had gained the impression that they were leaning heavily in this direction during his visit to Moscow in March. Bevin himself was quite ready to accept such a solution, provided that it could be worked out satisfactorily from the western point of view. However, the principal problem lay with the Americans and the possible conflict partition might have with any strategic aims Washington had in Trieste. This meeting concluded that one of the first priorities should be to ask the Chiefs of Staff whether Britain had strategic aims in Trieste, bearing in mind the relationship of the city to the whole strategic solution and, in particular, its relationship to the Austrian settlement. In addition, Cabinet approval was to be sought for the maintenance of British troops in Trieste 'for as long as necessary', while the views of both the United States and Italy would be requested regarding the appointment of a Governor.[22]

The problem of Trieste in British strategic planning was also due for review within the wider context of British regional interests, and was encompassed within the general review of British strategic interests conducted at the end of 1947 and early in 1948. During the spring of 1948 a series of papers was presented to the Defence Committee which discussed British strategic interests in the context of possible future expansion of communist – or Soviet – influence.[23] Of the European countries, only France, the Benelux and the western zones of Germany (excluding the British zone of Berlin), were considered to be ultimately vital to British survival. Austria was considered indefensible and Italy, though of utmost importance to secure communications with the Middle East, would be expected to mount its own resistance in the event of overt aggression by the Soviet Union in Europe. Similarly, while the defence of the British position in the Middle East required that Russian domination of the Iberian Peninsula, North Africa, Turkey, Iraq and South Iran be prevented, Greece, like Italy and Berlin was 'not absolutely vital to strategic interests'. As regards Trieste, a later submission to the Defence Committee by the Chief of the Imperial General Staff (CIGS), Bernard Montgomery, argued that in an emergency, the port might usefully be defended by a garrison made up of troops withdrawn from Austria. This would have considerable bearing on events in Italy and at worst would give the western forces a valuable port of re-entry into south Europe. From the British point of view, then, Trieste was strategically useful as a stronghold, but its defence in the event of the outbreak of war was not considered vital.

With this established, the best political and economic solution seemed to be to return to advocacy of partition, despite the fact that this would mean revising an integral part of the Italian peace treaty. The British hoped that by showing the Soviet Union and the Yugoslavs that the western powers would not vacate Trieste simply to let the Yugoslavs in, they hoped that Moscow would be encouraged, in time, to adopt a policy of permitting Trieste's reversion to Italy out of preference to having the Union Jack and Stars and Stripes flying permanently at the head of the Adriatic.[24] In order for such a policy to succeed however, the Foreign Office believed that the Russians would have to be 'manoeuvred' by some means into suggesting partition themselves, in order that they would be able to claim at least some face-saving benefit for Italian communism.[25] The western powers, in turn, could hope to offset this by claiming that western firmness had secured the reversion of Trieste to Italian sovereignty. The Americans, with whom this possibility was evidently discussed during December, were easily persuaded and there now began a period of highly secret exchanges with the British which continued during the winter of 1947–8 while simultaneously maintaining the public posture of holding out for a good governor.[26]

In the meantime, Yugoslav impatience with western procrastination boiled over, leading them to make a formal protest at the Security Council when they complained in general about Anglo-American administration of the Free Territory and requested in particular the establishment of a joint Anglo-American/Yugoslav

Headquarters.[27] The western powers were indeed vulnerable to these charges. Many of the actions and measures taken in Zone A, such as the restrictions on the freedom of movement of civilians between the two zones and the application of controls on exchange of goods between Trieste and Yugoslavia, would have been difficult to justify under normal circumstances and were particularly so since they were not covered by the Peace Treaty. The only reasonable defence which could be offered by the British and American authorities would have to take as its central argument that these actions were being forced upon AMG as a result of what the Yugoslavs themselves had done in Zone B, and in self defence against Yugoslav manoeuvres to eventually absorb the Free Territory. Indeed, the Security Council had not as yet been apprised of these Yugoslav activities and the difficulties which AMG was encountering, and the Foreign Office prepared a draft which was intended to respond to the Yugoslav charges and present the Anglo-American version of what had taken place.[28]

Responding to the Yugoslav charges, the Foreign Office draft reply covered in great detail the history of the Anglo-American administration of the Free Territory, including the legal and moral commitments of AMG, which it felt would contrast favourably with any account of Yugoslav activities. Meanwhile, the State Department had drafted a couple of texts of their own, but neither offered the full explanation of AMG's activities and their emphasis tended to suggest that Airey himself was responsible for the actions to which the Yugoslavs were objecting. Even the most impartial observers would be inclined to infer that there was much truth in the Yugoslav accusations that Britain and the United States were conspiring to unreasonably obstruct unification and development of the Free Territory.[29]

On the first day of January 1948, the Foreign Office replied to the State Department, indicating its preference for returning to their original draft.[30] Preoccupation with the pending Italian elections, which were due to be held in April 1948, combined with the increasing assertiveness and cohesion of the Soviet bloc, following establishment of the Cominform, had combined to heighten British concerns at the continued difficulty with Venezia Giulia. The removal of Anglo-American troops from Trieste was, the British argued, a major objective of communist policy not only for the Free Territory but also for their whole campaign in central Europe. The Foreign Office cited recent reports which suggested that the communists would attempt to precipitate a crisis in the industrial north of Italy during the winter, and were building up reserved arms in Ljubljana for use in Italy. The continued presence of Anglo-American troops in Trieste was, therefore, not only an encouragement to the Italian government and a reassuring element to the anti-communist population, but also a block across communist supplies and communications which must ordinarily flow from the eastern into the Latin world through Trieste.[31] The importance attached to this question is indicated in a letter written at the time by Charles Bateman to James Balfour in Washington in which he observed that next to Greece, 'Trieste is the area in which there is the greatest danger of the present Slav offensive moving the Iron Curtain further into the western world'.[32] Putting the question into the context of British, and indeed western interests in Italy, Bateman continued that in the view of the Italian people, 'Trieste had become a symbol of the trial of strength between east and west. Our ability to prevent Trieste from falling into Yugoslav hands will be, to Italy . . . a yardstick of our ability to stop Italy from being drawn into the communist bloc'.

The British were successful in persuading the Americans to moderate their policy. Trieste could not be saved from falling into Yugoslav hands by any Governor, no matter how strong his institutional powers, and that for the time being an appointment to this post had to be blocked. The Americans were inclined to agree, and both delegations to the United Nations were briefed accordingly to work at creating an atmosphere in which partition would gain popularity. If called upon to defend their procrastination in the Security Council, they would argue that it was the Yugoslavs who were creating a situation which precluded implementation of the peace treaty but this had to be accomplished without creating circumstances in which the Russians would be forced to use their veto, for the complications of Soviet prestige would then be added as a factor which would damage the chances of partition being accepted.[33]

Indeed the Soviet bloc were publicly, at least, stuck on the principle of seeking a solution within the framework of the Treaty, a position which was being bolstered in both the Soviet and Yugoslav press through a campaign designed to show that the western powers were opposing the appointment of a Governor in order to buy time to turn Trieste into a military base. Tito had even expressed feelings of outrage personally to Cavendish Cannon during an interview held in the first few days of January.[34] Loathly opposite in interests, the Italians would have little difficulty, if they had known, with the concept of partition which had been vigorously promoted by de Gasperi at the peace conference.[35] Evidence of continued Italian interest in such a scheme had subsequently accrued in London indirectly, although the Italian government had been reluctant to discuss it directly, probably because of their uncertainty as to the sort of partition which would then be arranged.[36] A Foreign Office minute prepared early in January outlined three possible means of achieving partition:[37] firstly, through amendment of the terms of the peace treaty by the CFM, accompanied by Four Power guarantees; secondly through an accommodation outside the treaty framework with an Anglo-American guarantee only; and thirdly, a private arrangement arrived at between the Italian and Yugoslav governments which the other treaty signatories could recognise but without giving any guarantee. Italy, it was believed, would accept either the first or second but not the third. Among those counselling caution in this was Geoffrey Wallinger who argued that British interests would be best served by not chivying either the Italians or the Americans towards partition. Events were already working in British favour, and the preferred conclusion might be arrived at without British diplomacy taking too active a role.

The lull which followed this activity was broken in the first week of March by the Americans who slightly startled their British counterparts by announcing that they were now of the opinion that not just Zone A but the whole Free Territory should be returned to Italy and, moreover, that an end should be put to the present double-think by making a public declaration to this effect. This change in American policy, which came a fortnight after the Czech coup, was motivated by State Department concern for the outcome of the Italian elections scheduled to be held on 17 April. The present indications suggested that a win for the Christian Democrats was uncertain, and that support for Togliatti's PCI was swelling. Democratic endorsement of the PCI through the ballot box was a prospect which was regarded as an exceptionally dangerous advance for the Cominform and all steps were taken to ensure that this did not occur.[38] The position of the players in the chess game for Trieste seemed in both American and British minds, somehow critical, and they accorded it perhaps an importance well beyond its true value as a factor in electoral terms. The logic of the game seemed to indicate that should the western governments come out publicly with a suggestion of partition, this would play to the Soviet advantage; but to come out strongly against the entire notion of a free territory and advocate the territory's return to Italy would provoke the Russians to turn the suggestion down flatly and would thereby put the PCI on the spot.[39]

De Gasperi himself, sensing that the moment was expedient for an advance of the Italian case in Venezia Giulia, expressed a preference for a declaration in favour of the return of the whole territory to Italy on the grounds that this would assist his government's election campaign.[40] Susceptible as the British and Americans were to this line of argument, the Americans sought now to draw the French into the subterfuge and in so doing attempted to appease French hubris by inviting them to make the announcement. Bidault was not so malleable, however, as to accept this ploy without a display of French chauvinism, and complained that France was being dragged in as an outside third party to suit the end of Anglo-American diplomacy. Viewed from the French perspective this was undoubtedly true, but France was hardly an unwitting pawn and Bidault, after his protest, agreed to make the move, though not before he had given the British cause for a chauvinistic display of their own, by venturing that he would announce the policy during his official visit to Turin later in the month. The Foreign Office, in a jealous outburst, protested that the French would be seen to take the credit for an initiative which was not theirs to take. These objections were wisely overruled, or perhaps overlooked, in Washington, and Bidault announced the policy change on 20 March during his visit to Turin to sign the protocol for the Franco-Italian customs union, a popular idea in Italy, the signing of which had been also been staged to influence the elections in favour of the pro-western parties.[41]

The Three Power Declaration on Trieste, or, as it was popularly known, the Bidault Initiative, was in practice, meaningless. Soviet agreement, required for such a revision of the treaty to take place, was not anticipated by its authors. Anthony Eden says in his memoirs that the proposal was not designed as an immediate signal for action, but only a recommendation for consideration by both sides.[42] The British and Americans probably feared that the Soviet Union would make a gesture of friendship in order to assist Togliatti's campaign, and moved to pre-empt this with a gesture of their own. This was certainly the view of the Italian Ambassador in Washington, Alberto Tarchiani.[43] However, it was a propaganda tool which had the desired effect, being warmly welcomed in the Italian press of both right wing and centrist persuasions.[44] In the United States it was described by the *Washingon Post* as 'statesmanship of High Order' in as much as it underlined for the Italians the significance of the choice before theme 'without limiting the freedom of that choice'. The *New York Times* went further, comparing Trieste to Danzig in 1939, describing it as 'a tinder box which can be made safe only by its return to Italy'. It emphasised that this move to revise the immediate post-war settlement in the light of the communist threat would be followed by similar action in Germany. This was indeed, the principal point. This action was setting a precedent in the departure it signalled from the peace treaty so shortly after it had been brought into force. When briefing the British press, the Foreign Office took pains to reinforce the arguments that it was Yugoslav behaviour in Zone B which had led to this change.

The Yugoslav Government wasted no time in preparing a response. During the afternoon of 20 March, just a few hours after Bidault's speech, the Yugoslav Ambassador in Washington, issued a statement refuting the claims made against them and attacking the American government for its support of the declaration. The Russians were silent. The timing was fortuitous for the western powers, however. As we have seen, Stalin was already attempting to rein in the Yugoslavs, and so far enjoying little success. Displeased with the present Yugoslav government in general and with its aggressive foreign policy in particular, they were not now going to support Yugoslav posturing over Trieste.[45] Unaware, however, of the Soviet–Yugoslav differences, the Americans sought to forestall any Russian initiative by suggesting to the British that the French be requested to address a Note to the Soviet Embassy in Paris, proposing, in the name of the three Western Governments, that a meeting be held in Paris for the Four Powers to draft a new protocol transferring the Territory to Italy. Despite strong objections in both King Charles Street and the Quai d'Orsay, this meeting was duly called, if only in an all too transparent attempt to demonstrate that the Bidault Initiative was not simply electioneering.[46] The Russians declined to join in on the grounds that neither the Italians or the Yugoslavs had been invited, or even consulted. But through the device of avoiding an outright refusal, or acceptance, either of which would have been an embarrassment, they probably hoped that the machinations of the western powers would also be frustrated.[47]

The Yugoslav Government, however, perhaps now aware of

the weakness of the their own international position in the event that Soviet support should be withdrawn, and increasingly preoccupied with the problem in their relations with Moscow, issued a twenty-eight page Note of their own, defending their administration of Zone B and renewing their charges against AMG in Zone A. This hasty and emotional response rather played into the hands of the western powers who saw a distinct advantage in getting maximum publicity for their viewpoint and thereby also for the Italian government, by precipitating if possible the Soviet veto in the Security Council. Public opinion, as the Foreign Office was increasingly realising, was a major factor in the cold war and the Bidault Initiative had come across as the cynical electioneering which it undoubtedly was.[48] Returning to the Soviet Note, the western powers replied on 16 April, pointing out that they had only visualised 'a preliminary meeting of the powers principally concerned,' and requested that the Soviet Government suggest an alternative procedure. The Soviet government did not reply and by the time the western powers returned to the charge, the issue had lost its immediate political importance for the Italian Christian Democrats had swept to victory with a large majority. The Bidault Initiative had undoubtedly contributed to the Christian Democrats' success, although it is likely that fears of communist takeover in Italy had become exaggerated as a consequence of events in eastern Europe.

Further notes were sent on 1 June requesting an early indication of the Russian views in the hope that such an action would at least make it clear to the work in general and the Russians in particular that the western powers were in earnest.[49]

The situation was unchanged when news of Yugoslavia's expulsion from the Cominform reached the west. It emerged early on that the Trieste question had been one of the causes of the dispute and that while Soviet policy had been intent simply on securing the removal of western troops from Trieste, their plans had been thwarted by Tito who had remained obstinately determined to achieve his territorial claims. In London, the Foreign Office recommended a policy of inactivity: perhaps, they reasoned, the Russians would now reply to the western proposal to return Trieste to Italy, not least since the Communist Party in the city of Trieste had, in the main, rushed to side with the Cominform against their heretical neighbour. This seemed particularly significant in view of the substantial financing they had hitherto received from Belgrade.[50]

The Yugoslav government also considered that the Cominform dispute might be used by the Soviet Union as an occasion for coming out more firmly in favour of Italian interests, and at the end of July moved to forestall this by delivering to the Security Council a long note which brought fresh charges of violation of the Peace Treaty against AMG. After referring specifically to financial and currency questions, they called upon the Security Council to declare that the arrangements made by the AMG constituted a violation of the Peace Treaty, and requested that Britain and the United States respect the international agreements which were intended to guarantee the continued existence of the Free Territory.[51] The Yugoslavs seemed to think that Stalin remained undecided about Trieste: by bringing an accusation against the British and Americans before the Security Council of breaching the Treaty, they were trying to force the Russians into publicly defending the FTT settlement, since the alternative was to approve the conduct of the Anglo-American administration.[52]

In London, these developments were welcomed. At last, so it seemed, the western powers would have the opportunity to apprise the United Nations, and thereby the world at large, of the difficulties under which the Anglo-American military administration had been labouring for some three years. Moreover, the fact that the Yugoslavs themselves had provoked the debate was an added bonus for presentational purposes. 'One of our main tasks in the Cold War', wrote one British official, is 'to expose the contradictions of communist ideology and methods . . . There is an excellent opportunity of exploiting the Tito–Cominform rift. The Security Council would be public and reported all over the world.'[53]

The Security Council debate took place during November. Immediately it began, the Russians attempted to embarrass Britain and the United States by accusing them of deliberately delaying the appointment of a Governor and a resolution tabled by the Ukrainian delegation called for an appointment to be made immediately. At the same time, the Soviet delegation took great care not to give a reply to the western proposal for the return of the FTT to Italy. While the methods which the western powers were proposing to revise the Italian Peace Treaty were stigmatised as illegal, the actual essence of the initiative was carefully not pronounced against. Nor was any reference made to the suggestion that a meeting be held to discuss the question and the Ukrainian Resolution did not demand one. When it came to the vote, the Security Council did not uphold the charges.[54]

However, the Russians were not prepared to let the matter rest: in a letter dated 8 February 1949, the Soviet representative requested that the question of the appointment of a Governor be considered by the Security Council in the near future.[55] More controversial was their suggestion that the Yugoslavs be permitted to put their case again regarding southern Carinthia, possibly hoping to provoke a direct clash between the West and Yugoslavia on this important issue in their relationship at a time when Yugoslavia was tending to gravitate towards the western camp.[56] The British still hoped to pin the Russians down to an outright rejection of the Three Power Declaration of the previous March, while avoiding involvement in a debate on the Yugoslav charges. Instead, they intended to argue in concert with the Americans that from experience they were convinced that the Peace Treaty settlement was unworkable and that the Soviet Union should be so informed. They could then argue that since the Russians had not replied to this communication, the situation would require further examination through the normal diplomatic channels.

The Security Council debate took place on 17 February and proceeded much as the British anticipated, apart from the Russian nomination of Colonel Herman Flueckiger for the Governorship.[57] Flueckiger, formerly Minister in the Swiss Embassy in Moscow, had been nominated initially by the British in September 1947 when the Russians had rejected the proposal. That they were now recommending one of the west's candidates was a clear signal that Moscow's purpose was to undermine Yugoslavia's neutrality. Since 1 January 1948, the western powers had deliberately avoided giving encouragement to those who still sought to appoint a Governor and thus perpetuate the idea of a Free Territory and now, after much persistence from both the British and American delegations, the Chinese President of the Security Council, Wellington Koo, was persuaded to assist in preventing the Soviet resolution from being put to the vote.

Until the summer of 1949, the cornerstone of British policy towards Trieste remained that of keeping the Anglo-American garrison of 10,000 troops in Zone A and ensuring that the Yugoslavs stayed out, with a view to the eventual return of both zones to Italy. This had not been altered by the Tito–Cominform dispute. However, as Yugoslavia's economy grew steadily worse, and Tito showed himself willing to compromise on the Greek question, so the British similarly reconsidered the Trieste problem. The further deterioration in Soviet–Yugoslav relations during the spring and early summer of 1949 found tangible expression in the Soviet abandonment of their support for Yugoslav claims regarding Carinthia. The Yugoslavs were unable to disguise the blow to their prestige which had thereby been struck and it seemed logical to assume that the Russians might now take a similar line with regard to Trieste. This had obvious implications for western policy for if the Soviet Union were now to accept the proposal to return the entire Free Territory to Italy, this would place Britain and the United States on the spot in respect to their attitude towards Yugoslavia. The interests of the West in the region had been complicated by Yugoslavia's dispute with the Cominform: they were no longer pursuing the interests of Italian democracy but had the problem of maintaining Yugoslav independence of the Soviet sphere. The Foreign Office concluded that this dilemma could best be resolved by a return to the policy of partition which they had followed throughout much of 1947.[58]

The difficulty lay in persuading the Italian and Yugoslav governments to come to a mutually satisfactory solution. Although Charles Peake suggested from Belgrade that the Italian government should be prompted to take advantage the presence of a Yugoslav Trade Delegation in Rome to make the first move, the Southern Department, revealing a subtle understanding of the delicate balance of the forces concerned, counselled caution: a fresh initiative, it was argued, could come more safely from the Yugoslav side since the Yugoslav Government would be in the best position to judge when the appropriate moment had arrived.[59]

Hopes of an early *rapprochement* between Rome and Belgrade were dashed, however. In early July, the Yugoslav government introduced the Yugoslav dinar into Zone B for 'economic reasons', but in British eyes this seemed to be intended to demonstrate that Yugoslavia was in possession of Zone B and was not about to be 'bounced' out of it.[60] Ever since the Yugoslavs had occupied the region they had operated a currency of their own called the Yugolira: they were required by the Italian Peace Treaty to negotiate with the Italian government for the introduction of the Italian lira into their zone but the Italians had refused to co-operate. The Yugoslavs themselves had aggravated the situation by claiming in a note to the UN Secretary General that their action had been forced upon them as a result of the Italian government's failure to furnish Zone B with Lira as the Treaty obliged.[61]

Over the previous few months, Italo–Yugoslav relations had

been steadily improving, with considerable progress in respect to economic relations, and this Yugoslav initiative seemed likely to threaten these advances. The Italians, quite reasonably, expressed their outrage and Sforza lost no time in making the British aware that the introduction of the dinar into Zone B was seen in Rome as a deliberate challenge which the Italian government felt unable to ignore. To reinforce the point, he handed an aidé-memoire to the British and American ambassadors in Rome which stated Italian intentions to slow down the negotiations for a commercial treaty, and expressing hope that similar action would be taken in London and Washington. It also hinted that the Italians intended shortly to propose further measures by which Zone A could be incorporated into Italy in the near future.[62]

This placed the British and Americans in an invidious position: a serious setback for Tito in foreign policy could seriously undermine his prestige at a critical juncture for Yugoslavia and at worst he needed to be in a position to save face over Trieste. Nonetheless, Bevin did not want to propose withdrawal of the Bidault Initiative and chose instead to play down the matter with a view to avoiding any difficulties in Yugoslav–western relations while simultaneously avoiding any appearance of condoning Yugoslav actions or of retreating from the position adopted the previous year.[63] Parallel British and American notes were delivered to the Yugoslav embassies in London and Washington which protested the Yugoslav action, but carefully avoided any suggestion that the Yugoslavs had actually committed an act which constituted a fresh breach of the peace treaty. Instructions were also sent to Belgrade and Rome to the effect that all efforts should be made to reduce the temperature in Italo–Yugoslav relations without prejudicing the case in either direction.[64]

This policy proved effective: at the end of August, Sforza conveyed to Bevin Italian keenness to establish good relations with Belgrade despite recent events. Accordingly the Italian government had decided not to proceed with the proposed protest to the United Nations concerning Trieste, although it remained possible that a note of protest might be addressed nevertheless to the Four Powers.[65] Towards the end of the year Ales Bebler, Tito's deputy foreign minister, approached the State Department with a request that the United States urge the Italians to accept a compromise solution for Trieste.[66] Such a move had been expected by the British since the Soviet Union had let the Yugoslavs down over southern Carinthia. Tito's concern to avoid receiving a rebuff from Italy, which would have been potentially damaging to his position at home, had contributed both to the delay in such an approach being made and to the fact that the State Department had been asked to assist. The latter had adopted the position, however, that it could not depart from the March 1948 Declaration, although the Yugoslavs were advised that should they be able to work out a mutually acceptable agreement with the Italians, then it would be duly considered by the United States in conjunction with the other signatories to the Treaty.[67]

It was quite clear that there would not be a satisfactory solution to the Trieste question without the Italians and Yugoslavs agreeing one with the other first. The British were prematurely optimistic, however, for despite this significant step forward in the attitudes of the protagonists, the deadlock was to continue for several years more. During 1952 and 1953, the Allied Military Government began to hand over military and civilian control in Zone A to the Italians provoking a Yugoslav threat to use force if the Italians were infiltrated into the administration of the disputed territory without Belgrade's agreement. However, a visit to Tito by Anthony Eden, who had returned to the Foreign Office after the conservative victory in the 1951 election, in September 1952, and a simultaneous re-opening of conversations on the question with the Italians, convinced the British that if a solution were to be implemented at all it would have to imposed from without. This was to be the basis of subsequent British planning.

Just over a year later, on 8 October 1953, an Anglo-American plan was announced, awarding Zone A to Italy with the termination of AMG, while Yugoslavia would continue to control Zone B. Essentially a revision of the Three Power Declaration, it pleased nobody. However, the way towards further negotiations had been opened. Highly secret discussions were subsequently held in Vienna between British and American representatives with active participation by the Italian and Yugoslav ambassadors in London. After a year of patient negotiation, a formula for the partition of Trieste was arrived at: with some minor frontier and population adjustments, the territory was divided between the two claimants in accordance with the existing zonal arrangements. Italy undertook to maintain Trieste as a free port and Yugoslavia received £20 million from the United States and £2 million from Britain to help her in her construction of a new port at San Nicola in Zone B south of Trieste.

Since it was legally impossible to alter the Italian Peace Treaty without approval of the Soviet Union, which had not been obtained, the western powers had adopted the device of emphasising the provisional nature of the solution. For this purpose the document was designated a 'Memorandum of Understanding', the word 'Agreement' being omitted; it was initialled in London on 5 October 1954.[68]

9

The Cold War and Yugoslav Unity

Soviet–Yugoslav antagonism was to persist until Stalin's death in 1953 and was only partially patched up thereafter. At the same time, western diplomatic support for Tito had become by the end of 1949 more overt: in September 1949, the British and Americans let it be known that they would regard an attack on Yugoslavia as an action which would require a western response (the terms of this response were left deliberately vague). In November, they supported Yugoslavia's election to the Security Council in preference to Czechoslovakia. Nevertheless, while Stalin lived, the Yugoslav leadership believed in and prepared for the possibility of military attack: in the spring of 1949, Belgrade had received a particularly threatening note from which they took seriously, and began making preparations for guerrilla warfare and defence of 'particular parts of the Adriatic Coast'.[1] There is evidence from the other side that Soviet war plans were indeed drawn up in this period. Major Bela Kiraly, commander of Hungary's infantry forces until his arrest on charges of treason in 1951, records that the war plan against Yugoslavia was completed in the summer of 1950: all Moscow's east European allies, particularly those which shared a border with Yugoslavia, were allotted a role. Kiraly claims that it was the Korean war which saved Yugoslavia from Soviet invasion because the Russians drew from that the conclusion that in Yugoslavia, as in Korea, the western powers 'would not have behaved like a paper tiger'.[2]

Despite western aid, Yugoslavia's economic situation in 1950–1 remained perilous: the summer drought of 1950 was disastrous and exacerbated the existing problems Yugoslavia had in the field of agriculture as a consequence of her collectivisation policies and the Soviet economic blockade. The government in Belgrade, facing economic collapse, sent Edward Kardelj to Washington in October

1950 to ask for extensive loans and grants. The drought had caused food shortages and dried up exports that otherwise would have financed development projects.[3] Acheson, now Secretary of State, warned him that the Administration was already having 'real trouble' in Congress over military aid, its policy towards China and its own domestic communist witchhunts being conducted in the name of McCarthyism. Kardelj was warned that the US could not therefore take on a major Yugoslav financial programme because of the ideological problems it would raise. In the present climate of hostility to all things communist, he believed that Congress would demand political concessions from Belgrade up front if approached directly on this question. Acheson was anxious to reassure Kardelj nonetheless that the United States would assist Yugoslavia in her present difficulties and advised him that they would 'muddle through with bits and pieces for the time being'. This process had yielded by August 1951 some $150 millions in economic aid which arguably did more than anything to confirm the occidentation of Yugoslav foreign policy. At the same time a new spirit of friendship in Anglo-Yugoslav relations was marked by the visit of the new Parliamentary Under Secretary for Foreign Affairs, Ernest Davies, to Bled in August 1950 and the establishment of the British Economic Mission in Belgrade which also had an American counterpart. However, Djilas came to London in the early spring of 1951 to lecture at Chatham House and took the opportunity to urge London to increase contact between the two countries without delay: rumours of Soviet military intervention were current and tension on the increase. The possibility of arms supplies from the west had been tested out by the Yugoslavs with Attlee in January when it received a positive response. This was followed up during August when Tito's Ambassador in Washington, Koca Popovic, went to Acheson to ask for arms, a request which the Americans answered with $60 million of military items in 1951 and a little more the following year. As Acheson reflected in his memoirs, this process of ad hoc aid 'carried Tito through his troubles'.[4]

However, for Tito this was purely a marriage of convenience. Following the split in 1948, and after an interval in which he affected a posture of being more sinned against than himself sinning, Tito took pains to demonstrate in speeches and in print, for the Yugoslav people and the world at large, that it was the Soviet Union which had diverged from the path of true socialism and that his interpretation of Marxist–Leninist teaching was the correct one. This was important: if he once allowed the ideology which legitimised his regime to be called into question within Yugoslavia, the whole process on which he had been engaged since 1942, of welding his country into a federation through imposing a supra-nationalist ideology, would degenerate into failure. This need to distinguish Yugoslavia ideologically from the Soviet Union, while also tailoring the rhetoric to suit the immediate needs of the country, led to the evolution of domestic and foreign policies which were designed to meet Yugoslavia's unique situation. The principal domestic tenant of 'Titoism' was the experiment with workers' self-management which began in 1950 and was intended to achieve, for the first time, true worker ownership of the factories, to which was added in 1953 the reversal of the policies of collectivisation. On the international front, Tito sought to carve out a role for Yugoslavia, and therefore for himself through the evolution of non-alignment, and he devoted much time subsequently to travelling the world promoting his alliances with similarly-minded statesmen such as Pandit Nehru. Such a policy was as much an expedient as were his domestic economic policies, and while non-alignment disintegrated during the 1970s when East–West détente removed much of its *modus vivendi*, so self-management socialism in its various incarnations, combined with the constitutional balancing acts which Tito performed to maintain the Yugoslav federation, brought Yugoslavia an illusion of unity and stability, the weaknesses of which became all too apparent once its creator – the cement which held the federation together – was dead. It can be no coincidence that implosion of Yugoslavia occurred once the end of the Cold War altered the balance of power in Europe, offering a new era of diversity and, so it seemed, the opportunity for the settling of some old scores and a revision of the post-war order.

Yugoslav unity was dependent then on the personality and vision of Tito, and on what Christopher Cviic in a recent study of the Balkans dubbed the 'Cold War corset'.[5] Tito was undoubtedly a natural leader of men, a born ruler, and also by nature an autocrat. His gift was a pragmatism which he exploited for statesman-like ends but with a statesman's eye on his place in history. That Tito was interested in power is self-evident, since being comfortable with power is essential for any politician and all the more so in eastern Europe where politics is traditionally conducted along more autocratic lines than in the culture of pluralism which has evolved in the West. A nationalist he may not have been in the sense of the promoters of Italian unity in the nineteenth century, but he developed an idea of Yugoslavia as a political unit, through cunning exploitation of ideology and recent Yugoslav history, and this provided the politician and statesman in him with a power base and sphere of action; in the words of Stevan Pavlowitch, one of Tito's critics, 'It was the inseparable association with the state that eventually made him identify with the life of the nation, as interpreted by him.'[6]

The importance of Tito was recognised by the West from 1943 onwards. The policies of any of the major powers, the Soviet Union included, were only effective so long as Tito willed them to be, and he exploited their various benefactions and patronages with the skill of the consummate politician which he undoubtedly was. As Charles Peake remarked in 1951, 'any attempt . . . to hasten the conversion of Yugoslavia into what might be called a liberal type of social democracy can in my opinion only lead to a porcupine display of bristling independence by Marshal Tito'.

Fitzroy Maclean had similarly remarked on this in 1943–4. In his report of November 1943, he argued that in the post-war world, much would depend on Tito and whether he saw himself in his former role of Comintern agent, or as the potential ruler of an independent Yugoslav state.[7] Maclean reflected shortly after the war that since his Comintern days, Tito had gone through the hazards and hardships of a bitter war fought for the independence of his country and speculated that whatever his sympathies and ideals before the war, the process of fighting must have made some impact on his outlook. It is worth bearing in mind that this was written in 1949 and that, as with so much of the literature on Yugoslavia, it was intended to develop a particular view of the problem (and possibly of the role of the author himself). Nonetheless, the essential contention is reasonable – Tito and his followers did not fight the war simply to further the cause of the Soviet empire, a point which is supported by the determination with which Tito sought to pursue Yugoslavia's foreign policy interests from the outset as an independent head of an independent state, and was prepared to state in public his resentment at the pressure being put on him by the Russians to conform to their outlook. The war-time struggle was clearly a battle for power in post-war Yugoslavia and having experienced the satisfaction of building up from nothing a powerful military and political organisation, of which 'he himself was the absolute master', to expect Tito to hand such power over to a foreign ruler would have been asking him to deny his own nature. Reflecting on the Tito–Cominform dispute some years later, Milovan Djilas, by then himself a sometime political prisoner of the Yugoslav regime, reflected that Moscow's disapproval of Yugoslavia served only to strengthen the nascent independence of Tito's government; his concern, Djilas recalled, 'was above all for the future of Yugoslavia, his own creation'.[8]

By the end of decade, Anglo-Yugoslav relations had come full-circle since the rejection of Britain by Tito in the spring of 1945. The Anglo-Yugoslav trade agreement, signed shortly before the end of 1949, was the first of its kind to be signed between a western government and communist state after the war, and it marked the beginning of a process which underpinned the region economically until the 1980s. In return, the border with Greece was closed, an action that effectively ended the civil war there.[9] Indeed, the emergence of the Cold War in Europe had made an independent Yugoslavia more valuable to the West than could have been envisaged in 1943–44 when the advantages of a securing a foothold with the Yugoslav regime were discussed in London. With Belgrade's neutrality, Italy could be defended against attack at the Ljubljana Gap, her natural point of defence, rather than on the Venetian Plain; Greece could be defended in the upper Vardar Valley, rather than at Salonika; the thirty-three divisions of the Yugoslav army were neutralised. Although Yugoslavia remained outside NATO, understandings were reached in the early 1950s with Greece and Turkey, which were part of this alignment. The purpose of British war-time policy – the search for stability and order in a notoriously troublesome and dangerous region – had been achieved. The problems still existed, however, and the inability of the major powers to ameliorate them remained the same. The 'Cold War' solution to the Yugoslav problem, which Tito supplied and the West supported, merely deferred the task of addressing the questions posed for European civilisation by this ethnic melting pot for solution by a subsequent generation.

Notes

Introduction

1. Vladimir Dedijer, *With Tito through the war. The Partisan diary 1941–44* (London: Alexander Hamilton, 1951); Milovan Djilas, *Wartime. With Tito and the Partisans* (London: Secker and Warburg, 1980); Edvard Kardelj, *Reminiscences: the struggle for recognition and independence. The New Yugoslavia 1944–57* (London: Blond and Briggs, 1982).
2. For example, Julian Amery, *Approach March* (London: Hutchinson, 1973); Stephen Clissold, *Whirlwind, an account of Marshal Tito's rise to Power* (London: Cressett Press, 1948); F. W. D. Deakin, *The Embattled Mountain* (Oxford: Oxford University Press, 1971), F. H. Maclean, *Eastern Approaches* (London: Jonathan Cape, 1949), and *Disputed Barricade. The Life and Times of Jozip Broz-Tito* (London: Jonathan Cape, 1957); Bickham Sweet-Escott, *Baker Street Irregular* (London: Methuen, 1965).
3. For example, Elisabeth Barker, *British Policy in South-East Europe in the Second World War* (London: Macmillan and SSEES, 1976) and from the American side, W. R. Roberts, *Tito, Mihailovic and the Allies 1941–1945* (New Brunswick: Rutgers University Press, 1973), which, though written from US archives without reference to the British record, remains a standard and reliable account. A detailed analysis of Britain and Yugoslavia during the first three years of the war was produced by Mark Wheeler, *Britain and the War for Yugoslavia 1940–1943* (Boulder, Colorado: East European Monographs, 1980); see also Elisabeth Barker, 'Fresh Sidelights on British Policy in Yugoslavia 1942–43', in *Slavonic and East European Review*, vol. liv (October 1976), pp. 522–85, and P. Auty and R. Clogg (eds), *British Policy Towards Wartime Resistance in Yugoslavia and Greece* (London: Macmillan & SSEES, 1975).
4. The introductory essay to Stephen Clissold's, *Yugoslavia and the Soviet Union 1939–73. A documentary survey* (London: Oxford University Press, 1975) is a case in point.
5. Among the more scholarly of these studies is Michael Deroc, *British Special Operations Explored. Yugoslavia in Turmoil 1941–43 and the British Response* (Boulder, Colorado: East European monographs, 1988) and K. St. Pavlowitch, 'Neither Heroes nor Traitors: suggestions for a

reappraisal of the Yugoslav Resistance', in Brian Bond and Ian Roy, *War and Society. A Yearbook of Military History* (London: Croom Helm, 1976). Nora Beloff, *Tito's Flawed Legacy* (London: Gollancz, 1985) is essentially a journalistic account. More recent works are David Martin, *The Web of Disinformation: Churchill's Yugoslav Blunder* (New York: Harcourt Brace Jovanovich, 1991), which develops the defence of Mihailovic first made by the same author in *Ally Betrayed: the uncensored story of Tito and Mihailovic* (New York: Prentice Hall, 1946), and expanded in *Patriot or Traitor: the case of Draza Mihailovic* (New York: Harcourt, Brace, Jovanovich, 1978); Ilija Jukic, *The Fall of Yugoslavia* (New York and London: Harcourt Brace Jovanovich, 1974) is a memoir by a member of the Yugoslav Government-in-Exile. See also Michael Lees, *The Rape of Serbia. The British role in Tito's grab for power* (New York: Harcourt Brace Jovanovich, 1991) essentially a memoir with some use of documentary sources, and Richard Lamb, *Churchill as War Leader: Right or Wrong?* (London: Bloomsbury, 1990) which devotes a chapter to the Yugoslav question.

6. *DBPO* (London: HMSO, 1984), Series I, vol. i, no. 102.

1 Britain in Search of an Ally, 1939–1942

1. The Yugoslav state, when it was recognised by the Allies at Paris in 1919 took the name the Kingdom of Serbs, Croats and Slovenes. This was changed to Yugoslavia, meaning South Slav, in 1929.
2. RG 226 E146B 156 F2223 OSS Report, Washington Research & Analysis.
3. Biographies of Tito abound from a variety of sources. Phyllis Auty's *Tito. A Biography* (London, 1970), is a lively read but has been justly criticised as hagiography; from the Yugoslav perspective, Vladimir Dedijer's *Tito Speaks: his self-portrait and struggle with Stalin* (London: 1953) is, as its title suggests, an ex-post facto justification of the rift with the Cominform; Milovan Djilas, *Tito: the Story from Inside* (London: 1981) published after Tito's death in 1980 is a personal memoir containing valuable insights from the communist perspective. Several biographies have appeared since Yugoslavia's break up: among the best is that by Steven Pavlowitch, *Tito: Yugoslavia's Great Dictator: a Reassessment* (London: C. Hurst & Co., 1992), and Richard West's *Tito and the Rise and Fall of Yugoslavia* (London: Stevenson, 1994).
4. *DGFP*, Series D, vol. xii, pp. 451–2, 480; *BFSP* 1941, vol. 144, pp. 878–9. See also Stephen Clissold, *Yugoslavia and the Soviet Union*, pp. 10–12, and G. R. Swain, 'Comintern in Southern Europe', in T. Judt (ed.), *Resistance and Revolution in Mediterranean Europe* (London, 1989). In his article 'The Cominform: Tito's International', *Historical Journal*, vol. 35, no. 3 (1992), Swain has noted that since 1985, the authorities in Belgrade have published a comprehensive collection of war-time communications from the Communist Party, the Partisan command and the liberation committee under the title, *Izvori za istoriju centralnih organa KPJ, NOR, I Revolucije 1941–1945*.

5. The best general account, still, of British policy towards the Balkans in this period is that by Elisabeth Barker, *British Policy in South East Europe during the Second World War*, but see also Mark C. Wheeler, *Britain and the War for Yugoslavia 1940–43*, which examines the detail of the personalities and early contacts with the Yugoslav government prior to March 1941.
6. See F. H. Hinsley, *British Intelligence during the Second World War*, vol. 1 *passim*; M. R. D. Foot, *SOE 1940–1946*; Christopher Andrew, *Secret Service. The Making of the British Intelligence Community*, pp. 665–6; see also Bickham Sweet-Escott, *Baker Street Irregular* (London: Methuen, 1965).
7. Accounts on this point differ. Julian Amery, who was instrumental in organising the mission claims in his autobiography, *Approach March* (London: Hutchinson, 1973), that Bullseye was 'a mission to Mihailovic'. But Bickham Sweet-Escott says that it was hoped Hudson would make his way to Colonel Mihailovic's Headquarters, which is not the same thing as a directive to report to the Cetnik leader exclusively. A detailed analysis of the origins and purpose of Operation Bullseye is contained in Michael Deroc, *Special Operations Explored*, pp. 53–83.
8. RG 226 B92 F60 Wash-Rgt-AD-7 The Soviets and Draza Mihailovic, 1 December 1942.
9. Fitzroy Maclean, *Eastern Approaches* (London, Jonathan Cape, 1949), p. 308.
10. Stephen Bailey, 'British Policy Towards Draza Mihailovic', in Auty and Clogg (eds), *British Policy towards Yugoslavia and Greece during the Second World War* (London: Macmillan, 1975), p. 64. For fuller analysis of the origins and objectives of the Cetnik movement see Matteo J. Milazzo, *The Chetnik Movement and the Yugoslav Resistance* (Baltimore and London: Johns Hopkins University Press, 1975) and Jozo Tomasevich, *The Chetniks. War and Revolution in Yugoslavia 1941–45* (Stanford: Stanford University Press, 1975).
11. Barker, *British Policy in South East Europe*, p. 159.
12. John Ehrman, *Grand Strategy*, vol. v (HMSO, London, 1956), p. 77.
13. FO 371 37583 R3346/3/92 Ploz series of telegrams.
14. Deroc, *British Special Operations Explored*, p. 214; FO 371 37583 R3346/2/92.
15. WO 204/8106 *op. cit.* The source for this was major Radoslav Djuric, then one of Mihailovic's most intimate collaborators. While commanding the Cetniks for Central and South East Serbia in the Spring of 1943, Djuric was ordered to set up separate Cetnik organisations in close liaison with the Nedic State Guard and Vojvoda Pecanac's 'legal' Cetniks 'to fight the Partisans'; Djuric and many of his men deserted to the Partisans in the spring of 1944.
16. FO 371 33470 *passim, qu* Barker, *British Policy in South-East Europe*, p. 158.
17. G. R. Swain, 'The Cominform Tito's International' pp. 641–83.
18. Vojtech Mastny, *Russia's Road to the Cold War: Diplomacy, warfare and*

the politics of Communism, 1941–45 (New York: Columbia University Press, 1979), p. 68.

19. Wheeler, *Britain and the war for Yugoslavia*, pp. 118–20; Hudson's account is contained in FO 371 37583 R3346/3/92.
20. Quoted in Bradley Smith, *The Shadow Warriors. OSS and the origins of the CIA* (London: André Deutsch, 1983), p. 84.
21. Barker, *British Policy in South East Europe*, p. 160. See also David Stafford, *Britain and European Resistance. A Survey of SOE with Documents* (London and Basingstoke: Macmillan for St Antony's College, Oxford, 1980).

2 Expedients of War: Tito or Mihailovic?

1. Llewellyn Woodward, *British Foreign Policy during the Second World War* (HMSO, 1971), vol. iii, p. 287 and FO 371 44276 R12712/11/92.
2. Mastny, *Russia's Road to the Cold War*, pp. 68–9.
3. Barker, Some factors in British Policy Making, in Auty and Clogg (eds), *British Policy towards resistance in Yugoslavia and Greece*, p. 34.
4. FO 371 33470 R5973/178/92 FO Minute.
5. WO 202/356 GESH no. 76, 22 October 1942.
6. FO 371 33470 R6363/178/92 FO Minute.
7. FO 371 33472, Howard minute, 25 November 1942, *qu* Barker, 'Some factors in British Policy Making', in Auty and Clogg (eds), *British Policy towards resistance in Yugoslavia and Greece*, p. 35.
8. Churchill, *The Second World War*, vol. iv, *The Hinge of Fate* (London: Cassell, 1951), p. 634; Deakin, 'The myth of an Allied landing', in Auty and Clogg (eds), *British Policy towards resistance in Yugoslavia and Greece*, pp. 102–3.
9. *Correspondence between the Chairman of the Council of Ministers of the USSR and the Presidents of the United States and Prime Ministers of Great Britain during the Great Patriotic War of 1941–1945. Correspondence with Winston Churchill and Clement Attlee* (Moscow: Foreign Languages Publishing House, 1957), pp. 99–102, 106; Mastny, *Russia's Road to the Cold War*, p. 75.
10. Basil Davidson, *Special Operations Europe. Scenes from the anti nazi war* (London: Gollancz, 1980), p. 140; M. R. D. Foot, *SOE, 1940–46*, p. 323.
11. Davidson, *Special Operations Europe*, pp. 156–7; F. H. Hinsley, *British Intelligence in the Second World War*, vol. iii, part I, pp. 144–6.
12. FO 371 37579 R1513/2/92. Cf. Michael Howard, *Grand Strategy* (London: HMSO, 1983), pp. 389–90. The note handed to Churchill by Keble was circulated to the Cabinet by Hollis as COS(43)44, 11 February 1943; Hinsley, *British Intelligence*, p. 141. Cf. Deakin, *The Embattled Mountain*, pp. 185–6, Churchill, *The Second World War*, vol. iv, p. 828; Deakin, 'The Myth of an Allied Landing in the Balkans', in Auty and Clogg (eds), *British Policy towards resistance in Yugoslavia and Greece*, p. 103; M. R. D. Foot, *SOE, 1940–46*, p. 239.

13. WO 202/356 Cairo to London BI 3192, 8 December 1942.
14. Deakin, *The Embattled Mountain*, pp. 178–81.
15. WO 202/357 Bailey telegram, 7 February 1943.
16. P. Hehn, *The German Struggle against Yugoslav Guerrillas in World War II. German counter-insurgency in Yugoslavia 1941–43* (Boulder and New York: East European Quarterly, 1979), pp. 3 and 34.
17. FO 371 37578 R1141/2/92 Rendel letter to Sargent, 1 February 1943; FO 371 37578 R1346/2/92 Howard minute (undated).
18. FO 371 37584 R3994/2/92 The specific record of the meeting, filed at R1503/2/92 has been withheld, but an SOE commentary on the paper discussed at the meeting on 18 February can be found at FO 371 37579 R1521/2/92. Cf. Barker, 'Some factors in British Policy Making', in Auty and Clogg (eds), *British Policy towards resistance in Yugoslavia and Greece*, pp. 36–7.
19. FO 371 37584 R3994/2/92, FO Memorandum, 23 April 1943, quoted in Elisabeth Barker, *British Policy towards South East Europe, ibid.*
20. FO 371 37583 R3031/2/92 Tel 1146 to Cairo, 8 April 1943. In March 1943, Cairo had just four aircraft at its disposal.
21. FO 371 37581 R2221/2/92 Summary of telegram from Glenconner to SOE London and passed to the Foreign Office by Charles Hambro, 11 March 1943.
22. Hinsley, *British Intelligence*, p. 143. Cf. FO 371 37581 R2091/2/92 Price letter to Sargent 7 March 1943.
23. FO 371 37583 R3346/2/92.
24. The phrase referring to the telegrams and their code name, *Ploz*, was deleted by SOE London from the copy sent to the Foreign Office. FO 371 37580 R1848/2/92 copy of telegram from Glenconner, 28 February 1943.
25. FO 371 37583 R3346/2/92 *op. cit.*
26. FO 371 37584 R3994/2/92 Howard Minute, 23 April 1943.
27. Woodward, *British Foreign Policy*, vol. iii, p. 292.
28. FO 371 37583 R3250/2/92 Letter from Clark Kerr to Sargent, 3 April 1943.
29. Churchill, *The Second World War*, vol. iv, pp. 839–40; Howard, *Grand Strategy*, p. 383; Deakin, *The Embattled Mountain*, pp. 104–5.
30. Robert Dallek, *Franklin D. Roosevelt and American Foreign Policy 1932–1945* (Oxford: Oxford University Press, 1979); Herbert Feis, *Churchill, Roosevelt, Stalin. The war they waged and the peace they sought* (Princeton: Princeton University Press, paperback edition, 1966), pp. 128–9.
31. Bailey, in Auty and Clogg (eds), *British Policy towards resistance in Yugoslavia and Greece*, p. 79.
32. Hinsley, *British Intelligence*, vol. 3, pt. 1, pp. 146–7; Deakin, *The Embattled Mountain*, p. 223.
33. Hinsley, *British Intelligence*, vol. 3, pt. 1, p. 153.
34. FO 371 37609 R5330/143/92; R5070/143/92 Letter from Morton to Sargent, 8 June 1943.
35. Woodward, *British Foreign Policy*, vol. iii, pp. 292–3.
36. FO 371 37613 R10561/143/92.

37. FO 371 37609 R5330/143/92 COS (43) 175 Mtg (O) Minutes from Chiefs of Staff to Foreign Office, Annex III, Yugoslavia: SOE Activities.
38. FO 371 37609 *ibid.*, Howard minute to Hollis, 21 June 1943.
39. FO 371 37609 *ibid.*, Howard minute, 23 June 1943.
40. FO 371 37609 R5651/2/92 Letter from Howard to Rendel, 3 July 1943.
41. Barker, 'British Policy towards wartime Yugoslavia', *South Slav Journal*, vol. 22, no. 2 (April 1979) .
42. FO 371 37612 R8513/143/92 nos 61–7 of 5/6 September 1943.
43. Sweet-Escott, p. 192; Deakin, *The Embattled Mountain*, p. 78.
44. Hinsley, *British Intelligence*, pp. 151–62 .
45. FO 371 37616 R12264/143/92 Armstrong–Bailey report summarised in Cairo tel. 108, 23 November 1943. WO 202/140 Rapier DDD, 18 November 1943; Rose Minute, 20 November 1943.
46. Hinsley, *British Intelligence*, p. 153.
47. FO 371 37619 R13486/143/92 SE/28 of 26 November 1943.
48. FO 371 37616 R12035/143/92 Stevenson tel. no. 100, 20 November 1943; letter from Sargent to Hollis and Stevenson tel. nos 102 and 103. Howard minute, 22 November 1943; Hinsley, *British Intelligence*, p. 155. Armstrong also suspected that Mihailovic had made some accommodation, FO 371 37617 R12760/143/92 Yugoslav Sitrep week-ending 16 November 1943. A detailed account of Cetnik–German relations is contained in Tomasevich, *The Cetniks*, pp. 321–58 and Milazzo, *The Cetnik Movement and Yugoslav Resistance*, pp. 162–81.
49. Barker, 'British Wartime Policy Towards Yugoslavia', *South Slav Journal*, vol. 2, no. 2 (April 1979).
50. Barker, *British Policy in South East Europe*, p. 167; Bailey, in Auty and Clogg (eds), *British Policy towards resistance in Yugoslavia and Greece*, p. 81.
51. The Foreign Office only became aware of this link when Stevenson made its discovery in mid-October: FO 371 37613 R10561/143/92.
52. PREM 3/66/2 MidEast to Air Min NOS/90, 3 October 1943 .
53. *Ibid.*, Churchill Minute to Eden, 4 October 1943; Letter from Ismay to Churchill, 4 October 1943.
54. Bradley Smith, *The Shadow Warriors.*, p. 239.
55. F. Maclean, *Eastern Approaches*, p. 308.
56. FO 371 37615 R11589/143/92 Minutes by Howard and Sargent, 17 November 1943; FO Minute, 16 November 1943.
57. FO 371 37609 R5502/143/92 Sitrep for week ending 18 June 1943; FO memorandum, 23 June 1943. .
58. FO 371 37616 R12759/143/92 GRAND no. 245, for Chiefs of Staff from Vice Chiefs, JIC(43)488 (O), 26 November 1943.
59. See Bradley Smith, *The Shadow Warriors*, pp. 238–9.
60. *FRUS* 1943, *The Conferences at Cairo and Tehran*, pp. 606–15.
61. FO 371 37614 R11248/2/92 Cairo telegram no. 42, 5 November 1943.
62. Clissold, *Yugoslavia and the Soviet Union*, p. 26; interview with Sir William Deakin, Spring 1987.

63. V. Dedijer, *Tito Speaks* (London, 1953), pp. 197–8, quoted in Clissold, *Yugoslavia and the Soviet Union* p. 26.
64. Roberts, *Tito, Mihailovic and the Allies*, pp. 106–12. See also Djilas, *Wartime: With Tito and the Partisans* (Secker and Warburg, 1980), pp. 229–45 and *Conversations with Stalin* (London: Rupert Hart-Davis, 1962), p. 9.
65. GFM 68/48 713, Hitler's remark to Pavelic, 27 April 1943.
66. Other than the fragmentary published accounts which appear in the memoirs of Deakin and Maclean, no record of this meeting exits.
67. Churchill, *The Second World War*, vol. v, *Closing The Ring* (London: Cassell, 1952), pp. 415–16; Deakin, *The Embattled Mountain*, pp. 262–3.
68. When Mihailovic was tried for treason by Tito's government in 1946, Churchill wrote to the then Foreign Secretary, Ernest Bevin, asking him to intervene to save Mihailovic's life: see Kenneth Harris, *Attlee* (London: Weidenfeld and Nicholson, 1982), p. 296. FO 371 59468 R 5505/170/92 Bevin to Attlee, 29 March 1946.

3 Expedients for Peace: the Politics of Yugoslav Unity

1. Stephen Clissold (ed.), *Yugoslavia and the Soviet Union 1939–1973*, p. 151. See also *Soviet foreign policy during the patriotic war* (USSR Government, 1946), vol. ii, p. 184.
2. FO 371 37618 R13107/143/92 Sargent minute, 11 December 1943; Draft telegram to Cairo, no. 126, 16 December and minute by Nichols 14 December 1943.
3. FO 371 44245 R840/8/92 *passim*; Woodward, *British Foreign Policy*, pp. 298–304.
4. Stephen Clissold, *Djilas: Progress of a Revolutionary*, p. 129.
5. Clissold, *Yugoslavia and the Soviet Union*, p. 27.
6. Following a sharp exchange with the Russians arising from the secret Partisan–German negotiations in March, Tito had radioed to Moscow: 'If you cannot understand what a hard time we are having and if you cannot help us, at least do not hinder us.' He then declared to his intimates that their first duty 'is to look after our own army and our own people'. Djilas later recalled that this was 'the first time anyone in the Central Committee openly stated that our interests might be different from Moscow's'. Quoted in Clissold, *Yugoslavia and the Soviet Union*, p. 26.
7. Djilas, *Wartime*, p. 317.
8. Churchill, *The Second World War*, vol. v, pp. 416–20.
9. *FRUS* 1944, vol. iv, p. 1353.
10. Bradley Smith, *The Shadow Warriors*, pp. 239–40.
11. RG 226 E146 B156 F2223, Wash Research and Analysis, 1 March 1945; E146 B156 F2223; E92 B253 F31 Wash-Reg-AD-7 General Mihailovic and his adversaries.
12. RG 226 E 144 B99 F1040, CAIRO-SO-OP-3–6, Mansfield Report and

covering letter, 13 May 1944.; E 146 B156 F2223, E92 B253 F31 Wash-Reg-Ad-7, General Mihailovic and his adversaries.
13. McDowell Report, 23 November 1944, in Martin, *The Web of Disinformation*, pp. 378–411.
14. *FRUS* 1944, vol. iv, p. 1362.
15. *FRUS* 1944, vol. iv, pp. 1370–3. Cavendish Cannon was appointed US Ambassador to Yugoslavia in August 1947.
16. FO 371 44309, Churchill minute to Eden, 1 April 1944; Stevenson minute of conversation between the Prime Minister and King Peter, 13 April 1944.
17. CAB 66/62 WP(44)304 716.44.
18. FO 371 44312 Broad to FO, 17 June 1944.
19. FO 371 44312, *passim*; FO telegram to Naples, Eden letter to Stevenson, 21 June 1944.
20. Eden, *The Reckoning*, p. 470.
21. Churchill, *The Second World War*, vol. vi, *Triumph and Tragedy*, p. 93; FO 371 44315, Eden letter to Stevenson, 21 August 1944.
22. FO 371 44317 Eden to Tito, 11 September 1944; FO telegram to Moscow, 11 October 1944.
23. Barker, *British Policy in South East Europe during the Second World War*, p. 143 .
24. Mastny, *Russia's Road to the Cold War*, pp. 207–8.
25. PREM 3/434/9 Churchill-Stalin meeting, minutes of 9 October 1943.
26. Much has been written on the so-called Percentages Agreement of 1944. Among the most enlightening are Barker, *British Policy in South East Europe*, pp. 140–7; P. G. Holdich, 'A Policy of Percentages? British policy in the Balkans after the Moscow conference of October 1944', *International History Review*, vol. 9, no. 1 (February 1987); Warren Kimball, 'The naked reverse right: Roosevelt, Churchill and Eastern Europe from Tolstoy to Yalta – and a little beyond', *Diplomatic History*, vol. iii, no. 2 (Spring 1979); A. Resis, 'The Churchill–Stalin Percentages Agreement', *American Historical Review*, vol. lxxxii (1978); Joseph Siracusa, 'The Meaning of Tolstoy: Churchill, Stalin and the Balkans. Moscow October 1944', *Diplomatic History*, vol. iii (1979).
27. PREM 3/434/2 Minutes of Eden–Molotov meeting, 11 October 1944. Mastny, *Russia's Road to the Cold War*, p. 209.
28. See Barker, *British Policy in South East Europe*, pp. 140–7.
29. Djilas, *Wartime*, pp. 406–7; E. Kardelj, *Reminiscences: the struggle for recognition and independence – the new Yugoslavia 1944–77* (London: Blond & Briggs, Summerfield Press, 1982), p. 65.
30. Kardelj, *Reminiscences*, pp. 50–60, 62.
31. This interpretation is advanced by Vojtech Mastny, *Russia's Road to the Cold War*, p. 210.
32. FO 371 44318 Cadogan Minute, 8 November 1944.
33. FO 371 44318 Dew minute, 1 December 1944.
34. FO 371 44319 Stalin to Churchill, 24 November 1944; FO 371 44318 record of conversation between Churchill and King Peter.
35. Harriman's growing concern for Stalin's intentions in Europe, which seems to date from the Warsaw Rising which left him 'badly shaken'

is charted his memoirs, W. Averell Harriman and Elie Abel, *Special Envoy to Churchill and Stalin 1941–1946* (London: Random House, 1975), p. 343ff.

36. Charles Thayer, *Hands Across the Caviar* (London: Michael Joseph, 1953), p. 89.
37. FO 44320 Halifax to FO, 23 December 1944.
38. FO 371 48860 King Peter to Churchill, 29 November 1944 and 4 January 1945; record of conversation between Churchill, Eden and King Peter, 9 Janury 1945.
39. *FRUS* 1945, *The Conferences of Malta and Yalta*, p. 278; FO 371 44860 Churchill to Stalin, 11 November 1945; *FRUS* 1945, vol. v, p. 1179.
40. *FRUS* 1945, *The Conferences of Malta and Yalta*, Conference Communiqué, p. 974.
41. FO 371 48861 FO to Washington, 23 January 1945; FO 371 48862 statement issued by the Yugoslav information office, 29 January 1945.
42. RG 226 E144 B97 F1010, Cairo-SO-op-3 Mihailovic mystery and Yugoslav government, 5 April 1943.
43. Paul Shoup, *Communists and the National Question* (New York, 1968) pp. 104–5; Hugh Thomas, *Armed Truce: the beginnings of the Cold War* (London: Hamish Hamilton, 1986), p. 434; Lindsay, *Beacons in the Night*, p. 13.

4 Yugoslavia between the Allies: Trieste and the Emergence of Cold War Europe, 1945–1946

1. The text of the Yalta Declaration is printed in *FRUS The Conferences of Malta and Yalta*, pp. 968–84.
2. FO 371 48812 Churchill minute to Eden, 20 April 1945.
3. See J. R. Whittam, 'Drawing the Line: Britain and the emergence of the Trieste Question, January 1941–May 1945', *English Historical Review*, vol. cvi, no. 419 (April 1991).
4. The standard works on Trieste are Geoffrey Cox, *The Race for Trieste* (London, 1977); J-B Duroselle, *Le conflict de Trieste, 1943–1954* (Brussels, 1966); G. Valdevit, *La questione di Trieste 1941–1954* (Milan, 1987) and Bogdan Novak, *Trieste, 1941–1954. The ethnic, political and ideological struggle* (Chicago: University of Chicago Press, 1970).
5. FO 372 50787 U 650/51/70 FO minute, 3 February 1945, quoted in J. R. Whittam, 'Drawing the Line', *English Historical Review*, vol. cvi, no. 419, April 1991. See also David Close, *The Origins of the Greek Civil War* (Longman, 1995).
6. FO 371 50788 U 1936/51/70 Rome tel. to FO, 19 March 1945, quoted in J. R. Whittam, 'Drawing the Line', *ibid.*
7. Bruce Arcidiacono, 'The Dress Rehearsal. The Foreign Office and the Control of Italy 1943–44', *Historical Journal*, vol. 29, no. 2 (1985); J. L. Harper, *America and the Reconstruction of Italy 1945–50* (Cambridge: Cambridge University Press, 1986), pp. 35–64, 146–48. See also Barker, *Churchill and Eden at War*, chap. 13, pp. 162–81.
8. Mastny, *Russia's road to the Cold War*, pp. 282, 288.

9. *FRUS* 1945, vol. iv, pp. 1103–6.
10. *FRUS* 1945, *The Conferences of Malta and Yalta*, p. 888.
11. FO 371 48812 R 7022/6/92 Washington tel. 2613, 17 April 1945.
12. FO 371 48812 R 7022/6/92 Churchill tel. to Eden contained in tel. 3850 to Washington, 18 April 1945.
13. Churchill, *The Second World War*, vol. vi, pp. 480–81.
14. FO 371 48813 R 8017/6/92 Churchill telegram to Alexander, 6 May 1945; R 7833/6/92 Macmillan telegram to FO, 4 May 1945.
15. FO 371 48813 R 7941/6/92 Stevenson tel. to FO, 4 May 1945.
16. FO 371 48813 *ibid.*, Sargent minute, 5 May 1945.
17. FO 371 48813 R 8038/6/92 Rome telegram to FO, 7 May 1945; 48814 R 8268/6/92 Sargent minute to Churchill (undated draft copy).
18. FO 371 48813 *ibid.* R 8023/6/92 Stevenson to FO, 7 May 1945.
19. FO 371 48815 R 8405/6/92 Belgrade telegram to FO, 14 May 1945; 48817 R 8734/6/92 Belgrade telegram, 18 May 1945.
20. WO 204/9790 Administration of North East Italy: political relations with Yugoslavia, May–July 1945; see also *FRUS* 1945, vol. iv, pp. 1176–7.
21. *FRUS* 1945, *ibid.*, pp. 1168–9 and pp. 1172–3.
22. Clissold, *Yugoslavia and the Soviet Union 1939–73*, pp. 83–4; FO 371 48827 R 9273/6/92 Belgrade tel. 771, 28 May 1945.
23. Clissold, *Yugoslavia and the Soviet Union*, p. 165–6.
24. Clissold, *Yugoslavia and the Soviet Union*, p. 45.
25. Mastny, *Russia's Road to the Cold War*, p. 282.
26. FO 371 48816 R 8428/6/92 Eden minute to Churchill, 18 March 1945.
27. FO 371 48812 R 10662/6/92 Cadogan minute to Churchill, 20 June 1946.
28. John Colville, *The Fringes of Power, Downing Street Diaries, 1941–April 1955* (London, 1987), vol. ii, p. 262.
29. J. W. Pickersgill and D. F. Forster, *The Mackenzie King Record*, vol. iii, 1945–1946 (Toronto, 1970), p. 71.
30. David Dilks, *The Diaries of Sir Alexander Cadogan, 1938– 1945* (London, 1971), p. 785; H. Thomas, *Armed Truce* (London, 1988), pp. 295–6.
31. *DBPO*, Series I, vol. ii, no. 19.
32. *DBPO*, Series I, vol. i, no. 102.
33. Lynn Etheridge Davis, *The Cold War Begins: Soviet–American conflict over Eastern Europe* (New Jersey: Princeton University Press, 1974), p. 314.
34. *DBPO*, Series I, vol. 1, no. 68.
35. Barker, *British Policy in South-East Europe*, p. 61.
36. *DBPO*, Series I, vol. i, no. 19, note 5.
37. FO 371/33154 Minutes by Howard, Warner and Sargent, 1–2 and 11 January 1943; cf. Barker, *Churchill and Eden at War*, p. 286.
38. FO 371/48636 PM's personal minutes M.487/4 and 498/4, 4 May 1944.
39. Barker, *Churchill and Eden at War*, pp. 290–1; Thomas, *Armed Truce*, pp. 309–10.
40. See pp. 47–8 above.

41. *DBPO*, Series I, vol. i, no. 102.
42. This theme is developed in Keith Hamilton and Ann Lane, 'Power, status and the pursuit of liberty, Britain and Eastern Europe 1945–46', in M. Dockrill (ed.), *Europe within the Global System* (Bochum: Brockmeyer, 1995), pp. 31–54.
43. *Parliamentary Debates*, 5th Series, House of Commons, vol. 413, cols. 291–3.
44. See *DBPO*, Series I, vol. i, no. 194; *FRUS* 1945, vol. ii, pp. 127–9; FO 371/48808, R 13445/6/92, Howard letter to Stevenson, 18 August 1945, FO Memorandum to Bevin, 'Status report on situation in Yugoslavia', August 1945.
45. *DBPO*, *ibid.*, telegram 8711 to Washington, 23 August 1945.
46. FO 371/45694, Foreign Office Memorandum, 'The effect of our External Financial Position on our Foreign Policy', 30 March 1945.
47. FO 371 45678 UE 4032/79/53, Coulson Memorandum, 23 August 1945.
48. FO 371 47857 N 15085/18/38, FO Memorandum for Bevin, 'Status Report on Situation in Yugoslavia', August 1945, R 13445/6/92; FO Memorandum, 25 October 1945.
49. FO 371 47857 *ibid.*, FO Memorandum (draft copy undated).
50. FO 371 48856 R 19949/104/92, Colville letter to Osborne, 27 November 1945.
51. For an account of British overseas information in the immediate post-war period see Philip M. Taylor, 'The Projection of Britain Abroad, 1945–51', in M. Dockrill and J. W. Young (eds), *British Foreign Policy 1945–56* (London, 1989); Warsaw telegram 250, 22 August 1945, N 10829/211/55.
52. See for example report from Yugoslavia by John Henniker-Major, December 1945, FO 371 48876 R 20477/130/92; Warner minute, 19 September 1945, FO 371 47611 N 12148/6/55; *DBPO*, Series I, vol. vi, no. 57.i.
53. FO 371 47611 N 14743/6/45, Warsaw telegram 217 Saving, 24 October 1945.
54. FO 371 48876, *op. cit.*
55. This argument is developed by David Holloway, 'The atomic bomb and the end of the Second World War', in Lane and Temperley (eds), *The Rise and Fall of the Grand Alliance*, pp. 207–25.
56. FO 371 48219 R 14797/5063/67, Washington tels 5850 and 6047, 25 August and 6 September 1945; J. Wheeler Bennett and A. Nichols, *The Semblance of Peace. The Political Settlement at the end of the Second World War* (London, 1975), p. 420; Gage minute, 21 August, FO 371 44537 AN 2505/4/45.
57. The text of the Yalta Declaration on Liberated Europe is printed in *FRUS* 1945, *The Conferences of Malta and Yalta*, pp. 971–2.
58. A. Bullock, *Foreign Secretary*, p. 134; Piers Dixon, *Double Diploma. The Life of Pierson Dixon* (London, 1975), p. 189.
59. Dixon, *Double Diploma*, p. 193.
60. Bullock, *Ernest Bevin*, p. 133; J. F. Byrnes, *Speaking Frankly* (New York, 1947), p. 92.

61. For example, Brimelow minute, 29 August 1945, FO 371 47938 N 11474/1407/38.
62. FO 371 47881 N 12165/165/38, Moscow Despatch no. 642, 6 September 1945.
63. Report by the Joint Intelligence Sub-committee of the Cabinet, 'Relations with the Russians', JIC (45) 299 (0) (Final), 18 October 1945, *DBPO*, Series I, vol. vi, no. 41.
64. FO 371 47881 N 15702/165/38, Moscow despatch no. 799, 31 October 1945.
65. *DBPO*, Series I, vol. vi, *op. cit.* Stewart minute, 22 November 1945 and cf. Williams minute, 5 November 1945.
66. FO 371 47881 N 14646/165/38 Brimelow minute, 27 October 1945.
67. *DBPO*, *ibid.*, no. 13.iii.
68. *DBPO*, *ibid.*, no. 13, note 2.
69. For example, Djilas, *Conversations with Stalin*, p. 181ff.
70. FO 371 48194 R 19541/81/67 Sargent letter to Houstoun-Boswall, 26 November 1945.
71. FO 371 48874 R 19610/130/92, Sargent letter to Stevenson, 24 November 1945.
72. *DBPO*, Series I, vol. vi, Appendix I, Memorandum by Coulson, 12 March 1946.
73. Barbara Jelavich, *History of the Balkans*, vol. ii, p. 322.
74. Interview with Lord Mayhew, spring 1988.
75. See chapter 5, note 68.
76. The debate about repatriation of the Yugoslavs by General Keightley's forces was stimulated in the first instance by publication of Nikolai Tolstoy's article, 'The Klagenfurt Conspiracy: War Crimes and Diplomatic Secrets', in *Encounter*, May–June 1983. This was followed by a full-length publication, *The Minister and the Massacres* (London, 1986). Tolstoy's allegations were challenged effectively by Robert Knight in 'Harold Macmillan and the Cossacks: was there a Klagenfurt Conspiracy?', *Intelligence and National Security*, I (1986).
77. *FRUS* 1945, vol. v, pp. 1289–91.
78. FO 371 48874 R 19610/130/92, Sargent letter to Ralph Stevenson, 24 November 1945.
79. FO 371 48898 R 19021/445/92 FO Minute, 11 December 1945.

5 Limited Objectives: Seeking a Balkan Foothold, 1946–1947

1. This was not the first use of the phrase 'Iron Curtain': In the middle of the Trieste crisis in May 1945, Churchill had used the phrase in a telegram to Truman dated 12 May. Churchill, *The Second World War*, vol. vi, pp. 498–9.
2. FO 371 47857 N 150/18/38 FO minute, 25 October 1945.
3. FO 371 47857 N15085/18/38 FO minute 25 October 1945.
4. FO 371 48852 RG197/104/92 Department of Trade paper, 15 May 1945.
5. FO 371 53016 UE 1050/413/53 'Soviet Economic Policy in central and south eastern Europe', 12 March 1946.

6. FO 371 53016 UE1597/413/53, *ibid.*
7. FO 371 62279 UE 1044 UK delegation brief for Moscow Conference of Foreign Ministers, March 1947.
8. See Donald Cameron Watt, *Succeeding John Bull: America in Britain's place* (Cambridge: Cambridge University Press, 1984), pp. 167–93, and Kathleen Burke, 'American Foreign Economic Policy and Lend Lease in Lane and Temperley' (eds), *The Rise and Fall of the Grand Alliance* (London: Macmillan, 1995), pp. 43–68. Richard N. Gardner, Sterling-Dollar Diplomacy in current perspective, W. Roger Louis and Hedley Bull (eds), *The Special Relationship: Anglo-American relations since 1945* (Oxford: Clarendon, 1986), pp. 185–200.
9. *DBPO*, Series I, vol. viii, nos 35 and 58.
10. *DBPO*, Series I, vol. vi, no. 80.
11. *DBPO*, Series I, vol. vi, no 78 and 90.
12. *DBPO*, Series I, vol. vi, no. 88.
13. *DBPO*, Series I, vol. vi, no. 82.
14. R. Merrick, The Russia Committee of the British Foreign Office and the Cold War, 1946–47, in *Journal of Contemporary History*, vol. 20, no. 3 (July 1985); FO 371 56763 N14151, FO Minute, 4 May 1946. John Zametica, Three Letters to Bevin, in John Zametica (ed.), *British Officials and Foreign Policy 1945–50* (Leicester: Leicester University Press, 1990).
15. FO 371 53017 UE 2812/413/53 FO Minute, 28 June 1946.
16. FO 371 59507/104 Colville Minute, 5 June 1946.
17. FO 371 59473/196 FO Minute, 12 February 1946; 59474 R3851/106/92 Treasury brief (undated copy).
18. FO 371 9477 R 5956/196/92 Somerville-Smith minute, 10 April 1946.
19. FO 371 59477 R 5956/192/92 Somerville-Smith minute, 10 April 1946.
20. FO 371 53017 UE 2217/413/53 Bevin Minute, 20 May 1946; 59481 R 8676/196/92 Colville Minute, 6 June 1946; 48851/104 Maclean telegram to FO, 14 January 1945; *FRUS* 1945, vol. v, p. 1300.
21. FO 371 48854 R 14722/104/92 FO minute; 48854 R 15897/104/92 FO to Belgrade, 19 September 1945; 58556 R 20528/105/92 Stevenson telegram to FO, 5 December 1945; R 20601/105/92 Colville Minute, 11 Dcember 1945; 59478 R 7202/196/92 Leonard telegram to FO, 2 February 1946.
22. Byrnes, *Speaking Frankly*, p. 132.
23. Acheson, *Present at the Creation*, p. 196.
24. C. M. Woodhouse, *British Foreign Policy since the Second World War* (London, 1961), cited in Bullock, *Ernest Bevin*, p. 309.
25. John Young, *France and the Cold War 1944–49* (Leicester: Leicester University Press, 1990), pp. 95–6.
26. Dean Acheson, *Present at the Creation* (London, 1970), p. 194.
27. *FRUS* 1945, vol. ii, pp. 135–45 and 179–81; FO 371 48838 R 15014/24/92 Aide-mémoire from Yugoslav Ambassador, 3 September 1945.
28. *FRUS* 1945, vol. ii, pp. 248–53.
29. FO 371 59337 R 530/3/92 Colville Minute, 11 January 1946.

30. FO 371 59337 R 530/3/92 Williams Minute, 13 January 1946.
31. FO 371 59341 R 4171/3/92 Colville Minute, 20 March 1946; Hayter Minute, 26 March 1946.
32. FO 371 59341 R 4171/3/92, Jebb Minute, 20 April 1946.
33. FO 371 59341 R 4171/3/92 Colville Minute, 2 April 1946.
34. FO 371 59341 *ibid.*
35. FO 371 59343/3 *passim.*
36. FO 371 59568 R 6409 UK delegation brief, April 1946.
37. Byrnes, *Speaking Frankly*, pp. 133–4.
38. FO 371 59345 R 7409/3/92 Sargent Minute, 15 May 1946.
39. Acheson, *Present at the Creation*, p. 195.
40. Byrnes, *Speaking Frankly*, p. 147.
41. FO 371 59355 R 11263/3/92 Waldock letter to Williams, 29 July 1946; R 10761/3/92 Colville Minute, 22 July 1946.
42. FO 371 59360 R 12856/3/92 Colville Minute, 2 September 1946.
43. FO 371 59360 R 12856/3/92, *ibid.*
44. FO 800/552 YU/46/8 Belgrade telegram to FO, no. 906, 18 June 1946.
45. *Parl. Debs.* 427 HC debs. cols. 1676–7.
46. *FRUS* 1946, vol. iv, pp. 840–7; FO 371 59355 R 11264/3/92 Colville Minute, 31 July 1946.
47. FO 371 59359 R 12705/3/92 Brief no. 10 for Peake, 16 August 1946.
48. FO 800/552 PM/46/153 YU/46/14 Sargent to Prime Minister, 31 October 1946; COS/333/6, Ismay Minute, 30 October 1946.
49. FO 371 59494 R 16533/210/92 Brown Minute, 15 November 1946; FO 800/552 YU/46/20 Bevin telegram to FO, 25 November 1946; C. Bohlen, *Witness to History 1929–69* (New York: W.W. Norton, 1959), pp. 255–6.
50. Byrnes, *Speaking Frankly*, p. 153.
51. FO 371 67325 R 691/10/92 FO minute, 31 June 1946.
52. FO 371 67324 R 150/10/92 Creswell and Colville Minutes, 1 Janaury 1947; 67326 R 2430/10/92 Belgrade telegram, 11 February 1947.
53. Ann Lane, 'Putting Britain Right with Tito: the displaced persons question in Anglo-Yugoslav relations 1946–7', *European History Quarterly*, vol. 22, no. 2 (April 1992), pp. 217–46.
54. See above p. 75, note 76.
55. FO 371 57735 WR 3897/6/48 Policy document, 29 March 1943.
56. FO 371 48892 R 15090/329/92 FO minute, 12 September 1945; see also 47734 WR 3897/6/48 letter to Representatives in London on UNWCC, 17 August 1945; *FRUS* 1945, vol. v, pp. 1265–6.
57. FO 371 49499 R 1288/58/92 Sargent to Stapleton (Offices of the Cabinet), 27 January 1946.
58. Interview with Lord Mayhew, 1987.
59. FO 800/552 YU/46/1 M110/46 Attlee minute to Bevin, 29 March 1946.
60. FO 371 57710 WR 1414/6/48 CO (46)204 FO memorandum to Cabinet, 23 May 1946.
61. *FRUS* 1946, vol. iv, pp. 797–800.
62. CAB 128/19 minutes of Meeting of 30 May 1945.

63. FO 800 66601 WR 1070/1/48 Denis Allen letter to Rendel, 14 March 1947.
64. Lane, 'Putting Britain right with Tito', p. 229.
65. Among those spirited out of Yugoslavia by the Church was Ante Pavelic who had been hidden in a Franciscan monastery in Rome, evading all attempts by the British and American authorities to find him. In January 1946 he was put on a boat at Genoa and went from there to Bueneos Aires. See Lane, 'Putting Britain right with Tito', p. 229.
66. Robert E. Herzstein, *Waldheim: the missing years* (London, 1988), p. 164. See also US Army Intelligence Center, *History of the Counter Intelligence Corps*, esp. vol. xxvi, *The CIC and the Occupation of Germany*, and vol. xxv, *The Occupation of Austria and Italy* (Baltimore, 1959). See also Guenther Reinhardt, *Crime Without Punishment* (New York, 1952).
67. FO 371 67440 R 13091/1430/92 Yugoslav refugee problem: discussions between Brigadier Maclean and Marshal Tito on the Yugoslav refugee problem, communicated in a letter from Brigadier Maclean, 23 June 1947.
68. Fitzroy Maclean, Tito–Maclean talks of 1947–48. An account given in a contemporary letter written by Brigadier Maclean of his discussions with Marshal Tito on the Yugoslav refugee problem, September 1947, *South Slav Journal*, vol. 4 (Winter 1981–2).

6 A New Cold War Perspective: Tito's Separate Road

1. Djilas, *Rise and Fall*, p. 127.
2. *FRUS* 1947, vol. iii, pp. 319–20.
3. Quoted in J. P. D. Dunbabin, *The Cold War. The Great Powers and their allies* (London: Longman, 1994), pp. 93–4; Nikita Khrushchev, *Khrushchev Remembers*, vol. iii, pp. 88–100; see also William Taubman, *Stalin's American Policy*, pp. 135–9.
4. Gioliano Procacci, et al. (eds), *The Cominform: Minutes of the three Conferences 1947/1948/1949* (Milan: Feltirnelli, 1994), pp. 36–461.
5. Eugenio Reale, *Avec Jaques Duclos au Banc des Accuses a la reunion Constitutive du Kominform*, tr. P. Bonuzzi (Paris, 1960) *passim*.
6. See M. McCauley (ed.), *Communist Power in Europe, 1944–49* (London: Macmillan, 1977).
7. Peter Calvocoressi, *Survey of International Affairs 1947–48* (Oxford: Oxford University Press, 1953), pp. 147–68.
8. Translations of the various statements made by the Yugoslav communist party and the Cominform in June 1948, are published together with a translation of the six published letters between Stalin and Tito as *The Soviet-Yugoslav Dispute* (London: RIIA, 1948).
9. RIIA, *The Soviet-Yugoslav correspondence*, *ibid*.
10. Clissold, *Yugoslavia and the Soviet Union*, p. 51.
11. See in particular Ivo Banac, *With Stalin against Tito* (Cornell University Press, 1988), who accepts the claims of Tito that there was no ideological dispute and argues instead that the crisis in Soviet–Yugoslav relations can be traced to Yugoslav policy towards Greece. Geoffrey

Swain, while accepting the importance of the Greek issue in the origins of the dispute argues in 'The Cominform, Tito's International', *The Historical Journal*, vol. 35, no. 3 (1992) that there was indeed an ideological dispute in so far as it was Tito's determination to establish the popular front from below, that is he wanted a clear communist offensive in Europe, particularly in Greece, Italy and France which Tito wanted to lead. This theme is also developed by Charles Gati who suggests in 'The Democratic Interlude in Post-war Hungary: Eastern Europe before Cominform', *Survey*, vol. 28 (Summer 1984), pp. 99–134, that the Yugoslavs had been used as critics of the other European communist parties at the founding meeting of the Cominform in September 1947 in order to isolate them so that when, in 1948, Stalin called the Yugoslav leadership to account, they found themselves friendless among eager zealots keen to demonstrate their loyalty. This was how Stalin divided his rivals during the power struggles in the Soviet Union in the 1920.

12. Clissold, *Yugoslavia and the Soviet Union*, p. 165; Dunbabin, *The Cold War*, p. 409, note 7.
13. Hamilton Fish Armstrong, *Tito and Goliath* (London: Victor Gollancz, 1951), pp. 61–2; Koni Zilliacus, *Tito of Yugoslavia* (London: Michael Joseph, 1952), p. 227.
14. Dunbabin, *The Cold War*, p. 414; Clissold, *Yugoslavia and the Soviet Union*, pp. 194–7; Dedijer, *The Battle Stalin Lost*, p. 109.
15. Ulam, *Titoism and the Cominform*, p. 93ff; Dedijer, *Tito Speaks*, p. 323; Djilas, *Conversations with Stalin*, p. 155; see also FO 371 72162 R 1349/4/97 Moscow tel. 162, 29 January 1948.
16. See pp. 20–1 above.
17. See Elisabeth Barker, *Macedonia, Its place in Balkan Power Politics* (London, 1950).
18. Clissold, *Yugoslavia and the Soviet Union*, p. 105, note 160.
19. Clissold, *Yugoslavia and the Soviet Union*, p. 46.
20. Djilas, *Rise and Fall*, pp. 227–8.
21. Barker, *Macedonia*, p. 117.
22. Charles G. Stefan, 'The emergence of the Soviet-Yugoslav break: a personal view from the Belgrade Embassy', *Diplomatic History*, vol. 6, no. 4 (Fall 1982), p. 390.
23. The fullest account of this meeting is that by Djilas, *Conversations with Stalin*, pp. 156–68.
24. Clissold, *Yugoslavia and the Soviet Union*, p. 55.
25. D. Volkogonov, *Stalin: Triumph and Tragedy*, trans. Harold Shukman (London: Weidenfeld & Nicholson, 1991), p. 538.
26. FO 371 72579 R 7655/407/92 Belgrade tel. no. 656, 29 June 1948; 72578 R 1645/407/92 Sykes minute, 9 February 1948. Stefan, 'The emergence of the Soviet-Yugoslav break', p. 390.
27. FO 371 58566 R 10748/2124/7 F. A. Warner minute, 27 July 1946; see also 58520 R 9504/10/7.
28. See in particular Ivo Banac, *With Stalin against Tito*, see also David Close, *The Origins of the Civil War in Greece* (Longman, 1995).
29. L. S. Wittner, *American Intervention in Greece*, pp. 250–2.

30. Djilas, *Wartime*, p. 426.
31. Djilas, *Conversations with Stalin*, p. 161.
32. Dedijer, *The Battle Stalin Lost*, p. 105ff.
33. For a discussion of the role of ideology in the dispute see Swain, 'The Cominform: Tito's International'.
34. Djilas, *Tito. The Story from Inside*, p. 125; Dedijer, *Tito Speaks*, pp. 343–4; Stefan, 'Emergence of the Soviet–Yugoslav break', p. 397; Clissold, *Yugoslavia and the Soviet Union*, pp. 54–5, 197–8.
35. FO 371 72583 R 8197/407/92 FO minute, 1 July 1948.
36. FO 371 72578 R 5917/407/92 Peake telegram no. 477, 12 May 1948.
37. FO 371 72578 R 5912/407/92 Watson minute, 18 May 1948.
38. *FRUS* 1948, vol. iv, p. 1070. See also Stefan, 'The Emergence of the Soviet-Yugoslav Break'.
39. *FRUS* 1948, vol. iv, *ibid.*
40. FO 371 72579 R 7655/407/92 Belgrade tel. to FO, 29 June 1948.
41. *FRUS* 1948, vol. iv, pp. 1073–5.
42. *FRUS* 1948, vol. iv, p. 1073.
43. FO 371 72587 R 413/407/92 Brief concerning the Cominform Headquarters in Belgrade, 10 January 1948.
44. FO 371 77624 N 9737/1052/38 RC/147/49, Russia Committee minutes of 8 November 1948. Papers of Sir Charles Peake.
45. FO 371 72583 R 8197/407/92 FO minute, 1 July 1948.
46. Roy Medvedev, *Let History Judge* (New York: Alfred A. Knopf, 1971), p. 475.
47. FO 371 72583, *ibid.*
48. Bullock, *Ernest Bevin*, p. 599; FO 800/502 SU/48/8 PM/48/63 Bevin to Attlee, 28 July 1948.
49. DEFE 4/16 COS (18) 135, 24 September 1948; JIC (48) 81 (0) F. Report on the Tito–Cominform dispute.
50. *FRUS* 1948, vol. iv, pp. 1088–98.
51. *FRUS* 1948, *ibid.*, pp. 1076–7.
52. FO 371 72579 R 7657/407/92 Washington tel. no. 3207, 30 June 1948.
53. *FRUS* 1948, vol. iv, pp. 1070–81.
54. John Lewis Gaddis, *Strategies of Containment. A critical appraisal of postwar American National Security Policy* (Oxford: Oxford University Press, 1982), pp. 67–70.
55. *FRUS* 1948, vol. iv, pp. 1079–81.
56. FO 371 72584 R 8418/407/92 Watson minute, 17 July 1948; 72579 R 7055/407/92 tel. to Washington, 30 June 1948; *FRUS* 1948, vol. iv, p. 1078.
57. Gaddis, *Strategies of Containment*. See also Beatrice Heuser, *Western Containment Policies in the Cold War: the Yugoslav case 1948–53* (London: Routledge, 1989). FO 371 72196 R 10197/8476/179 FO Paper, 20 July 1948.
58. FO 371 71687 N 13016/761 RC/6/48.
59. FO 371 71632A N 13467/1052/38 RC/25/48 Russia Committee minutes, 14 December 1948.
60. FO 371 71632A N1727/1052/38 Russia Committee minutes, 15 Feb-

ruary 1949.

61. FO 371 78715 R 2260/10345/92 Bateman minute to Sargent, 19 February 1949; N 5326/1052/38 RC/54/49 Russia Committee minutes, 10 June 1949.
62. FO 371 71632A N 2694/1952/38 Russia Committee minutes, 15 March 1949.
63. FO 371 78715 R 2160/10345/92 Wallinger minute, 17 February 1949.
64. Nicholas Bethell, *The Last Betrayal. The Untold Story of Kim Philby's Biggest Coup* (London: Hodder & Stoughton, 1984), p. 33.
65. Verne Newton, *The Butcher's Embrace. The Philby Conspirators in Washington* (London: Macdonald & Co., 1991), p. 248; Anthony Verrier, *Through the Looking Glass. British Foreign Policy in an Age of Illusions* (London: Jonathan Cape, 1983).

7 Limited Commitments: Keeping Tito Afloat, 1948–1949

1. FO 371 72580 R 7786/407/92 Belgrade tel. to FO, 30 June 1948.
2. *Khrushchev Remembers*, vol. i, p. 544.
3. FO 371 77624 N 9737/1052/38 Russia Committee Minutes, RC/147/49, 8 November 1949.
4. Djilas, *Rise and Fall*, pp. 235–6.
5. FO 371 72582 R 8163/407/9 Wallinger letter to Sappington, 10 July 1948.
6. FO 371 72582 R 8050/407/92 Sykes Minute, 8 July 1948; Belgrade tel. no. 698, 5 July 1948.
7. Jelavich, *History of the Balkans*, vol. ii, pp. 326–7; Clissold, *Yugoslavia and the Soviet Union*, pp. 213–14.
8. FO 371 72580 R 7861/407/92 Washington tel. no. 3275; 72582 R 8163/407/92 Sappington (London: US Embassy) letter to Wallinger, 8 July 1948; *FRUS 1948, ibid.*, p. 1084.
9. FO 371 72582 *ibid.*, Wallinger letter to Sappington, 10 July 1948.
10. FO 371 72583 R 8234/407/92 Rob minute, 7 July 1948, Wallinger minute (undated).
11. *FRUS* 1948, vol. iv, pp. 1088 and 1092.
12. Inernationalisation of the Danube is discussed by T. G. Patterson in 'Eastern Europe and the early Cold War: the Danube Controversy', in *The Historian* (1983), pp. 237–47. For a contemporary account see J. C. Campbell, 'Diplomacy on the Danube', *Foreign Affairs* (January 1949).
13. FO 371 70230 W 3913/676/803 Stewart minute, 15 June 1948; Freese–Pennefather minute, 18 June 1948.
14. FO 371 50404 W 4028/142/803 Cheetham minute 26 March 1948; *FRUS* 1948, vol. iv, pp. 1100–92.
15. FO 371 70231 W 4421/676/803 Stanley–Fordham minute, 28 July 1948.
16. *FRUS* 1948, vol. iv, pp. 1100–2; FO 371 72586 R 9206/407/92, and see pp. 107–8 above.
17. FO 371 72591 R 14134/407/92 FO minute, 6 December 1948.

18. *FRUS* 1948, vol. iv, pp. 1106–10; FR 371 72589 R 10968/407/92 Wallinger minute, 22/9/48.
19. See p. 89 above.
20. FO 3671 72554 R 1341/9/42 Trevelyan Minute, 23 January 1948.
21. FO 371 72555 R 5134/9/42 Belgrade telegram no. 399, 22 April 1948.
22. FO 371 72555 R 5231/9/42 Belgrade telegram no. 407, 26 April 1948.
23. FO 371 72555 R 5851/9/42 Sykes minute, 12 May 1948.
24. *FRUS* 1948, vol. iv, pp. 1058–63.
25. *FRUS* 1948, *ibid.*, p. 1093 Editorial note.
26. Department of State, *Bulletin*, pp. 137–40, 1 August 1948.
27. *FRUS* 1948, vol. iv, pp. 1084–5.
28. *FRUS* 1948, *ibid.*, pp. 1085–7.
29. *FRUS* 1948, *ibid.*, pp. 1088–92.
30. *FRUS* 1948, *ibid.*, p. 1088.
31. Lorraine M. Lees, 'The American decision to assist Tito', *Diplomatic History*, vol. 2, no. 4 (Fall 1978), p. 409.
32. *FRUS* 1948, vol. iv, pp. 1092–3.
33. *FRUS* 1948, *ibid.*, pp. 1097–8.
34. *FRUS* 1948, *ibid.*, pp. 1092–3; 1099.
35. *FRUS* 1948, *ibid.*, p. 1099.
36. FO 371 72556 R 8046/9/42 Wallinger Minute, 2 July 1948.
37. FO 371 72556 R 8550/9/42 Watson minute, 8 July 1948.
38. FO 371 72556 R 8609/9/42 Wallinger minute, 17 July 1948; Bevin minute (undated).
39. FO 371 72556 R 8046/9/42 Campbell minute, 2 July 1948.
40. FO 371 72556 *ibid.*, Wallinger minute, 2 July 1948.
41. FO 371 72556 *ibid.*, Sargent minute, (undated).
42. See above pp. 127–8
43. FO 371 72557 R 10352/9/42 Wallinger letter to Stacy (Board of Trade), 7 September 1948.
44. FO 371 72557 R 11655/9/42 FO minute; 72558 R 11904/9/42 Wallinger minutes, 12 and 13 October 1948.
45. F0 371 87830 R 1585/1153/92 Bevin's reply in House of Commons, 9 February 1949.
46. FO 371 72557 R 11760/9/42 Wallinger minute, 21 October 1948.
47. FO 371 72557 R 11760/9/42 Wallinger minute, 21 October 1948.
48. FO 371 72557 *ibid.*
49. *FRUS* 1948, vol. iv., pp. 1105–6; FO 371 71924 UR 5268/1844 OEEC Paris (UK delegation) telegram no. 554, 15 September 1948.
50. *FRUS* 1948, *ibid.*, pp. 1098–9.
51. *FRUS* 1948, *ibid.*, pp, 1105–6.
52. *FRUS* 1948, *ibid.*
53. *FRUS* 1948, *ibid.*, p. 1106.
54. *FRUS* 1948, *ibid.*, pp. 1106–10.
55. *FRUS* 1948, *ibid.*, pp. 489–98.
56. FO 371 71925 UR 6545/1841 *op. cit.*, *FRUS* 1948, vol. iv, pp. 527–8.
57. *FRUS* 1948, vol. iv, pp. 536–42.

58. *FRUS* 1948, vol. iv., pp. 562–3; FO 371 71923 UR 4183/1841 Makins minute, 16 August 1948.
59. FO 371 71924 UR 6508/1841 McDermott minute for Secretary of State, 13 October 1948.
60. FO 371 71925 UR 6747/1841 FO telegram to UK delegation to OEEC Paris, 27 October 1948; UR 6929/1841 Record of meeting held by Secretary of State, 23 October 1948.
61. FO 371 77789 UR 411/45/98 UK paper, 14 January 1949.
62. FO 371 77793 UR 2609/1841 Rob brief for Secretary of State, 14 March 1949; EPC (48) 8th meeting.
63. FO 371 77790 UR 1128/45/98 FO minute, 2 February 1949.
64. FO 371 71924 UR 5565/1841/98 Welch letter to Rowan, 17 September 1948.
65. *FRUS* 1948, *ibid.*, pp. 585–8.
66. FO 371 78729 R 305/1152 FO paper, 6 January 1949.
67. FO 371 78729 *ibid.*
68. FO 371 78729 *ibid.*
69. FO 371 77792 UR 1963/45/98 FO paper.
70. *FRUS*, 1949, vol. v, pp. 854–6.
71. *FRUS*, 1949, *ibid.*, p. 856.
72. *FRUS*, 1949, *ibid.*, pp. 866–9.
73. FO 371 77792 UR 1962/45/98 Henniker minute, 25 February 1949.
74. FO 371 77791 FO paper prepared for under-secretaries meeting, 'Economic relations between the United States and Yugoslavia', 14 February 1949.
75. FO 371 78729 R 305/1152 FO paper, 'Yugoslavia', 6 January 1949.
76. FO 371 77792 UR 1963/45/98 FO paper.
77. FO 371 78731 R 2184/1153 Draft brief, 23 February 1949.
78. FO 371 78732 R 2540/1153 Belgrade telegram no. 169, 5 March 1949.
79. FO 371 78733 R 3055/1153 FO tel. 250 to Belgrade, 17 March 1949; Wallinger minute, 7 March 1949; 78735 R 3475/1153 Morland memorandum, 29 March 1949; R 3750/1153 FO telegram no. 347 to Belgrade.
80. See p. 2 above.
81. FO 800/468/GRE/48/2 Alexander to Bevin, 11 February 1948. See also Alan Bullock, *Ernest Bevin*, p. 598.
82. FO 371 72196R 10197/8476/679 FO paper, 'Review of the European Situation', 20 July 1948.
83. Interview with Sir Fitzroy Maclean, London, Spring 1988; FO 371 78769/1634 *passim*; 78739 R 4828/1153 Campbell minute, 12 May 1949.
84. FO 371 78741 R 5994/1153 Minutes by Campbell and Rumbold, 21 June 1949; 78743 R 6516/1153 Washington tel. no. 3186, 1 July 1949.
85. L. S. Wittner, *American Intervention in Greece, 1943–49* (New York: Columbia University Press, 1982), pp. 250–2.
86. FO 371 78741 R 5530/1153 Brief for McNeil, May 1949; R 5950/1153 Morland minute, 14 June 1949.
87. FO 371 78744 R 6933/1153 Campbell minute, 19 July 1949.

88. FO 371 78747 R 8232/1153 Talbot minute, 24 August 1949; R 8443/1153 Wilson to Attlee, 29 August 1949.
89. FO 371 78747 R 82232/1153 Talbot minute, 25 August 1949; R 8443/1153 Wilson minute to Attlee, 25 August 1949.
90. M. Charlton, *The Eagle and the Small Birds* (London: BBC, 1984), p. 78 cited in Dunbabin, *The Cold War*, p. 415.

8 Trieste: Frontier Making in Cold War Europe

1. FO 371 67331 R 4743/19/92 Warner minute, 3 January 1947.
2. FO 371 67331 *ibid.*
3. FO 371 67331 R 4188/10/92 tel. to Washington, no. 3163, 1 January 1947.
4. FO 371 67331 R 4767/10/92 Warner minute, 10 April 1947.
5. FO 371 67332 R 5276/10/92 Warner minute, 22 April 1947.
6. FO 371 67339 R 9740/10/92 Warner minute, 18 July 1947.
7. FO 371 67339 R 9322/10/92 FO minute for Bevin, 16 July 1947.
8. FO 371 67341 R 12626/10/92 FO minute for Bevin, 11 September 1947; 67342 R 12495/10/92 Washington telegram no. 5010, 18 September 1947; *FRUS* 1947, vol. iv, pp. 95–6.
9. FO 371 67342 R 12797/10/92 Anderson minute, 16 July 1947; *FRUS* 1947, vol. iv, pp. 98–9.
10. FO 371 67342 R 12837/10/92 Trieste (Political Adviser) tel. to FO, no. 291, 18 September 1947.
11. FO 371 67342 *ibid.*
12. *FRUS* 1947, vol. iv, pp. 108–10.
13. FO 371 67343 R 13153/10/92 Warner minute, 30 September 1947.
14. Bogdan Novak, *Trieste, 1941–54*, pp. 259–67.
15. FO 371 67344 R 14290/10/92 FO minute, 16 October 1947.
16. FO 371 59359 R 12705/10/92 Brief no. 10, 'Viability of Free Territory of Trieste', for Peake, 16 August 1947; 67344 R 14290/10/92 FO minute 16 October 1947; 72482 R 380/44/70.
17. FO 371 67344 R 14290/10/92 FO minute, 16 October 1947.
18. FO 371 67344, *ibid.*
19. FO 371 67344, *ibid.*
20. FO 371 67342 R 13109/10/92 FO tel. to New York, no. 3198, 26 September 1947; *FRUS* 1947, vol. iv, p. 102.
21. FO 371 67344 R 14717/10/92 FO minute, 24 October 1947.
22. FO 371 67344 R 14290/10/92 *ibid.*
23. DEFE 5/10 COS (48) 74 (0) 6 April 1948.
24. DEFE 5/11 COS (48) 156 (0), 19 July 1948: 'The role of British troops in Austria and Trieste in an emergency', Note by CIGS.
25. FO 371 67346 R 17007/10/92 Watson minute, 28 November 1947.
26. FO 371 67344 R 14717/10/92 Washington tel. to FO, no. 6159, 3 November 1947; 67345 R 15229/10/92 FO minute (top secret).
27. FO 371 72482 R 44/44/70 FO minute, 29 December 1947.
28. FO 371 72482 *ibid.*
29. FO 371 67471 R 15893/10882/92 FO tel. to Washington, no. 2357, 29

November 1947; 67346 R 16582/10/92 Washington tel. to FO; 67479 R 16584/14063/92.

30. FO 371 72482 R 139/44/70 FO tel. no. 11 to Washington, 1 January 1948.
31. FO 371 72482 *ibid.*, FO tel. no. 33 to Washington, 1 January 1948.
32. FO 371 72482 R 155/44/70 Bateman letter to Balfour, 13 January 1948.
33. See above p. 152.
34. FO 371 72483 R 703/44/70 FO tel. no. 231 to New York, 17 January 1948 and tel. 631 to Washington, 13 Janaury 1948; 72484 R 1519/44/70 FO minute, 8 January 1948.
35. FO 371 72483 R 1286/44/70 FO tel. 398 to New York, 29 January 1948.
36. FO 371 72483 *ibid.*
37. FO 371 72483 *ibid.*, Wallinger minute, 30 January 1948.
38. FO 371 72485 R 3665//44/70 Wallinger minute, 8 March 1948; Washington tel. 1080, 6 March 1948; 72487 R 3606/44/70 FO minute 13 March 1948; *FRUS*, 1948, vol. iii, p. 513, note 1.
39. FO 371 72487 *ibid.*
40. *FRUS* 1948, vol. iii, p. 514.
41. *FRUS* 1948, *ibid.*, pp. 515–16; Department of State, *Bulletin*, vol. 18, p. 425. Young, *France and the Cold War*, p. 187.
42. Anthony Eden, *Full Circle. The memoirs of Anthony Eden* (Boston, 1960), pp. 198–9.
43. Alberto Tarchiani, *Dieci anni tra Roma e Washington* (Verona, 1955), p. 143, cited in Novak, *Trieste 1941–54*, p. 282.
44. FO 371 72487 R 3735/44/70 Rome tel. 538 to FO, 21 March 1948.
45. FO 371 72487 R 3799/44/70 Washington tel. 1380 to FO.
46. FO 371 72489 R 4555/44/70 Wallinger Minutes, 2 and 8 April 1948.
47. FO 371 72489 R 4707/44/70 FO tel. 4143 to Washington, 14 March 1948; 72493 R 7051/44/70 Wallinger minute, 3 June 1948.
48. FO 371 72491 R 5153/44/70 Watson minute, 30 April 1948.
49. FO 371 72493 R 7051/44/70 Wallinger minute.
50. FO 371 72495 R 8416/44/70 Campbell minute, 5 July 1948.
51. FO 371 72523 R 8867/44/70 New York tel. no. 130 to FO, 28 July 1948.
52. FO 371 72496 R 9945/44/70 Campbell minute, 22 August 1948.
53. FO 371 72525 R 18220/8867/76 FO minute, 20 November 1948.
54. *FRUS* 1949, vol. iv, pp. 498–99, Editorial note; FO 371 72525 *ibid.*
55. FO 371 78636 R 1593/10111 Campbell minute, 11 February 1949.
56. FO 371 78636 *ibid.*, Talbot minute, 11 February 1949; R 1635/10111 Washington tel. 845 to FO, 11 February 1949; Wallinger minute, 14 February 1949.
57. FO 371 78636 R 1932/10111 Campbell minute, 21 March 1949; FRUS 1949, vol. iv, pp. 499–500.
58. Fo 371 78638 R 6479/10111 Belgrade tel. 554 to FO, 8 July 1949.
59. FO 371 78638 R 6072/10111 Belgrade tel. 516 to FO, 20 June 1949.
60. FO 371 78649 R 6736/10111 Rumbold minute, 9 July 1949; R 6572/10111 Campbell minute, 6 July 1949.

61. FO 371 78649 R 6572/10111 Rumbold minute, *op. cit.*
62. FO 371 78649 *ibid.*
63. Fo 371 78639 R 8152/10111 Campbell minute, 22 August 1949.
64. *FRUS* 1949, vol. iv, p. 515, note 1.
65. FO 371 78639 R 8235/10111.
66. *FRUS* 1949, vol. iv, pp. 522–4.
67. *Ibid.*
68. J. Wheeler Bennett and A. Nicholls, *The Semblance of Peace*, pp. 448–50 and note p. 450. See also, J. C. Campbell (ed.), *Successful Negotiation Trieste 1954* (New Jersey: Princeton University Press, 1976).

9 The Cold War and Yugoslav Unity

1. Gabriel Partos, *The World that Came in From the Cold* (RIIA, 1993), pp. 21–2.
2. Bela Kiraly, 'The aborted Soviet Military Plans against Tito's Yugoslavia', in Wayne S. Vucinich (ed.), *At the Brink of War and Peace: the Tito–Stalin Split in a Historic Perspective* (New York: Brooklyn & Mega Press, 1992), pp. 273–88; Partos, *The World that Came in From the Cold.*
3. Acheson, *Present at the Creation*, p. 333.
4. Acheson, *Present at the Creation*, *ibid.*; Djilas, *Rise and Fall*, pp. 273–4; Larson, *US Policy towards Yugoslavia*, pp. 240–1.
5. Christopher Cviic, *Remaking the Balkans*, 2nd edn (London: Pinter, 1995).
6. Pavlowitch, *Yugoslavia. The Improbable Survivor*, p. 41.
7. Maclean, *Eastern Approaches*, p. 341.
8. Djilas, *Tito The Story from Inside*, p. 332.
9. Jelavich, *History of the Balkans*, vol. ii, p. 328.

Bibliography

AFHQ	Allied Forces Headquarters, Mediterranean
AMG	Allied Military Government
AVNOJ	Anti-Fascist Council of National Liberation
BBC	British Broadcasting Corporation
CCS	Combined Chiefs of Staff
CFM	Council of Foreign Ministers
CIGS	Chief of Imperial General Staff
Cominform	Communist Information Bureau
Comintern	Communist International
COS	Chiefs of Staff
ECA	Economic Co-operation Administration
ECGD	Export, Credits and Guarantees Department
ERD	Economic Relations Department
ERP	European Recovery Programme
EAM	Ethnikon Apeleftheretikon Metopon (Greek National Liberation Front)
FPRY	Federal People's Republic of Yugoslavia
FTT	Free Territory of Trieste
GCCS	Government Code and Cipher School
HSS	Hrvatska seljacka stranka (Croat Peasant Party)
JIC	Joint Intelligence Sub-committee
JVO	Jugoslovenska vojska u otadzbini (Yugoslav Home Army)
KPJ	Kommunisticka partija Jugolsavije (Communist Party of Yugoslavia)
MEDC	Middle East Defence Committee
NDH	Nezavisna Drzava Hrvatska (Independent State of Croatia)
NKVD	Narodnyi Kommissariat vnutrennikh del (People's Commissariat for International Affairs)
NOP	Narodnooslobo-dilacki pokret (People's Liberation Movement)
NSC	National Security Council

OEEC	Organisation of European Economic Co-operation
OSS	Office of Strategic Services
PCI	Communist Party of Italy
PPS	Policy Planning Staff (US)
SACMED	Supreme Allied commander, Mediterranean Theatre
SIS	Secret Intelligence Service, also referred to as MI6
SOE	Special Operations Executive
Tass	Telegrafnoe agentstvo Svoetskogo Soviza (Telegraph Agency of Soviet Union)
UDBa	Yugoslav state security service
UNRRA	United Nations Relief and Rehabilitation Administration
UNGA	United Nations General Assembly
UNSC	United Nations Security Council

Archives

I Public Record Office, Kew, London

Board of Trade

BT 60	Department of Overseas Trade. Corresp. & papers 1943–46
BT 225	Export Promotion Department Files, 1945–50
BT 241	Commercial relations and export division policy files

Cabinet Office

CAB 78	War Cabinet committee miscellaneous and general series, 1941–47
CAB 79	Minutes of the Combined Chiefs of Staff
CAB 80	Memoranda of the Combined Chiefs of Staff
CAB 84	Minutes of the Joint Planning Committee
CAB 128	Cabinet Minutes 1945–50
CAB 129	Cabinet Memoranda 1945–50

Foreign Office

FO 371	General Correspondence
FO 536	Embassy and Consular archives: Yugoslavia Correspondence
FO 800	Private Collections. Various ministers and officials files
FO 934	Potsdam Conference
FO 954	Avon Papers
FO 1007	Allied Commission, Austria

Ministry of Defence

DEFE 4	Minutes of the Chiefs of Staff
DEFE 5	Memoranda of the Chiefs of Staff
DEFE 11	Chiefs of Staff Committee files

Prime Ministers' Official Papers

PREM 3	Operations papers
PREM 4	Confidential papers
PREM 7	Private Collections
PREM 8	Correspondence and papers

War Office

WO 201	Military Headquarters Papers: Middle East Papers
WO 202	Military Headquarters Papers: Military Mission
WO 204	Allied Forces Headquarters papers
WO 216	Chief of Imperial General Staff papers
WO 259	Private Office papers, Secretary of State
WO 263	Quarterly Historical Reports, British Zone, Austria
WO 264	Quarterly Historical Reports, British Zone, Trieste

II National Archives and Records Centre, Washington DC

Record Group (RG) 226 Records of the Office of Strategic Services

III Private papers

Sir Charles Peake; Ernest Davies

Interviews

Sir William Deakin; Sir Fitzroy Maclean; Lady Peake; David Floyd; Lord Mayhew; Sir Denis Wright

Published documents

German

Documents on German Foreign Policy, 1918–1945, Series D, abbreviated in notes as DGFP

Soviet Union

Sovetckii soyuz na mezhdunarodnykh konferentsiyakh perioda velikoi otechestvennoi voiny, 1941–1945 gg. Sbornik dokumentov, 6 vols, Izdatel'stvo politicheskoi literatury, Moscow, 1978–79, abbreviated in notes as SSNMK

Correspondence between the Chairman of the Council of Ministers of the USSR and the Presidents of the USA and the Prime Ministers of Great Britain during the Great Patriotic War of 1941–45, 2 volumes, Moscow, 1957.

Soviet Foreign Policy during the Great patriotic War, Moscow, 1946.

United Kingdom
Allied Military Government, *Trieste 1945–46, 1947, 1948–49.*
Allied Military Government, *Venezia Giulia, September 1945–September 1947.*
Basic Handbook, *Yugoslavia.*
British Foreign and State Papers, London, 1941–1977, cited in notes as *BFSP*.
E. L. Woodward *et al.* (ed.) *Documents on British Foreign Policy, 1939–1945*, London: HMSO, 1949 ff, 1949–1985, abbreviated in notes as *DBFP*.
Rohan Butler *et al.* (ed.) *Documents on British Policy Overseas*, Series I, London: HMSO, 1984– , abbreviated in notes as *DBPO*.
Parliamentary Papers (Hansard) 1945.
Royal Institute of International Affairs, *The Soviet-Yugoslav dispute. Text of the published correspondence*, London, 1948.

United States
Department of State, *Bulletin*, USGPO.
Department of State, *Foreign Relations of the United States. Diplomatic Papers*, vols for 1942–1950, USGPO: Washington, 1965–1980, abbreviated in notes as *FRUS*.
United Nations, *Official Records of the Security Council, New York, 1946–1949*, abbreviated in notes as *UNSC*.

Memoirs

Dean Acheson, *Present at the Creation: My years at the State Department*, New York: W. W. Norton, 1969.
Svetlana Allilueva, *Twenty Letters to a Friend*, trans. Priscilla Johnson Macmillan, New York: Harper & Row, 1967.
Julian Amery, *Approach March*, London: Hutchinson, 1973.
Sir Roderick Barclay, *Ernest Bevin and the Foreign Office 1932–69*, Great White End: Latimer, 1975.
Charles E. Bohlen with Robert H. Phelps, *Witness to History 1929–1969*, New York: W. W. Norton, 1973.
James Byrnes, *Speaking Frankly*, New York: Harper & Row, 1948.
——, *All In One Lifetime*, New York, Harper & Row, 1956.
Alexander Cadogan, *The Diaries of Sir Alexander Cadogan*, ed. David Dilks, London: Cassell, 1971.
John C. Campbell (ed.), *Successful Negotiation, Trieste, 1954. An appraisal by the five participants*, New Jersey: Princeton University Press, 1976.
Georges Catroux, *J'ai vu tomber le Rideau de Fer – Moscou 1945–1948, Recits et Souvenirs*, Paris: Hachette, 1952.
Winston Churchill, *The Second World War*, 6 vols, London: Cassell, 1948–54.
R. Colakovic, *Winning Freedom*, London: Lincolns-Praeger, 1962.
John Colville, *The Fringes of Power. Downing Street Diaries*, London: Hodder & Stoughton, 1985.
Basil Davidson, *Special Operations Europe. Scenes from the anti-nazi war*, London: Gollancz, 1980.
Vladimir Dedijer, *The Battle Stalin lost. A Memoir of Yugoslavia, 1948–1953*, New York: Grosset & Dunlap, 1971.

——, *With Tito through the war. The Partisan Diary 1941–44*, London: Alexander Hamilton, 1951.
F. W. D. Deakin, *The Embattled Mountain*, London: Oxford University Press, 1971.
Milovan Djilas, *Conversations with Stalin*, trans. Michael B. Petrovich, London: Hart-Davis, 1962.
——, *Wartime. With Tito and the Partisans*, London: Secker and Warburg, 1980.
——, *Tito. The Story from Inside*, trans. Vasilije Kojic and Richard Hayes, London, 1981.
Anthony Eden, *The Reckoning*, London: Cassell, 1965.
——, *Full Circle*, London: Cassell, 1960.
Lord Gladwyn, *The Memoirs of Lord Gladwyn*, London: Weidenfeld & Nicolson, 1972.
Alexander Glen, *Foothold against a Whirlwind*, London: Hutchinson, 1975.
Andrei A. Gromyko, *Pamyatnoe*, 2 vols, Moscow: politizdat, 1988, trans. Harold Shukman as *Memories*, London: Hutchinson, 1989.
W. Averell Harriman and Elie Abel, *Special Envoy to Churchill and Stalin, 1941–46*, New York: Random House, 1975.
William G. Hayter, *A Double Life*, London: Hamish Hamilton, 1974.
Edward Kardelj, *Reminiscences: the struggle for recognition and independence – the new Yugoslavia, 1944–1977*, London: Blonds & Briggs, Summerfield Press, 1982.
George F. Kennan, *Memoirs, 1925–1950*, Boston: Little, Brown, 1967.
Michael Lees, *The Rape of Serbia: the British role in Tito's grab for power*, San Diego: Harcourt Brace Jovanovich, 1990.
Franklin Lindsay, *Beacons in the Night. With the OSS and Tito's Partisans in wartime Yugoslavia*, Stanford: Stanford University Press, 1993.
Fitzroy Maclean, *Eastern Approaches*, London: Jonathan Cape, 1949.
Harold Macmillan, *The Blast of War 1939–45*, London: Macmillan, 1967.
Rene Massigli, *Une Comedie des Erreurs, 1943–1956*, Paris: Plon, 1978.
Eugenio Reale, The Founding of the Cominform, in Milorad M. Drachkovitch and Brankko Lazitch (eds), *The Comintern: Historical highlights*, New York: Praeger for the Hoover Institute, 1966.
George Rendel, *The Sword and the Olive*, London: Murray, 1957.
Frank Roberts, *Dealing with Dictators. The destruction and revival of Europe, 1930–70*, London: Weidenfeld & Nicolson, 1991.
Walter Bedell Smith, *Moscow Mission, 1946–49*, London: Heinemann, 1950.
Bickham Sweet-Escott, *Baker Street Irregular*, London: Methuen, 1965.
Charles Thayer, *Hands across the caviar*, London: Michael Joseph, 1953.
Josip Broz Tito, *Le Front Populaire*, Paris: Eds. Sociales, May 1948.
Harry S. Truman, *Year of Decisions, 1945*, Garden City, NY: Doubleday, 1955.
Svetozar Vukmanovic (Tempo), *How and Why the People's Liberation Struggle of Greece met with defeat*, London: Merlin, 1975.

Secondary sources

G. M. Alexander, *Prelude to the Truman Doctrine: British Policy in Greece, 1944–47*, Oxford: Clarendon, 1982.

T. H. Anderson, *The United States, Great Britain and the Cold War, 1944–1947*, Columbia: University of Missouri Press, 1981.

Christopher Andrew, *Secret Service: the making of the British Intelligence Community*, London: Heinemann, 1985.

Hannah Arendt, *The Origins of Totalitarianism*, 3rd edn, New York, 1966.

Drago Arsenkjevic, *Un Voyage Oublié*, ed, France Empire, Paris, 1976.

Phyllis Auty, *Tito. A biography*, London: Longman Group, 1970.

Phyllis Auty and Richard Clogg (eds), *British Policy towards wartime resistance in Yugoslavia and Greece*, London: Macmillan for the School of Slavonic and East European Studies, 1975.

Lars Baerentzen, John Iatrides and Ole Smith (eds), *Studies in the History of the Greek Civil War, 1945–49*, Copenhagen: Tusculanum Press, 1987.

Ivo Banac, *The National Question in Yugoslavia. Origins, history, politics*, Ithaca, New York: Cornell University Press, 1984.

——, *With Stalin against Tito: Cominformist splits in Yugoslav communism*, Ithaca, New York: Cornell University Press, 1988.

Elisabeth Barker, *British Policy in South East Europe during the Second World War*, London: Macmillan, 1976.

——, *Churchill and Eden at War*, London: Macmillan, 1978.

——, *Macedonia: its place in Balkan power politics*, London and New York: RIIA, 1950.

——, *Britain between the Superpowers, 1945–1950*, London: Macmillan, 1986.

Robert Bass and Elizabeth Marbury (eds), *The Soviet-Yugoslav controversy: a documentary record*, New York: Prospect Books for the east European Institute, 1952.

Nora Beloff, *Tito's Flawed Legacy: Yugoslavia and the West, 1939–84*, London: Gollancz, 1985.

Nicholas Bethell, *The Minister and the Massacres*, London, 1986.

——, *The Last Betrayal. The Untold Story of Kim Philby's Biggest Coup*, London: Hodder & Stoughton, 1984.

F. Borkenau, *European Communism*, London, 1953.

Zbigniew Brzezinski, *The Soviet Bloc: unity and conflict*, Cambridge, MA: Harvard University Press, 1967.

Alan Bullock, *Ernest Bevin, Foreign Secretary*, London: Heinemann, 1983.

J. R. M. Butler, *History of the second World War*, UK Military Series, 6 vols, London: HMSO, 1956.

R. N. Carew Hunt, *The theory and practice of communism*, Penguin, edn, 1963.

Michael Charlton, *The Eagle and the small birds*, London: BBC, 1984.

Henry M. Christman (ed.), *The Essential Tito*, Newton Abbot, Devon: David & Charles, 1971.

Anton Ciliga, *La Yougoslavie sous la Menace Interieure et Exterieure*, Paris: Iles d'Or, 1951.

Stephen Clissold (ed.), *Yugoslavia and the Soviet Union, 1939–1973. A documentary survey*, London: Oxford University Press for RIIA, 1975.

Robert Conquest, *Stalin. Breaker of Nations*, London: Wiedenfeld & Nicholson, 1991.

Geoffrey Cox, *The Race for Trieste*, London, 1977.

Christopher Cviic, *Remaking the Balkans*, 2nd edn, London: Pinter for RIIA, 1995.

Robert Dallek, *Franklin D. Roosevelt and American Foreign policy, 1932–45*, New York: Oxford University Press, paperback 1981, first published 1979.

Louis Dalmas, *Le Communisme Yougoslave depuis la Rupture avec Moscou*, Paris: Terre Des Hommes, 1950.

Peter Danylow, *Der Aussenpolitischen Beziehungen Albaniens zu Jugoslawien und zur USSR, 1944–61*, Munich: Oldenbourg Verlag, 1982.

William Deakin, Elisabeth Barker and Jonathan Chadwick, *British political and military strategy in central, eastern and southern Europe in 1944*, London: Macmillan, 1988.

Diego De Castro, *La Questione di Trieste: l'Azione Politica e Diplomatica Italiana dal 1943 al 1954*, 2 vols, Trieste: Lint, 1982.

Michael Deroc, *Special Operations Explored. Yugoslavia in Turmoil 1941–43 and the British Response*, Boulder, Colorado: East European Monographs, 1988.

Aleksa Djilas, *The Contested Country. Yugoslav unity and the communist revolution, 1919–53*, Cambridge, MA: Harvard University Press, 1991.

Milovan Djilas, *The New Class. An analysis of the Communist system*, London: George Allen & Unwin, 1957.

Milovan Djilas, *Rise and Fall*, Vlast, 1985.

Dominique Desanti, *Les Staliniens, 1944–1956, une Expérience Politique*, Paris: Antheme Fayard, 1975.

Isaac Deutscher, *Stalin: a political biography*, Harmondsworth, Pelican Books, 1966; first published by Oxford University Press, 1949.

Veselin Djurdjevac, *La Yougoslavie: Socialisme et Non-alignment*, Paris: le Sycomore, 1983.

Robert J. Donovan, *Conflict and Crisis: the presidency of Harry S. Truman 1945–48*, New York: W. W. Norton, 1977.

Roy Douglas, *From War to Cold War 1941–1948*, London: Macmillan, 1981.

Jean Baptiste Duroselle, *Le Conflict de Trieste, 1943–1954*, Brussels: Eds. de l'Institute de Sociologie de l'Université Libre de Bruxelles, 1966.

Robin Edmonds, *The Big Three, Churchill, Roosevelt and Stalin in Peace and War*, London: Hamish Hamilton, 1991.

——, *Setting the Mould: the United States and Britain 1945–50*, Oxford: Clarendon, 1986.

John Erickson, *The Road to Berlin. Stalin's War with Germany*, London: Harper & Row, 1981.

Thomas H. Etzold & John Lewis Gaddis, *Containment: documents on American policy and strategy, 1945–50*, New York: Cambridge University Press, 1978.

R. Barry Farrell, *Jugoslavia and the Soviet Union, 1948–1956. An analysis with documents*, Hamden Ct: Shoestring Press, 1956.

Herbert Feis, *Churchill, Roosevelt, Stalin: the war they waged and the peace they sought* Princeton, NJ: Princeton University Press, 1957.

——, *From Trust to Terror. The onset of the Cold War*, Princeton, NJ: Princeton University Press, 1970.

Louis Fischer, *The Road to Yalta: Soviet foreign relations 1941–1945*, New York: Harper & Row, 1972.

M. R. D. Foot, *Special Operations Executive, 1940–1946*, London: BBC, 1984.

William T. R. Fox, *The Superpowers: the United States, Britain and the Soviet Union - their responsibility for peace*, Harcourt, Brace: Yale University Institute of International Studies, 1944.

John Lewis Gaddis, *The United States and the Origins of the Cold War, 1941–47*, New York: Columbia University Press, 1972.

——, *Strategies of Containment – a critical reappraisal of post-war American National Security Policy*, New York: Oxford University Press, 1982.

A. A. Gromyko and B. N. Ponomarev (eds), *Soviet Foreign Policy 1945–1980*, 2 vols, Moscow: Progres, 1981.

Thomas T. Hammond (ed.), *The Anatomy of communist Takeovers*, New Haven: Yale University Press, 1975.

Frazer J. Harbutt, *The Iron Curtain: Churchill, America and the origins of the Cold War*, New York & Oxford: Oxford University Press, 1986.

John L. Harper, *America and the Reconstruction of Italy, 1945–48*, Cambridge: Cambridge University Press, 1986.

Kenneth Harris, *Attlee*, London: Weidenfeld & Nicolson, 1982.

Jonathan Haslam, *The Soviet Union and the Struggle for Collective Security in Europe 1933–39*, London: Macmillan, 1984.

William Hayter, *The Kremlin and the Embassy*, London: Hodder & Stoughton, 1966.

P. Hehn, *The German struggle against Yugoslav guerrillas in world war II: German counter insurgency in Yugoslavia, 1941–43*, Boulder, Colorado: East European Quarterly, 1979.

Irena Reuter-Hendrichs, *Jugoslawische Aussenpolitik 1948–1968*, Cologne: Carl Heymanns Verlag, 1976.

Peter Hennessy, *Never Again*, London: Cape, 1992.

Beatrice Heuser, *Western Containment policies in the Cold War: the Yugoslav case, 1948–53*, London: Routledge, 1989.

F. H. Hinsley, *British Intelligence in the Second World War*, vols i–iii, HMSO 1979–84.

——, *Nationalism and the International System*, London: Hodder & Stoughton, 1973.

Adolf Hitler, *Hitler's Table Talk 1941–44*, London: Weidenfeld & Nicolson, 1953.

George Hoffman and Fred Warner Neal, *Yugoslavia and the New Communism*, New York, 1962.

J. Hoptner, *Yugoslavia in Crisis 1934–1941*, New York: Columbia University Press, 1962.

Michael Howard, *The Mediterranean Strategy in the Second World War*, London: Weidenfeld & Nicolson, 1968.

Ghita Ionescu, *The Breakup of the Soviet Empire in Eastern Europe*, Harmondsworth: Penguin, 1965.

Barbara Jelavich, *History of the Balkans*, vol. 2, Cambridge: Cambridge

University Press, 1983.
A. Ross Johnson, *The Transformation of Ideology: the Yugoslav case 1945–53*, Cambridge Mass: The MIT Press, 1972.
Richard Kindersley (ed.), *In Search of Eurocommunism*, London: Macmillan, 1981.
Gabriel Kolko, *The Politics of War. the world and US foreign policy 1943–45*, London: Weidenfeld & Nicolson, 1968.
J. and G. Kolko, *The Limits of Power*, New York, Harper & Row, 1972.
Dimitrios G. Kousoulas, *The Price of Freedom: Greece in World Affairs, 1939–1953*, Syracuse: Syracuse University Press, 1953.
Bruce R. Kuniholm, *The origins of the Cold War in the Near East: Great Power conflict and diplomacy in Iran, Turkey and Greece*, Princeton, NJ: Princeton University Press, 1980.
Richard Lamb, *Churchill as war leader: right or wrong?*, London: Bloomsbury, 1991.
David D. Larson, *United States Foreign Policy twoards Yugoslavia, 1943–1963*, Washington DC: University Press of American, 1979 (1st edition, 1965).
Melvyn Leffler, *A Preponderence of Power: National Security, the Truman Administration and the Cold War*, Stanford: Stanford University Press, 1992.
William Roger Louis, *The British Empire in the Middle East 1945–51: Arab nationalism, the United States and psotwar imperialism*, Oxford: Clarendon Press, 1984.
Geir Lundestadt, *The American Non-Policy towards Eastern Euorpe 1943–1947 – Universalism in an area not of essential interest to the United States*, Tromso: Universitetsforlaget, 1978.
William O. McCagg, *Stalin Embattled, 1943–1948*, Detroit: Wayne State University Press, 1978.
Martin McCauley (ed.), *Communist Power in Eastern Europe 1944–49*, London: Macmillan and SSEES, 1979.
Fitzroy Maclean, *Disputed Barricade: the life and times of Josip Broz Tito, Jonathan Cape, 1957.*
William H. McNeill, American, Britain and Russia: their co-operation and conflict 1941–46, London and New York: Oxford University Press, 1953.
Lilly Marcou, *Le Kominform: le Communisme de guerre Froide*, Paris: Presses de la Fondation nationale des Sciences Politiques, 1977.
David Martin, *The Web of Disinformation, Churchill's Yugoslav blunder*, New York: Harcourt, Brace Jovanovich, 1991.
Vojtech Mastny, *Russia's road to the Cold War. Diplomacy, warfare and the politics of communism 1941–45*, New York: Columbia University Press, 1979.
Matteo J. Milazzo, *The Chetnik movement and Yugoslav resistance*, Baltimore and London: Johns Hopkins University Press, 1975.
Czeslaw Milosz, *The Captive Mind*, trans. Jane Zielonko, London: Secker & Warburg, 1953.
Kenneth O. Morgan, *Labour in Power: 1945–51*, Oxford and New York: Clarendon Press and Oxford University Press, 1984.
Bogdan Novak, *Trieste 1941–1954: the ethnic, political and ideological struggle*, Chicago: University of Chicago Press, 1970.

Ritchie Ovendale, *The Foreign Policy of the British Labour Government 1945–51*, Leicester: Leicester University Press, 1984.

Stevan Pavlowitch, *Tito. Yugoslavia's Great Dictator A Reassessment*, London: C. Hurst & Co, 1992.

——, *The Improbable Survivor. Yugoslavia and its problems 1918–1988*, London: C. Hurst & Co, 1988.

——, *Unconventional Perceptions of Yugoslavia, 1940–1945*, East European Monographs, no. CLXXVIII, New York: Columbia University Press, 1971.

Mosha Pirjevic, *Tito, Stalin e l'Occidente*, Trieste: Editoriale Stampa Triestina, 1985.

Mosha Piyade, *About the Legend that the Yugoslav Uprising owed its existence to Soviet assistance*, London: Yugoslav Information Service, 1950.

R. Rabel, *Between East and West: Trieste, the United States and the Cold War, 1941–1954*, London, 1988.

Robert Rhodes James, *Anthony Eden*, London: Weidenfeld & Nicolson, 1987.

Walter R. Roberts, *Tito, Mihailovic and the Allies 1941–45*, New Jersey: Rutgers University Press, 1973.

Graham Ross (ed.), *The Foreign Office and the Kremlin*, Cambridge: Cambridge University Press, 1984.

Dennis Rusinow, *The Yugoslav Experiment, 1948–1974*, London: C. Hurst for RIIA, 1977.

Henry Butterfield Ryan, *The vision of America: the US-UK alliance and the emerging Cold War 1943–46*, Cambridge: Cambridge University Press, 1987.

O. A. Rzheshevsky, *Istoriya vtorogo fronta: voina i diplomatiya*, Moscow: Izdatel'stvo Znanie, 1988.

George Schopflin, *Politics in Eastern Europe*, Oxford: Blackwell, 1993.

Hugh Seton-Watson, *Eastern Europe Between the Wars, 1918–1941*, Cambridge: Cambridge University Press, 1946.

——, *The East European Revolution*, London: Methuen, 1956, 3rd edn.

Paul Shoup, *Communism and the Yugoslav National Question*, New York, 1968.

Martin D. Shulman, *Stalin's Foreign Policy Reappraised*, Cambridge: Harvard University Press, 1963.

Ljubo Sirc, *Between Hitler and Tito: Nazi occupation and communist oppression*, London: André Deutsch, 1989.

Bradley Smith, *The Shadow Warriors. OSS and the origins of the CIA*, London: André Deutsch, 1983.

J. V. Stalin, *Dialectical and historical Materialism*, Moscow: Foreign Languages Publishing House, 1951.

David Stafford, *Britain and European Resistance. A survey of SOE with documents*, London: Macmillan for St Antony's College, Oxford, 1980.

Mark Stoler, *The Politics of the Second Front*, Westport, 1977.

William Taubman, *Stalin's American Policy*, New York: Norton, 1982.

Hugh Thomas, *Armed Truce: the beginnings of the Cold War, 1945–46*, London: Hamish Hamilton, 1986.

Nikolai Tolstoy, *The Minister and the Massacres*, London, 1986.

Joso Tomasevich, *The Cetniks. War and Revolution in Yugoslavia 1941–45*, Stanford: Stanford University Press, 1975.

Robert C. Tucker (ed.) *Stalinism: essays in historical interpretation*, New York: W. W. Norton, 1977.

Adam Ulam, Expansion and co-existence: Soviet foreign policy 1917–1973, London: Secker & Warburg 1968.

——, *Stalin: the man and his era*, New York: Viking Press, 1972.

——, *Tito and the Cominform*, Cambridge, MA: Harvard University Press, 1952.

G. Valdevit, *La questione di Trieste 1941–1954*, Milan, 1987.

Dmitri A. Volkogonov, *Stalin. Triumph & Tragedy*, ed. and trans. Harold Shukman, London: Weidenfeld & Nicolson, 1991.

Wayne Vucinich (ed.), *At the Brink of War and Peace: the Tito-Stalin split in an Historical Perspective*, New York, 1982.

Donald Cameron Watt, *Succeeding John Bull: America in Britain's Place 1900–1975*, Cambridge and New York: Cambridge University Press, 1984.

——, *Personalities and Policies. Studies in the formation of British foreign policy in the Twentieth Century*, London: Longman, 1965.

Evelyn Waugh, *Unconditional Surrender*, Penguin, 1957.

Rebecca West, *Black Lamb, Grey Falcon. A journey through Yugoslavia*, London: Macmillan, 1942.

Richard West, *Tito and the Rise and Fall of Yugoslavia*, London: Sinclair Stevenson, 1994.

John Wheeler-Bennett and Anthony Nichols, *The Semblance of Peace. The Political Settlement after the Second World War*. London: Macmillan, 1972.

Mark Wheeler, *Britain and the War for Yugoslavia, 1941–1943*, Boulder, Colorado: East European Monographs, 1980.

Duncan Wilson, *Tito's Yugoslavia*, Cambridge: Cambridge University Press, 1979.

L. S. Wittner, *American Intervention in Greece, 1943–49*, Columbia University Press, 1982.

C. M. Woodhouse, The Struggle for Greece, 1941–49, London: Hart Davis, McGibbon, 1976.

E. L. Woodward, *British Foreign Policy in the Second World War*, 5 vols, London: HMSO, 1970–76.

Stephen Xydis, *Greece and the Great Powers 1944–1947: Prelude to the 'Truman Doctrine'*, Thessaloniki: Institute for Balkan Studies, 1963.

Daniel Yergin, *Shattered Peace. The origins of the Cold War and the National Security State*, London: Pelican, 1980.

Charles Zalar, *Yugoslav Communism – a critical study*, Washington DC: USGPO, 1961.

K. Zilliacus, *Tito of Yugoslavia*, London: Michael Joseph, 1952.

Articles

Ivo Banac, Historiography of the countries of eastern Europe: Yugoslavia, *American Historical Review*, October 1992.

Elisabeth Barker, British wartime resistance towards Yugoslavia, *South Slav Journal*, vol. 12, no. 2, April 1979.

——, Yugoslav policy towards Greece, 1947–1949, in Lars Baerentzen, John Iatrides and Ole Smith (eds), *Studies in the History of the Greek Civil War, 1945–1949*, Copenhagen: Museum of Tusculanum Press, 1987.

Robert Blum, Surprised by Tito: the anatomy of an intelligence failure, *Diplomatic History* XII, 1 (Winter 1988).

Peter G. Boyle, The British Foreign Office and American foreign Policy 1947–48, *American Studies*, XVI, 3, 1982.

Henry W. Brands, Jr, Redefining the Cold War: American policy towards Yugoslavia 1948–1960, *Diplomatic History*, XI, Winter 1987.

Kathleen Burke, American foreign economic policy and lend-lease, in Ann Lane and Howard Temperley (eds), *The Rise and Fall of the Grand Alliance*, London: Macmillan, 1995.

I. Crmcanin, General Dusan Simovic and the 1944 Royal Regency, *South Slav Journal*, vol. 4, no. 3, Autumn 1981.

Hugh de Santis, In search of Yugoslavia: Anglo-American policy making 1943–45, *Journal of Contemporary History*, vol. 16, no. 3, July 1981.

David Dilks, The British view of security: Europe and the wider world, 1945–48, in Olav Riste (ed.), *Western Security: The formative years. Europe and Atlantic Defence, 1945–53*, Oslo: Norwegian University Press, Universitetsforleget, 1985.

John Lewis Gaddis, The United States and the question of a sphere of influence in Europe 1945–49, in Olav Riste (ed.), *Western Security: the formative years. Europe and Atlantic defence, 1945–53*, Oslo: Norwegian University Press, Universitetsforleget, 1985.

——, Was the Truman Doctrine a real turning point? *Foreign Affairs*, LII, January 1974.

——, Containment, a reassessment, *Foreign Affairs*, LV, 1976–77.

Richard N. Gardner, Sterling-Dollar diplomacy in current perspective, in W. Roger Louis and Hedley Bull (eds), *The Special Relationship: Anglo-American relations since 1945*, Oxford: Clarendon, 1986, pp 186–200.

Robert A. Garson, The role of Eastern Europe in America's containment policy, 1945–48, *Journal of American Studies*, XIII, 1979.

Keith Hamilton and Ann Lane, Power, status and the pursuit of Liberty: Britain and Eastern Europe, 1945–46, in Michael Dockrill (ed.), *Britain within the global system 1938–60: Britain, France, Italy and Germany: from Great Powers to Regional Powers*, Bochum: Brockmeyer, 1995, pp. 31–54.

Jonathan Haslam, Soviet war aims, in Ann Lane and Howard Temperley (eds), *The Rise and Fall of the Grand Alliance*, London: Macmillan, 1995.

Robert Hathaway, Truman, Tito and the politics of hunger, in William Leavantrosser (ed.), *Harry S. Truman: the Man from Independence*, Westwood CT: Greenwood Press, 1986.

Beatrice Heuser, Western diplomatic perceptions of the origins of the Tito-Cominform split, *South Slav Journal*, vol. 10, no. 3, Autumn 1988.

P. G. Holdich, A Policy of Percentages? British policy in the Balkans after the Moscow conference of October 1944, *International History Review*, vol. 9 no. 1 February 1987.

Robert Strausz-Hupe, Yugoslav counter offensive in the Cold War, *The Yale Review*, XL, December 1950.

——, The United States and Yugoslavia: a reappraisal, *The Yale Review*, XLV, December 1955.

Warren Kimball, Naked reverse right: Roosevelt, Churchill and Eastern Europe from Tolstoy to Yalta and a little beyond, *Diplomatic History*, vol. III, no. 2, Spring 1979.

Robert Knight, Die Kartner Grenzfrage und der Kalte Krieg, *Carinthia* I, 1985.

Dimitrios Kousoulas, The Truman Doctrine and the Stalin–Tito rift: a reappraisal, *South Atlantic Quarterly*, LXXII, Summer 1973.

Ann Lane, Coming to terms with Tito, in Richard J. Aldrich and Michael F. Hopkins (eds), *Intelligence, Defence and Diplomacy. British policy in the post-war world*, London: Frank Cass, 1994.

——, Putting Britain right with Tito: the displaced persons question in Anglo-Yugoslav relations 1946–47, *European History Quarterly*, vol. 22, no. 2, April 1992.

——, Personalities in diplomacy: Eastern Europe 1945–46, in FCO, *Historical Branch Occasional Paper* no. 4, *Eastern Europe*.

Lorraine M. Lees, The American decision to assist Tito, 1948–49, *Diplomatic History*, Fall 1978, vol. 2, no. 4.

Melvyn P. Leffler, National Security and United States foreign policy, Melvyn P. Leffler and David S. Painter, *Origins of the Cold War: an international history*, London: Routledge, 1994, pp. 15–52.

Michael McGwire, National Security and Soviet foreign policy, in Melvyn P. Leffler and David S. Painter, *Origins of the Cold War: an international history*, London: Routledge, 1994, pp. 15–52.

Fitzroy Maclean, Tito–Maclean talks of 1947–48. An account given in a contemporary letter written by Brigadier Maclean of his discussions with Marshal Tito on the Yugoslav refugee problem, September 1947, *South Slav Journal*, vol. 4, Winter 1981–82.

——, Tito: a study, *Foreign Affairs*, vol. 28, no. 2, January 1950.

Edouard Mark, The question of containment: a reply to John Lewis Gaddis, *Foreign Affairs*, LVI, January 1978.

Stephen Markovich, American foreign policy and Yugoslav foreign policy, in Peter Potichnyj and Jane Shapiro (eds), *From Cold War to Detente*, New York: Praeger, 1976.

Vojtech Mastny, Stalin and the militarization of the Cold War, *International Security*, IX, Winter 1984–85.

S. M. Max, Cold War on the Danube: the Belgrade Conference of 1948 and Anglo-American efforts to re-internationalise the river, *Diplomatic History*, vol. 7, no. 1, pp. 55–77.

Ray Merrick, The Russia Committee of the British Foreign Office and the Cold War 1946–47, in *Journal of Contemporary History*, vol. 20, no. 3, July 1985.

Paul Nitze, The development of NSC68, *International Security*, IV, 4, 1979–1980.

Thomas G. Patterson, Eastern Europe and the early Cold War: the Danube controversy, *The Historian*, 1983, pp. 237–47.

Stevan K. Pavlowitch, Neither heroes nor traitors: suggestions for a reappraisal of the Yugoslav resistance, Brian Bond and Ian Roy (eds),

War and Society: a yearbook of military history, London: Croom Helm, 1976.
——, The Grey Zone in NATO's Balkan Flank, *Survey*, XXV 3, Summer 1980.
——, Out of context. The Yugoslav government in London, 1941–45, *Journal of Contemporary History*, vol. 16, no. 1, January 1981.
Bradford Perkins, Unequal Partners, The Truman Administration and Great Britain, in W. Roger Louis and Hedley Bull (eds), *The Special Relationship: Anglo-American relations since 1945*, Oxford: Clarendon, 1986, pp 43–64.
Joze Pirjevec, Die Auseinandersetzung Tito–Stalin im Spiegel britischer diplomatischer Berichte, *Sudostforschungen*, XL, 1981.
P. Radan, The British, Mihailovic and Tito, *South Slav Journal*, vol. 4, issue 3, Autumn 1981.
Albert Resis, The Churchill–Stalin percentage agreement, *American Historical Review*, lxxxii, 1978.
David Reynolds, Roosevelt, Churchill and the wartime Anglo-American alliance, 1939–45: towards a new synthesis, in W. Roger Louis and Hedley Bull (eds), *The Special Relationship: Anglo-American relations since 1945*, Oxford: Clarendon, 1986, pp. 17–42.
——, The European dimension of the Cold War, in Melvyn P. Leffler and David S. Painter, *Origins of the Cold War: an international history*, London: Routledge, 1994, pp. 125–38.
——, A Special Relationship? America, Britain and the international order since the Second World War, *International Affairs*, LXII, 1, Winter 1985–86.
K. St Pavlowitch, Yugoslav–Soviet relations 1939–43, as seen from British sources, *Slavonic and East European Review*, vol. 56, no. 3, July 1978.
George Schöpflin, Nationality in Yugoslav Politics, *Survey*, XXV, 3, Summer 1980.
Avi Shlaim, Britain, the Berlin Blockade and the Cold War, *International Affairs*, Winter 1983–84.
Joseph Siracusa, The meaning of Tolstoy: Churchill, Stalin and the Balkans, Moscow, October 1944, *Diplomatic History*, vol. III, 1979.
Raymond Smith and John Zametica, The Cold Warrior: Clement Attlee reconsidered, 1945–47, *International Affairs*, LXI, 1985.
Raymond Smith, Ernest Bevin, British officials and British Soviet Policy 1945–47, in Anne Deighton, *Britain and the First Cold War*, Cambridge: Cambridge University Press, 1990.
Charles G. Stefan, The emergence of the Soviet–Yugoslav break: a personal view from the Belgrade Embassy, *Diplomatic History*, Fall 1982, vol. iv, no. 4.
Zara Steiner, Decision-making in American and British foreign policy: an open and shut case, *Review of International Studies*, XIII, 1, 1987.
Geoffrey Swain, The Cominform: Tito's International, *Historical Journal*, vol. 35, no. 3, 1992.
Philip M. Taylor, The projection of Britain abroad, 1945–51, in M. Dockrill and J. Young (eds), *British Foreign Policy 1945–56*, Basingstoke: Macmillan, 1989.

M. Vauhnik, the last days of the Kingdom of Yugoslavia, *South Slav Journal*, vol. 3, issue 2, June 1980.

Geoffrey Warner, The study of Cold War origins, in David Armstrong and Erik Goldstein (eds), *The End of the Cold War*, London: Frank Cass, 1990.

Mark Wheeler, Crowning the revolution: the British, King Peter and the path to Tito's cave, in Richard Langhorne (ed.), *Diplomacy and Intelligence in the Second World War*, 1985.

J. R. Whittam, Drawing the Line: Britain and the emergence of the Trieste question, January 1941–May 1945, *English Historical Review*, vol. cvi, no. 419, April 1991.

Index